"Jessica Pryce-Jones establishes happiness as more than a fleeting feeling; she argues that it is a critical resource for successful work and a good life. She brings her years of experience to bear on this important topic and provides practical tools for achieving more happiness at work. The book is wonderfully written."

> *Robert Biswas-Diener, author of* Positive Psychology Coaching

"We all want to be happy in every area of our lives, including work. This book offers the secret of finding happiness at work for us all, which in turn helps us to experience a more meaningful and healthy life."

> *Lynne Franks, businesswoman and author of* The Seed Handbook

"Illustrated with fascinating and diverse interviews, this book is understandable and easy to read. Jess Pryce-Jones has definitely created a great guide for anyone who wants to improve their working life."

> *Cathy L. Greenberg, PhD, New York Times Best Selling author of* What Happy Working Mothers Know, *and Managing Partner of h2c Happy Companies Healthy People*

For David, Jack, Harry, and Kitty – with love and thanks

Happiness at Work

Maximizing Your Psychological Capital For Success

Jessica Pryce-Jones

A John Wiley & Sons, Ltd., Publication

This edition first published 2010
© 2010 Jessica Pryce-Jones

Wiley-Blackwell is an imprint of John Wiley & Sons, formed by the merger of Wiley's global
Scientific, Technical, and Medical business with Blackwell Publishing.

Registered Office
John Wiley & Sons Ltd, The Atrium, Southern Gate, Chichester, West Sussex, PO19 8SQ, UK

Editorial Offices
The Atrium, Southern Gate, Chichester, West Sussex, PO19 8SQ, UK
9600 Garsington Road, Oxford, OX4 2DQ, UK
350 Main Street, Malden, MA 02148-5020, USA

For details of our global editorial offices, for customer services, and for information about how
to apply for permission to reuse the copyright material in this book please see our website at
www.wiley.com/wiley-blackwell.

The right of Jessica Pryce-Jones to be identified as the author of this work has been asserted in
accordance with the UK Copyright, Designs and Patents Act 1988.

Wiley also publishes its books in a variety of electronic formats. Some content that appears in
print may not be available in electronic books.

Designations used by companies to distinguish their products are often claimed as trademarks.
All brand names and product names used in this book are trade names, service marks,
trademarks or registered trademarks of their respective owners. The publisher is not associated
with any product or vendor mentioned in this book. This publication is designed to provide
accurate and authoritative information in regard to the subject matter covered. It is sold on the
understanding that the publisher is not engaged in rendering professional services. If
professional advice or other expert assistance is required, the services of a competent
professional should be sought.

Library of Congress Cataloging-in-Publication Data is available for this title

HB: 978-0-470-68942-4
PB: 978-0-470-74946-3

A catalogue record for this book is available from the British Library.

Set in 10.5 on 13 pt Minion by Toppan Best-set Premedia Limited
Printed and bound in United States of America
by Sheridan Books, Inc.

2   2010

γνῶθι σεαυτόν

Contents

Prologue

In the Beginning was the H Word

I am in a wood-paneled boardroom of a large multinational waiting to make a pitch. The coffee's delicious but I can't swallow a single mouthful: I'm too nervous. I'm waiting for the Chief Executive Officer and his acolytes to appear. They're late. My stomach lurches as I anticipate having to use the "H" word. It just feels too New-Agey to associate with the hard-numbered world of business.

Right now I know that the easier option facing me would be to talk about morale. But I also know both from my experience and our research that morale is not the right word for the issue we're there to address.

My mind flashes back to lots of conversations with executives, friends, and acquaintances, several of whom had roared with laughter when we'd talked about what we were doing. I'll never forget one Senior Vice-President putting his arm around my shoulder in a bar and saying condescendingly, "It will never catch on – don't waste your time, sweetie. It's a joke, an idea without a future."

Across the polished table the executives are now waiting. I take a deep breath and, going with it, I say, "We're here today to talk about happiness. Happiness at work." The words sound so flaky: "happy clappy" and "happy hippy" ping into my mind even though the numbers tell their own powerful story. I explain how people who are really happy at work are nearly twice as productive as those who are not, and what that might mean for this organization.

I glance at one of my colleagues nodding with encouragement. No-one else is. Everyone is polite but non-committal as I end my pitch. And then the CEO asks everyone to leave but indicates that I should stay behind. The palms of my hands start to sweat gently and I'm expecting an ear-bashing for wasting his time. I try to breathe deeply and marshal my thoughts. I think to myself, "I'll just be polite and pretend to scribble down some comments he makes."

The heavy mahogany door shuts behind the last person and I am completely gobsmacked as he says, "When you said that word, 'happiness,' it really resonated with me. I'm so unhappy in my job, I hate what I do and I can barely bring myself to come in every day. Every time I see my Chairman I think about resigning. I really need to talk to you about all this."

This was the first sign that happiness mattered as a concept to be talked about in boardrooms, even when times were good. If he got it, offices, institutions, and businesses everywhere would too.

That was the start of the journey. You are the next part.

Who's This Book For?

This book is for you. If you've picked it up, maybe you'd like things to be better in some way at work. Perhaps you're looking for a starting point. Or wondering about a change of direction. It's written for you whatever kind of job you're in, and whatever level of seniority you're at. And it will help you if you are supporting other people who are not happy at work.

Reading this will tell you what happiness at work is, why it matters, and how you go about getting more of it. Plus it will explain what that means in terms of what we call psychological capital.

What's Its Underlying Approach?

The fundamental point of being happy at work is to enable you to achieve your full potential and to make the most of the highs and manage the lows on the way. There are some basic principles on which this book is based:

- You are responsible for your own levels of happiness.
- You have much more room for maneuver than you think.
- There is always a choice.
- Self-awareness is an essential first step.

What Was My Aim?

I wanted to write something based in recent research but that's practical and accessible too. Often research psychology takes 10–20 years to become mainstream, by which time things have changed and it's not as useful as it could have been. This book is based on up-to-the-minute findings, including ours.

It's written in a way that should work for any reader, whether you like to dip in and out, read end-to-end, or want to flick through for the stories and case studies. If you like lots of facts and references, you'll find the sources all in the back.

What's It All About?

Chapter 1 sets the scene with some key research findings; Chapter 2 outlines what we set out to do and explains the research journey; Chapters 3–8 tell you about the core of happiness at work – what we call the five components, or 5Cs: Contribution, Conviction, Culture, Commitment, and Confidence. Pride, Trust, and Recognition underpin all the 5Cs and you'll read about them in Chapter 9. Chapter 10 investigates achieving your potential.

You'll have noticed already that I'm using capital letters to describe, for example, each of the 5Cs. This is to highlight the fact that when I use these terms I'm using them not in a lay sense but specifically in the context of happiness at work interpreted through our research. So if you read them and think, "That's not precisely what I understand that word to mean," I'd agree with you. Meanwhile, in terms of happiness at work, I hope you'll agree with me.

What Are the Case Studies?

Chapters 3–8 contain mini-case studies to illustrate issues and how they play out in the real world. These case studies are real, come from our consulting and coaching practice, and, although identities are altered and businesses changed, they illustrate issues that we have helped others work through.

Who Are the Interviewees?

Over 80 people were interviewed for this book; from lawyers through to lamas their stories, observations, and experience will give you deeper insights than I ever could. For a little more about them take a look at the *dramatis personae* at the end.

And Finally ... How Happy Are You?

If you would like to find out exactly how happy you are at work before you start reading this book, complete our questionnaire by going to www.iopener.com/ippqreport. Within 24 hours you'll have received your free report.

I hope you enjoy what you read and, most importantly, that it enables you to be happier at work.

Jessica Pryce-Jones
Oxford, October 2009

Acknowledgments

First I owe a huge debt of gratitude to my interviewees. It was a real privilege and a delight talking to all of them. Diane Scott, Barbara Fölscher, Kalpana Morris, Gulrez and Sarah Arshad, Nathaniel de Rothschild, Zvi Limon, and Boaz Keysar and Linda Ginzel variously opened their homes, contact books, and many doors for me: this book would have been very different without their help.

Stephan Chambers at Oxford (Saïd) Business School helped me move the project from an idea into a proposal; Claire Andrews's patient and supportive guidance saw it to fruition. Antony Read at Jaine J Brent Personal Management and Casting as well as Andy Peart, my agent and publisher, need a particular mention for taking me on; so does Brigitle Lee Messenger for holding my hand through the production process.

Meanwhile at iOpener, Julia Lindsay and David Solomon were wonderful listeners, thought clarifiers, and debaters. Dr. Laurel Edmunds, Simon Lutterbie, and Lucia Nyiriova crunched the numbers and helped me stay on track; Philippa Chapman, Melissa Sharp, Diane Lytollis, Ben Woodgates and Ian Hitchcock found time to offer invaluable input and help.

Nisha Pillai and Andrew Robshaw gave me really useful feedback especially in the early stages; Michael Gilson helped with reference checking at the end. I am also immensely grateful to Ciaron Murphy and Alan Kemp, both of whom sharpened up my thinking at exactly the right moments.

I'd also like to thank friends and colleagues at London Business School over many years, especially Michael Hay, Lynn Hoffman, JoEllyn Prouty McLaren, Mike Nowlis, and Lorraine Vaun Davis. Test-driving ideas on participants and students has been more helpful than they'll ever know.

I do want to make one thing plain: although this book was a big collaborative effort, any mistakes are of course mine and mine alone.

Finally, I'd like to dedicate this to my husband David and children Jack, Harry, and Kitty: without your love, teasing, cooking, and back-up I'd still be stuck in the prologue.

1

Why Happiness at Work? Why Now?

It Started for Me When ...

I was in my early twenties and I'd landed what I thought was a dream job. An interesting financial institution, well-paid and in a prestigious location.

I hated every minute of it.

As I walked up the marble staircase on the first day, I knew I should have been excited. Thrilled to be there, expecting to grab the world and launch a successful career. But my head, heart, and guts were all screaming that I was doing the wrong thing.

Every day my stomach lurched with the dread of going into work. My office was located in a small basement with no windows. My boss didn't know what he wanted and would tell me to do something only to contradict himself a few hours later. One day his boss sent us all a memo which said, "When I come out of my office I expect to see your heads bent. When your heads are bent you're working and when they are not, you're not. This is not a holiday camp." For the 11 months that I lasted in that role, I was miserable.

My unhappiness at work spilt over into my personal life too. I was permanently exhausted and moody. One day trying to keep a cool head, I went for a run at lunchtime. As I pounded round the square under the lime trees, this thought popped into my head. "I wonder if I could get a little bit run over by a bus? Because if I could get a little bit run over, I could take three weeks out and not have to be here." Once I'd had that revelation I knew I had no option. I had to find something else to do.

Hunting for the next job, reality set in. I wondered if it was ever possible to achieve happiness at work. I'd had an education I hadn't much enjoyed, so didn't really see why a job should be any different. Then I thought about what it might be like to hate most of my daytime hours for the next 45 years of my life. It was too ghastly to contemplate.

But were my expectations unreasonable? Was it possible to be happy at work?

Why Happiness at Work Matters

If you're not concerned about happiness at work, you should be. Because there are huge downsides when you don't have it and upsides when you do: you know that without me telling you. If you've ever hated your job I'd put hot money that you knew what the negative effects were in terms of your effort, energy, and enthusiasm. But what about the upsides of being happy?

If you're happy at work you:

- Get promoted faster.
- Earn more.
- Get more support.
- Generate better and more creative ideas.
- Achieve your goals faster.
- Interact better with colleagues and bosses.
- Receive superior reviews.
- Learn more.
- Achiever greater success.
- Are healthier.

This last benefit is a big one. The higher your happiness levels, the stronger your immune system. You'll be less affected by stress hormones, develop 50 percent more antibodies to flu vaccines, be less likely to get heart disease, diabetes or have lung problems. In fact happiness looks as if it makes the same difference to your health as smoking or not smoking does. And that may add more than a decade to your overall life span.

And here's what our research has found. When we compare the un-happiest and happiest people at work, we've found that if you're really happy, you:

- Are 180 percent more energized.
- Are 180 percent happier with life.

- Are 155 percent happier in your job.
- Are 108 percent more engaged at work.
- Love your job 79 percent more.
- Are 50 percent more motivated.
- Have 40 percent more confidence.
- Achieve your goals 30 percent more.
- Contribute 25 percent more.

Too good to be true? Got it all back-to-front? Maybe you're thinking that all these marvelous things lead to happiness at work. Not so. Happiness leads to all these positive outcomes, not the other way round.

Happiness pays especially when you're under pressure. It's a valuable resource which not only generates career success but differentiates you from your colleagues too.

Now you know why it's so vital.

What Is Happiness at Work?

Philosophers, commentators, and religious leaders have been arguing for millennia about what happiness actually is. Is it an end in itself or a by-product of what you do? Does it disappear if you focus on it? Is it part of who you are, what you do, or where you find yourself in life? Is it about the journey and the goal, as Aristotle says, or the high points on the way, as Epicureans argue? Or perhaps it's using reasoning to overcome negative emotions like the Stoics believed? Maybe it's the more Buddhist way of detaching and getting over it?

There's one thing that happiness at work absolutely isn't – as pop psychology has it. It isn't about always smiling, thinking positively, or about being in a permanently sunny mood: that's patently absurd. Nor does it work.

Based on our research as well as years of consulting and coaching inside large and small organizations, we've found that happiness at work can't be tied to any one single approach. It incorporates everything I've just mentioned. And it's not something you do on your own, you need others to help you achieve it.

It involves a mix of high moments accompanied by some low ones, a journey in which you grow and flourish, and at the same time overcome your negative emotions. And you can do that best when you use insight and reason to help you. Sometimes the tasks, resources, outcomes, and time-frames are clear and comfortable, sometimes they're not. But the tough stuff results in learning. Because that's when you have to struggle to perform at your best, or make a breakthrough in what you're doing. So you extend yourself and fulfill your potential. It's hard and takes time. But moving from struggle to success – and repeating that cycle – is how you grow, develop, and achieve more.

It's how you become happy at work.

Happiness at Work: A Definition

Here's what we think it is.

Happiness at work is a mindset which allows you to maximize performance and achieve your potential. You do this by being mindful of the highs and lows when working alone or with others.

There are three important points to this definition of happiness at work.

The first key to happiness at work is your approach and being aware of it. And that awareness needs to extend not just to the lows, which are obvious, but to the highs as well. Being mindful allows you to have perspective on a situation, which means you'll manage it better.

Secondly, broadly speaking the "Western" cultural approach holds that life and work are all about the individual not the group, while the "Eastern" approach is exactly the opposite. Our definition of happiness focuses not only on the individual but also on their role within a group because that's where most work takes place.

Thirdly, it's important to recognize the "yin and yang" effect. Growth of any sort involves accepting that discomfort and difficulty are part of the process. Happiness at work doesn't mean that you have to feel good 100 percent of the time. Or that you shouldn't feel the usual negative emotions you do at work. Like anger, frustration, disappointment, failure, jealousy, or shock. Those are the emotions that will propel you to take different actions to get back on your happiness track. They're not to be avoided but actively explored on your career journey. Just like the times when you feel so stretched that you aren't sure how you'll cope. Those are the moments that help you achieve your potential. The times that you look back at with a sense of accomplishment and achievement because you know you can deliver.

For example, I took part as an expert in a BBC TV series called "Making Slough Happy." Our aim was to see if we could improve the happiness levels of a small industrial town just outside London. The town's only claim to fame was that a well-known comedy, *The Office*, was filmed there.

It was an awful project to deliver. The hours were immensely long and the pressure to perform was huge. Not to mention the tension both on and off camera. Yet on the last day, filming at the huge festival that everyone taking part had organized, I was really pleased I'd done it. I'd experienced the fact that happiness is about stretching yourself to achieve your potential and you only do that by doing difficult things.

So do the highs matter? Of course they do. The moments when you make a breakthrough, have a brainwave, connect with someone, or simply experience a strong positive emotion are important. These are the internal signals that you're doing the right thing. You're on track. And if you don't have enough of them, it's time to reconsider what you're doing. Right now. If you continue to put up with what you've always had, that's what you'll always get. And if we all do that, nothing will change.

And the world of work needs something different.

Now's the Time for a New Approach

Over the past few years a plethora of happiness books has burst on to the market. Psychologists, philosophers, and even the Dalai Lama have been adding to the literature. And although many of them disagree about how to build happiness, everyone agrees it's worth a go. But most of them were written when the world economy looked stable. When the money-go-round felt secure.

More recently confidence has been shaken and trust battered. Many of the global business values, theories, practices, and processes have been called into question. And more than ever leaders and employees are looking for answers to tough questions. Like: "What should our organization stand for?" "How do we reward employees?" "How do we find clarity in the complexity?" "What does sustainable mean in the largest sense?" "How do we build a future?" "What are we expecting from our people?"

The answers to these questions will shape the organizations that survive and thrive over the next decade and more. They'll affect our working practice and the global economy as a result.

So how do we find the answers? We need to make a fundamental shift to work that brings together some of the key recent findings in organizational research, psychology, neurology, behavioral economics, psycholinguistics, and anthropology. To create new models, new practices, and a new approach.

To bring that about everyone's got to be involved. Regardless of sector, nationality, product, service, role, or status. The only way to do this is to galvanize people around something that's practical, that's compelling for individuals as well as organizations, and that produces real results. Results of real and long-lasting value.

Understanding Real Value

All organizations talk about "added value" and look for ways to measure it too. But when you hear this term the only aspect that's being addressed is the financial one. It's part of what's been an obsessive focus on shareholder value. I know that executive directors have a fiduciary duty to deliver this. But it's idiotic to suppose that it's a strategy: it's not. It's the outcome of a strategy.

By the way, looking for value beyond financial value isn't new thinking. Frederick Taylor, one of the first and toughest of management consultants who founded the Efficiency Movement, in his 1912 testimony before US Congress cautioned against putting financial objectives at the heart of an organization's mission and purpose. He believed that sound financial performance is the consequence of good business. When even Jack Welch, the former General Electric Chief Executive who ushered in the reign of shareholder value, thinks that "shareholder value is the dumbest idea in the world," you know an era is under question.

Now of course capital matters. The question is what kind. Because the organizations and individuals who will be most successful over the next decade are people who'll be actively pursuing a new sort of capital. The kind of capital that has been overlooked in the past which benefits the many, not just the few: psychological and social capital.

Myth 1: Financial Capital Is All That Counts

I'd like to be really clear about one thing. Financial value is crucial to every organization. But driving any workplace from this standpoint alone is putting the cart before the horse. Look at it in simple accounting terms. If you've ever read a set of accounts, you'll know that goodwill is worth something. It's an asset. But the goodwill that's embedded within individuals and groups is also a valuable resource that needs to be accounted for too. And nurtured because it's precious. Financial value is reduced or increased as a direct consequence of the relationships that individuals have with themselves and with others at work. Moreover, it's something that every individual and their organization benefits from. People come first. For sound financial reasons: how they feel has a direct effect on the bottom line.

Here's how it works.

Human capital

Human capital isn't new; it's a term that was coined by Adam Smith in 1776. What it refers to is an individual's skills, talents, education, experience, and knowledge which in today's economy need constant upgrading. Human capital is an essential component for delivering financial value because the sum of it enables any organization to deliver on its strategy. That means it's important for every workplace to constantly think about how it manages its human capital.

But you can't optimize human capital without two other things first. Social and psychological capital. Social capital leads people to want to be in a group and learn from it, while psychological capital gives them the wherewithal to do so.

Social capital

Social capital is a multilayered and dynamic concept that takes time to build. It consists of:

- Relationships and connections you have with others.
- A group, community, or society that you belong to.
- Interactions that flow from all the various relationships.

High social capital means you have shared values, goals, aims, and aspirations which in turn lead to common ways of thinking, understanding, and acting. You know it's in place when you have good working relationships; that means you'll be willing to take a risk within a group, commit yourself to its members, and in turn you can rely on them for their support. And they on you.

But you'll only really contribute to that group when you have strong psychological capital.

Psychological capital

Psychological capital encompasses the mental resources that you build when things go well and draw on when things go badly. These resources include resilience, motivation, hope, optimism, self-belief, confidence, self-worth, and energy. All of which are key elements of happiness in a working context.

If you don't have a high level of psychological capital because you aren't happy at work, you'll only be going through the motions.

Yet very few people are aware of this.

In doing over 80 interviews for this book, I've found only two people who knew the term psychological capital. However, I'm certain that within the next ten years everyone will be talking about, measuring, and managing it too. Because it makes such an enormous difference not only to how you feel, but also to what you do.

Despite the fact that standard economic theory takes no account of feelings, emotions really do matter. They affect your personal investment, effort, and therefore your output too. And that of those around you. Psychological capital matters particularly in a pressured and stressed service economy which requires motivation, creative thinking, and perseverance, all of which happier employees have more of.

In other words, organizations do better when employees feel good about themselves and the colleagues they work with. Like financial capital this takes time, effort, and energy to build. Unlike financial capital it endures much better when institutions and markets crash and burn.

Myth 2: Happiness is Job Satisfaction or Engagement in Another Guise

Of course there are a few overlaps and similarities between these concepts. But there are a couple of important differences between happiness and everything else. Before I get to them, let's briefly define and discuss some terms.

Job satisfaction

Most job satisfaction theories propose that it comes from one of three components. These include who the employee is, what their working environment is like, or what kind of conditions they work in. There are a couple of problems with all of them. Firstly, all the approaches were developed in a working world which was much more static. The very institutional and context-specific notion of how job satisfaction arises is much less relevant in a world where more and more people work when they want, where they want, and how they want.

Secondly, because job satisfaction is about making sure that you have the right person in the right place, there's very little room for maneuver. The only way to improve matters is to "fix the environment or fire the employee." It's an ideal approach for a command-and-control structure, but it's a very disempowering way of measuring or managing individuals because there's so little an employee can do. And it's very expensive.

Engagement

Engagement in its purest sense refers to the relationship you have with your working environment and the strength of your connection to it. Thought to be the opposite of burnout, it's been broadly defined as "vigor, dedication, and absorption" and has been widely used by organizations and consultants for improving retention. But there are issues with engagement as a concept: it's even been described as "not theoretical, valid or unique." At its best engagement has been researched through using the concept of flow at work (which you can read about in more detail in Chapter 5).

But here's the central issue: in crunching through all our statistics – and we now have over 300,000 data points – we can see that engagement relates to 10 percent fewer items than happiness at work does. However, there are two more important details to draw your attention to. Firstly, engagement doesn't link to all our five components in as strong a way as happiness does; we can tell that because we've run sophisticated statistical modeling tests to check. These have revealed that although it's something that matters – who doesn't want to feel engaged at work? – it's not as "large" a concept as happiness at work is. This leads to the second point:

those modeling tests reveal that engagement – and job satisfaction – is something which happiness appears to encompass.

Happiness: the crucial differences

There are three key differences which tell us why happiness at work is so important.

Happiness is DIY

The starting point of happiness at work is that it's self-initiated: we know that you want to make your working world better and enjoy contributing to it if you are given that opportunity. It doesn't work from the top-down: being happy at work operates best from the ground-up because you know most about managing and affecting your world. We know this because it's what our research statistics clearly indicate and that's backed up by our work inside organizations. Happiness is strongly linked to the idea of agency, but that's not widely accounted for in the satisfaction or engagement approaches.

Moreover, because the focus is on the individual rather than the workplace, it's easier, cheaper, and more flexible for organizations to implement.

Happiness is strongly connected to productivity

Unlike job satisfaction or engagement, we've found – and this is really crucial – that happiness at work is strongly related to productivity. And it's the only concept that is linked to productivity both consistently and progressively. That means the happier you are, the more productive you are. In other words, more job satisfaction doesn't mean more productivity and in the same amounts. Nor does more engagement.

Happiness does.

Happiness is a bigger concept

If happiness indicates job satisfaction and engagement but they don't work the other way round, the automatic implication is that they are both smaller concepts. That's backed up by statistical modeling that we've done which shows that happiness encompasses both job satisfaction and engagement and includes them within it. And because it's a broader concept, happiness gives you richer and deeper insights.

Job satisfaction or engagement vs. happiness?
Be honest: would you rather be satisfied, engaged, or happy at work? You decide.

Myth 3: You're Born Happy or Sad and There's Nothing You Can Do

Twin studies show that our genes are responsible for a hefty 50 percent of our emotional experience and about the same chunk of our personalities too. We know that because David Lykken and Auke Tellegen, famous for their research in Minnesota, worked with 69 pairs of identical twins who were raised apart. They were all asked about their happiness twice over a nine-year period. What the researchers found was not only were their scores closely related, but also one twin's score pretty much predicted another's. So they concluded that a lot of who we are and what we feel is gene-driven and responsible for a happiness "set point."

Except that new and exciting neuroscience showing how malleable emotions are made David Lykken completely shift his thinking.

He said, "It's now clear we can change our happiness levels widely." Because there is now a lot of data which show that emotional levels fluctuate, sometimes quite extensively, over time. Think about quitting one job and landing another. You'll be delighted to be leaving one place and starting somewhere fresh and you may well experience what's called the honeymoon effect. Weeks or months later that may be followed by what's called the hangover effect – the point at which you realize what you're truly facing. This fluctuation suggests less of a fixed happiness point and more of a range.

That's backed up by research which began in Germany in 1984; studies were started to investigate what happens to happiness over the long term. People were asked to rate their happiness at various times and over the years those data have been compared and contrasted. What's interesting is that there have been substantial changes in some participants' happiness over 15–20 years – both positive and negative. That's backed up by further research into people who become disabled: unsurprisingly, their happiness levels don't get back to what they were when they were able-bodied.

What about the positive end of the spectrum? A recent study in the USA asked students to practice deliberate strategies to increase their overall happiness. Researchers wanted to take personality into account and see which had the stronger effect: who they were or what they did. And they found that "doing" greatly outweighed "being." Interestingly, the most important happiness-boosting behavior was finding support, while the second was helping others.

All this research points to the fact that we have a happiness range rather than a set point. Some peoples' ranges will be more extensive (anyone who is bipolar can confirm that), while the range itself will depend on your usual levels of optimism or pessimism. But the exciting thing is that you can take action to manage that range and you don't have to stay miserable because you are "born like that." Simply by changing behavior and doing things differently you can have a big effect on how happy you are and push yourself up to the top of your range. Increasing your level of happiness at work is just about analyzing then applying the right personal strategy for you.

That means your happiness at work doesn't have to be a haphazard by-product of what you do but something that you can get more of if you choose to. That's why understanding what affects it, why, and what you do to manage it are so important.

Are You Leading the Life You Choose or Managing the One You've Got?

That's the question that Commander Dr. Mike Young of the Royal Navy asks. From time to time maybe you can only manage the life you've got at work. But over a long period, is that enough?

Now let's assume that you're an average person who's working from the age of about 20 to retirement at, say, 65. And let's also assume you take three weeks holiday a year. I know this number might shift depending where in the world you're located – just go with it for a moment. Then let's imagine you work about a 40-hour week, a number that looks conservative from our database. That means over a lifetime, you'll probably spend at least 90,000 hours at work. This figure doesn't take into account those emails answered during evenings, weekends, or holiday; or time spent thinking about work issues when you're at home – either on purpose or by accident; or the occasions you get in early and stay late. The fact of the matter is, workplace issues probably take up many more hours of mental engagement than you realize.

Those long hours had better add to your overall sense of purpose, well-being, and happiness rather than subtract from it. Because you won't get them back once they're gone. If you're going to make sure you get the best out of what you put in, you'll need to reflect on how you want to spend those 90,000 hours.

So that you are as happy as you can be at work.

Top take-aways for Chapter 1

This chapter:

- Starts with the big personal benefits for happiness at work which include faster promotions, more pay, greater creativity, better feedback, and better health. And more happiness with life as well.
- Suggests that financial value is too limited a measure of success in times of economic and financial uncertainty.
- Sets out that a new focus on psychological and social capital could fundamentally change the way we work and what we value.
- Shows that happiness is different from satisfaction and engagement.
- Demonstrates that we have happiness ranges which can be maximized rather than set-points which are fixed.

2

The Research Journey

The Initial Seeds

In Dubai the management team held hands, in Moscow they became emotional, in London cynical, and in Milan irritated; in Tel Aviv the shouting was unbelievable and in Jo'burg they were plain distracted. The issue? Managing and measuring motivation and performance. I and a colleague were running a series of seminars around the world for the leadership teams of a global IT organization and the same conversations kept coming up. Something was missing.

But right now I was at the gate for the last flight leaving Warsaw. It was an hour late and everything was shut; there wasn't even water for sale. At the end of a grueling day with plenty more travel to come, I was tired and my mood wasn't helped by an uncommunicative ground crew.

Watching the sullen and unhelpful staff I wondered what it would take to put a smile on their faces. To make them happier to be there.

Half an hour later it was time to get on the plane.

A couple of weeks later at the end of a long meeting, I was mulling over a throw-away comment which had made me prick up my ears. That happiness word had come up again: I had a hunch it had to matter. Might it be a missing piece of the jigsaw? Could it be connected in some way to being really productive at work? That hunch had to be worth pursuing.

In talking to a colleague and asking her what she thought, I decided that the only way to find out would be by taking a good long look at the research literature.

I spent three days in one of the only libraries in the world with a copy of almost every single book ever printed. The Bodleian Library in Oxford. With a degree and a sponsor anyone can work there after signing a declaration promising not to light a fire amongst other things. Biking there takes me past the honey-colored stone colleges with their manicured lawns and rose-beds, over the cobbles and down tiny lanes. Walking in through the massive wooden gates from bright sunlight to the dark book-filled shelves always makes me blink. I love the fusty smell and old-fashioned atmosphere: very little other than a stray mobile phone and occasionally whispering student ruffles the quiet calm.

Hunting about I found lots of studies with fascinating data about the effects of general happiness in the workplace. But a definition, a fully blown investigation of the effects, a theory and a means of measuring and managing it just didn't exist. Nor had anyone shown that a happy employee was a productive one too. In fact it seemed to be a concept that was deeply out of fashion.

There was only one thing for it: getting serious about happiness would mean working it out from the ground up.

And a lot of hard graft.

First of All, Focus Groups ...

The first priority was to try to find out what the components of happiness at work were. I quickly realized that if my colleagues and I were going to undertake such a massive task we needed to do this really well. That meant working to robust and rigorous academic research standards and in such a way that when scrutinized or challenged, we'd be on solid ground. I'd spent some time looking at psychological research methodology: it was time to dig out the books and review them all.

The literature was fragmented and piecemeal; it was unclear what the theoretical background was, how to join things together, or even how to identify a starting point. First principles at iOpener include "when in doubt, ask other people." And start at the bottom. If you want to know what's good or bad in any organization, you don't begin at the top where the view is often sunnier. Smelling the coffee means talking to receptionists, people who work in admin, the post room, or the "back office." Doing that in detail would involve focus groups, and lots of them.

Working in a small team, three of us put together a protocol which consisted of questions, exercises, and precise statements, so that what participants say isn't influenced by the person leading the session. The data collection began. I sat in to watch the first focus group, forcing myself to be quiet in a corner: I knew that my eagerness and enthusiasm would not be helpful. And it was gripping to watch. It was clear that while no-one had ever thought about what happiness at work was, everyone was intrigued. In fact it was almost impossible to stop conversations once they'd started: a group of British lawyers were the most garrulous.

After each focus group there was the painful task of typing up all flip charts and audio tapes to extract the information and gather the key themes.

And the results were fascinating for two reasons.

Firstly, people found it hard to articulate what made them happy at work. They knew exactly what made them unhappy and tended to home in fast on what was wrong, rather than on what was right. Which just showed that what's broken is always more obvious than what works.

Secondly, we started to see that there were some really big questions associated with this. For example, what is the difference between feeling and being happy at work? Was unhappiness the opposite of happiness? Was a person more important than the culture or vice versa? How could we account for individual differences? What were we missing or failing to tap into?

At that point we started to experience major doubts about what we were undertaking. This was immense. How on earth would we get to the bottom of it? But when you're climbing a mountain there's only one thing to do. Keep putting one foot in front of another. Focus on the detail and the rest will fall into place. Which is what we did until we had data from 14 focus groups: then we decided we'd done enough. It was time to think about what next.

... Then One-to-One Interviews

Once we'd collated everything we identified major themes which we decided to cross-check by doing one-to-one interviews. We needed to see if people had different responses in another setting. So once more it was develop a protocol, test, refine and then use it.

At that point we were facing the problem that all researchers face: where to find people to take part. A regular supply of undergraduate students is a marvelous research aid and available to any academic. But the drawback with students is that most of them haven't spent any considerable time at work. Which means that they aren't really representative of an average employee. We wanted to develop research which was rooted in the real working world so we identified 67 leaders, managers, and employees to help push the project further.

Once we'd confirmed our previous themes in these one-to-one interviews, we were able to put 33 of them into a questionnaire. The aim was to ask people how happy they were at work, and get them to rate their actual job against their ideal job. Doing this would help us really understand what contributed to overall happiness at work.

That stage involved asking 418 executives, many of whom were doing part-time MBA programs at London Business School and Oxford Business School, if they would help us with our research. Executive MBA students are generally aged around 36, are in full-time jobs, and squeeze their degrees in at weekends and during holidays. And they are highly international and mobile as a group. We wanted to test them because that way we knew our research would work in as wide a context as possible. And we'd get really interesting data.

Finally, we had something that felt solid.

And Hey Presto, the First Set of Findings

The top five reported items that people wanted in an ideal job were, in ranked order, to:

1. Progress in their careers.
2. Be good at their jobs.
3. Do something worthwhile.
4. Have control over what they did.
5. Have a boss they can respect.

But what did it all mean?

Standing back and just eyeballing this you can see that the great news is that the world doesn't divide into the workers and the shirkers. Most people want a feeling of getting somewhere at work because they're good at what they do.

Moreover, a sense of purpose matters. Almost everyone I've interviewed at any point in this research has told me that they want to add to or enhance something bigger than just themselves. So it's easy to see how making progress in your career, being good at your job, and doing something worthwhile walk hand-in-hand.

What about control? Well if you've ever read your horoscope you're probably curious about what life might have in store for you. Time and again psychological research over 40 years has shown how important a topic control is.

I was intrigued by number 5 – having a boss you can respect. I thought that *being* respected by your boss would be more important. But if you respect your boss, you're happy to make an effort on his or her behalf. And as a result you probably feel that, in turn, he or she will help you progress your career. Because you perceive you have something to learn from your boss, and your boss therefore has something of real value to you.

The gender differences we found made me smile wryly: men were more interested in status and didn't mind doing a lot of overtime, while women didn't care about status but did want lunch breaks. *Lunch breaks.* As an 80s feminist who started work in the days of big hair, big shoulders, and big drinks, I'm part of a group of women who thought we could have and do it all. But when you ask women why lunch breaks, it's obvious – that's when all the other non-work responsibilities get managed.

Now we started to trial our questionnaire with our coaching clients. It was incredibly exciting to use our own research-based instrument which instantly allowed us to gauge how happy coachees were at work and where their personal gaps lay. The analysis was simple, which should have been a warning sign. It was too simple.

Here's why.

The Cold Hard Truth

Firstly, the data didn't cluster into any overall factors. For anyone who isn't a statistician, a factor consists of a group of questions which clump together under a common theme. What we had was just a meaningless mess. Every single chart or graph we looked at was an unintelligible mass of dots which were unrelated to the 1–10 happiness scale we'd used. In other words, we'd got some answers, but answers to the wrong questions. We should have been heading down a different track.

Secondly, we hadn't established whether we were really testing happiness at work. Frankly we could have been assessing anything – contentment, commitment, satisfaction, engagement – we simply didn't know. Because we didn't have a definition, a proven way of testing happiness, a theory or any real outcomes.

Thirdly, we hadn't any way of assessing happiness at work and connecting it to performance.

And finally, we didn't really have anything that was earth-shatteringly new.

By now I was working with two incredibly capable business partners, Philippa Chapman and Julia Lindsay. When Julia first looked at the data we'd collected she responded with a characteristic down-to-earth "no shit Sherlock." Which shortly afterwards became our mantra.

We'd clearly arrived at a major crossroads and had a difficult choice to make. The world around us didn't exactly support what we were doing; many people said things like, "It's great but can't you call it something else?" Some made more cynical remarks such as, "a bunch of women talking about happiness at work?" and simply raised an eyebrow or two. A few commented, "I couldn't even say the word 'happiness' to my executive team." And "that word really sticks in my throat." Meanwhile, the economic climate was still booming and money seemed to be driving everything. Were we totally out of step with the times?

We needed to reassess what we were doing and decide what to do. Cutting our losses seemed like the best possible decision we could come to.

Lose It or Use It

Sitting round our boardroom table fortified with coffee and croissants on a gorgeous spring day, we had a critical meeting. We argued the pros and cons and thought through all the "what ifs." What if we continued for another year and still had nothing to really show for it? What if we did find amazing results but the business world wouldn't take it seriously anyway? What if someone else beat us to it? But on the other hand, what if we could make this work? What if we could find the happiness–productivity link? What if we could create something really simple and practical too?

We had a difficult decision to make.

Philippa, Julia, and I all had to decide whether or not we really believed in what we were doing and if we did, whether we were capable of seeing it through. We had plenty of other commitments to clients and colleagues. And more than enough to keep all of us occupied twice over. But the thought of abandoning what we'd started seemed like a lost opportunity. One that we'd look back on and regret.

We simply had to keep going.

What we really needed was to plan our next steps carefully. Which included re-examining all the data we had, establishing some serious happiness measures, finding a way of linking happiness and productivity, developing and testing a theory, and building a diagnostic tool. And getting the right person to lead the research too. Elementary, my dear Watson. But enough to keep me awake at 3 a.m. in the morning, wondering what kind of voyage we'd embarked on.

Building the Next Steps

It quickly became clear that we needed to find someone much more experienced to help direct the research. Although Oxford is a small town it's full of big talent and Dr. Laurel Edmunds was interested in the role. She already had an interest in positive psychology and experience in developing the sort of diagnostic questionnaire we wanted to create. Most importantly, she was extremely clear about the next steps and how to go about them.

Laurel explained that developing a new questionnaire was like designing a building: there was both a science and an art to it. We'd need to plan what we did really carefully, test everything, and make sure that there'd be as little wasted effort as possible. But we'd keep having to craft and hone what we did.

And there were some vital elements to developing a questionnaire that we had to get right. Like our outcome measures.

Developing Outcome Measures

Measures are the proof of the pudding. You know that your recipe works when you have strong and reliable measures. It's all very well asking people if they are happy but you need to tie that to outcomes that matter. We thought through what that might be and decided that if you were happy at work you would:

- Work more discretionary hours.
- Take less sick leave.
- Stay longer in your job.

To test our assumptions we carried out two surveys on two different groups of 193 and 403 people respectively. And now we had some really serious data. We then divided the answers into five groups using a validated general happiness scale and, holding our breath, we looked to see what we'd got. This was a crucial and critical moment. If we couldn't tie the results to measures that mattered, it was the end of the research road for us.

Here's exactly what the numbers told us, in a table if you like numbers and a graph if you prefer a visual.

Table 2.1 Happiness and outcome measures

Groups 1 = low, 5 = high	Happiness rating 1–7	Staying in role	Discretionary hours	Days off sick
1	3.0–3.9	0–6 months	6.5 hours per week	5
2	4.0–4.9	6–12 months	6 hours per week	2
3	5.0–5.9	12 months	7 hours per week	2.5
4	6.0–6.9	18 months	7 hours per week	2
5	7	25 + months	8 hours per week	1.5

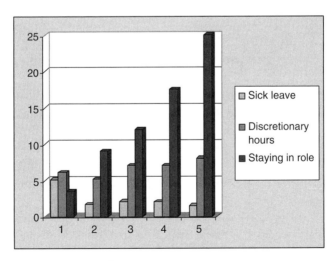

Figure 2.1 Happiness and outcome measures.

I breathed a huge sigh of relief: although it seems obvious that happier employees should show different effects from their unhappier colleagues, now we had the data to show it. We could easily see that they tended to do more overtime, take less time off sick, and stay longer in their jobs. It was time to celebrate and crack open a bottle of champagne. Although they weren't sophisticated, we had our first results which showed that happiness was associated with some tangible measures.

But we hadn't yet nailed productivity. We needed a way of assessing that too.

One weekend I was catching up with my reading and I came across an article in the *Wall Street Journal* about productivity. It was by Edmund S. Phelps, the Nobel Prize winner and Professor of Economics at Columbia. And it got me thinking. Gauging productivity would ideally be done by looking at output. But how do you assess knowledge workers' output? Involving other people would be ideal – but too complicated as everyone's output is different. We needed a simple self-assessed measure.

Then it came to me. If we could ask people what percentage of their time they were focused on their tasks, and link that to their rating for happiness at work, we'd have the happy–productive link. Best of all, it would be easy to test.

That was the next phase.

Launching the First iOpener People and Performance Questionnaire: The iPPQ

Now we had some clear outcome measures which told us we were on the right path, we were in a position to start to develop what was to be called the iOpener People and Performance Questionnaire (iPPQ).

Laurel had suggested that we review all our data to make sure we captured everything that had ever come up anywhere in any of the previous research. She was really pleased that we had done focus group work, one-to-one interviews, and had robust findings about ideal job perception. She told us that the process we'd followed was what was becoming best practice for capturing concepts that are difficult to define. This bottom-up approach means that the questionnaire is grounded in employees' reality rather than "expert" opinions of what that reality might be. And it means you start with content that has validity from the outset.

In short, we'd done a great job. But it was now time to assess exactly what we had.

In all we found we had 70 themes. To find out which topics mattered most we created a questionnaire and beefed up the demographic data too. Because we wanted to make sure we could investigate country, industry, and nationality differences as well as age and gender.

Then we had to pilot it. It's toe-curling to ask someone to complete 125 questions, it really is. Most people are bombarded with questionnaires. So why do yet another one? The only thing we could do was beg favors as we asked people to give up their valuable time to complete it. I've never begged so shamelessly. The first time I asked a group of about 50 international senior executives at London Business School, I felt cold sweat prickle in my armpits and heard a universal groan when one of them asked how many questions there were. But I was delighted to get 12 back. That's a terrific response rate.

To make it easier for all our associates we ran in-house sessions so that they could practice the "please do us a huge favor and thank you so much" technique to persuade people to participate.

It still took months to get 200 of them completed.

Now we were in a position to get to the nub of happiness at work. To see if the data analysis would show whether we had clear themes or factors. And to find out if the holy grail existed. Now was our moment of truth for the happiness–productivity link.

The 5Cs

Laurel crunched the numbers while we held our collective breath again. What we found has been further consolidated by over 3,000 respondents from 79 countries in both face-to-face and online viral campaigns.

Here's how it's structured.

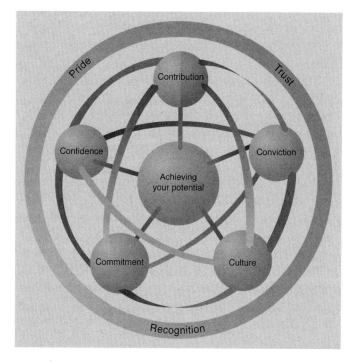

Figure 2.2   The structure of happiness at work. Copyright © iOpener Ltd.

There are five clear factors which we call the 5Cs that make up the core of the structure. Each of these 5Cs plays a major role in your happiness at work and is constructed in turn from a group of questions. Here's how they rank and what they mean:

- Contribution – is about the effort you make and your perception of it.
- Conviction – is about the motivation you have whatever your circumstances.
- Culture – is about how well you feel you fit at work.
- Commitment – is about the extent to which you are engaged with your work.
- Confidence – is about the sense of belief you have in yourself and your job.

Once you have them all there's another outer tier that consists of three important attributes. We know they really matter because they are connected to of the each of the 5Cs too.

They are Pride, Trust, and Recognition.

Pride and Trust in your organization work hand-in-hand. That means if you're proud of where you work, you'll also trust your workplace and its leaders. And vice versa. Pride in this case is an internal positive connection with what you're doing and its overall value to you here and now. Trust is about the faith you currently have in your organization.

Recognition works differently. Recognition is about having the effort you make noted and expressed by people you respect. It's about what you think your organization gives you in return for the work you've done. So it's more rooted in the past than Pride and Trust.

In summary, Pride and Trust are what you have in your workplace; Recognition is what you get back from it.

Finally, lying at the heart of all of this is achieving your potential. If that's what you think you're doing, you'll be happy at work.

But this still left us with the happiness–productivity connection to find.

And the Happiness–Productivity Link

Once we'd collected all the data we divided people into different groups ranging from most to least happy. Then we looked at the relationship between happiness and focus on task. It's strong. Incredibly strong. If people are more focused on what they're doing, they are being more productive.

Here's what the data looked like by happiness group and focus on task. You can see just how clear that relationship is in the table below or the graph if that's what you prefer.

Table 2.2 Happiness and its relationship to time on task

	Lowest happiness group	Lower happiness group	Middle happiness group	Higher happiness group	Highest happiness group	Significance: p
% of time on task at work	53%	63%	69%	73%	78%	.000

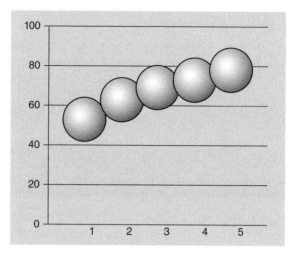

Figure 2.3 Happiness and time on task.

Let's just think about these astonishing numbers. They mean that people who are happiest at work are focusing on their work 78 percent of the time. People who are not are focusing on what they need to do 53 percent of the time, so half their day is without real aim or focus. That works out to a phenomenal 47 percent difference between the least happy and the most happy group in terms of productivity. That *p* or probability is .000 means that these results are extremely statistically significant – the kind of result that gets any statistician or psychologist smiling. Especially when dealing with something as potentially difficult to define as happiness at work.

Now let's think about the percentage difference between the two groups. The 25 percent difference between the top group and the bottom group. In concrete terms what that means is that the happiest employees are doing a whole day and a quarter's worth of effort more than your least happy colleagues – *per week*. Put another way, that's about 60 extra days a year. This is a phenomenal finding. Especially when you attach a cost to that like salary. Or sales. Or extra projects delivered. The cost of "low morale" is very big, very real, and it's quantifiable.

Now look at this from the other perspective. Think about 25 percent as part of the unhappiest employees' overall effort. That 25 percent represents just under half their *total* working effort. You don't want to work with an unhappy colleague or team member because they won't get enough done and you'll have to pick up the slack. Happier people are more productive and we're not the only people to have recently reached this conclusion.

When we've dug into the data we've also noticed some interesting gender differences. According to our findings women are on average 7 percent more on task than men. In other words, they seem to work an extra 16 days a year in terms of productivity – assuming a 40-hour week. And even when women are less happy at work, they still remain more on task than men.

Now take a look at the percentage of people who fall into each of the happiness categories (the following numbers account for 95 percent of our data – as most standard deviations do):

Table 2.3   Happiness groups by standard deviation

	Lowest happiness group	Lower happiness group	Middle happiness group	Higher happiness group	Highest happiness group
Total %	7%	23%	35%	26%	4%

If organizations started to think about how to attract, manage, and retain people by focusing on happiness at work, they'd immediately increase output. Because if everyone in the middle three groups moved up by just one group, there would be about a 5 percent increase in time on task. Five percent extra from 84 percent of a workforce works out as about a potential extra 12 days a year. Per person.

These results show why being happy at work matters on a daily basis. Not just to individuals but to employers too. Happiness isn't just a flaky, nice-to-have, feel-good aspiration. It's a need-to-have business fundamental because it has a massive impact on you and all your colleagues' output every single day.

When organizations are wondering how to account for every red cent, building happiness at work automatically increases financial value too. Focusing on financial value alone will never build psychological and social capital: focusing on both of these by targeting happiness at work will. The service–profit chain is now well known and taught all over the world. I'm absolutely certain that in a couple of years we'll be talking about the happiness–profit chain too.

For us these results were a fabulous vindication that we'd been on the right track all along.

Ten Top Findings That Really Matter

Here are our ten most important findings:

1. People who are happiest at work are 47 percent more productive than their least happy colleagues. In concrete yet conservative terms they are contributing a day and a quarter more than their least happy colleagues. Per week.

2. Those who are happiest at work take only 1.5 days off sick a year. In the UK and the USA the average employee takes 6 days off sick a year but in the public sector that ranges from 11 up to a staggering 20 days. We know that happiness is the cause of this because of the way we constructed our questionnaire – and because other researchers' findings corroborate this too. However you look at it, the happiness multiplier effect across any organization is enormous.

3. Employees in the top happiness group have 180 percent more energy than those who are most unhappy at work. Everyone wants to be around people with energy because it's so enthusing and motivating – as well as being a really good indicator of happiness at work.

4. When you are in the highest happiness group, you'll have 155 percent more happiness at work when compared to people in the lowest happiness group. And your overall happiness with life score will be 180 percent more too.

5. Engagement is something that many organizations measure and manage: the happiest employees report that they are 108 percent more engaged than their least happy colleagues. And they have 82 percent more job satisfaction too.

6. Without motivation nothing gets done: employees who are most happy are 50 percent more motivated than people who are least happy at work.

7. People in the top happiness category feel that they achieve their potential 40 percent more than unhappy employees. That's probably because they embrace goals 30 percent more and they're up for 27 percent more in terms of challenges too.

8. Happier employees report that they experience 28 percent more respect from their colleagues and 31 percent more from their bosses than their least happy colleagues.

9. People who are happier are 25 percent more effective and efficient than those who are least happy. And they have 25 percent more self-belief too.

10. Your working environment doesn't contribute to how happy you feel in your job. Shiny new offices, beautiful carpets, and high-tech offices, just like pay rises, cause a temporary hike in happiness, after which people will return to their usual level.

What about critics who think that these results were obtained because you might say one thing while thinking quite another, especially about your workplaces? Might you want to appear happier in case your boss finds out or could you just be kidding yourself?

Firstly, it's tough to fake your results when doing our questionnaire because the structure of happiness isn't that transparent. For example, the question "Do you get things done at work?" is not part of Contribution, which you might expect. In other words, it's hard to manipulate the outcome.

Secondly, other researchers have found that happiness is an area in which people don't fake good results to appear "better" than they are.

Finally, you are likely to be a good judge of sensitive issues about your working life. For example, if you're asked to assess how much time you've had off sick, you'll be pretty accurate about it. In short, do we think our findings are robust?

Absolutely.

Concluding the End of the Beginning

Although a research journey is never done, after four years we had defined what happiness at work was, analyzed the factors that it's made of, developed a model, built a robust and valid diagnostic questionnaire, got some fascinating findings, and gone through every process necessary to check our work. We knew that we were looking at the same concept whoever you were and wherever you worked because our research told us that – as do other researchers' findings. And by now we had the same amount of data as a large university study.

But what did that all mean? What were the five components all about? How do they work? And what can you do about them anyway? That's what you'll read about next.

Top take-aways for Chapter 2

- Building a questionnaire from the bottom up involved focus groups, one-to-one interviews, and lots of verification to develop a reliable and robust working instrument.
- Crunching the numbers showed us we had five really clear components that were important to happiness at work: Contribution, Conviction, Culture, Commitment, and Confidence.
- Recognizing that Pride, Trust, and Recognition were vital sub-themes of the 5Cs gave us an additional perspective to our findings.
- Achieving your potential lies at the heart of the happiness map.
- Proving that productivity was strongly associated with happiness at work was a huge and important win.

3

Contribution from the Inside-Out

Introduction to Contribution

Once we'd collected the data and started to look at it, we could see that Contribution was the most important of the five components that make up happiness at work. And Contribution says what it is on the tin: it's about what you put into your work. Now here's the great news for those of you who know you work hard. Hard work leads to happiness. We know that because the numbers tell us: people who contribute the most report that they are happiest at work. In fact we can see that they are contributing 25 percent more than their least happy colleagues.

Here's how that works in practice.

I was bored. So bored that every day I really struggled to stay awake despite copious cups of coffee. I was working in a summer vacation job managing a hot and airless shop that sold Victoriana in a fashionable part of London. While the contents – lace, materials, clothes, dolls, artifacts, and kitsch pictures – were fascinating, the customers were few and far between. There was only so much stock management and tidying up that I could do. The highlight of my entire job was when a tourist tried to buy the very unVictorian dress I was wearing. I needed to do more.

A few weeks later, I found myself on an archaeological dig. Because of the heat, we were up at 4 a.m. to start work half an hour later when the sun rose, finishing the day with supper, which we took turns to cook at sunset. The job was physically tough and very dirty. The only running water came through a hosepipe and we were living in army tents miles from anywhere. Our work involved moving rocks, heaving buckets of earth, sifting the contents, and occasionally finding precious treasures. And of course drawing and cataloguing everything. I can still strongly recall the immense thrill of finding a small, delicately carved amber bead that hadn't seen the light of day for 2,000 years.

Where was I happier working? Without doubt the dig. I loved the hard work, the learning, and the fellowship. I truly felt that I'd given my best effort to the progress and understanding of the site we were uncovering. In fact, I got so much out of it that I went back there the following two summers.

My experience reflects the fact that most of us are hard-wired to be industrious. You only have to look at a busy 3-year-old to understand that evolution designed us to want to acquire skills, to work, and to accomplish useful tasks in groups. Because doing this would mean you'd be much more likely to survive natural selection. Constructive and productive effort is gratifying in and of itself. That's why so many of our pastimes involve what others are paid to do. Lots of people love gardening, craftwork, or car, bike, and house maintenance, all of which involve intense work and effort.

But what are the pieces of the puzzle that means that happens?

Contribution: Inside-Out and Outside-In

"Happiness is a combination of the inner and the outer which have to be in balance. People want to do good for themselves and everyone around them and they want it back. If you can tap into that your success is guaranteed."

Dr. Iqbal Surve, doctor, social entrepreneur, CEO Sekunjalo Investments Ltd, Cape Town, South Africa

When we looked at all our statistics, we could see that there were eight critical elements that grouped tightly together under the heading Contribution. On investigating them more closely, we realized that these eight clustered into two groups. One group consisted of the elements you want from and within your working world; the other of elements your working world offers you.

Inside-Out
- Achieving your goals
- Having clear objectives
- Raising issues that are important to you
- Feeling secure in your job

Outside-In
- Being listened to
- Getting positive feedback
- Being respected by your boss
- Being appreciated at work

When you examine the contents of both groups, you can see that they flow from items that are more concrete to those that are more abstract. For example, achieving your goals or having clear objectives is more tangible, and therefore more actionable, than feeling secure in your job. And this is really useful and practical information: if you want to extend or develop your happiness at work, start to focus on things that are clear and doable first. Success here will mean you'll be ready to think about and develop some of the other more difficult elements later. Because people who are happiest at work have lots of all of them.

The rest of this chapter deals with how all these Inside-Out elements work; Chapter 4 will explore the Outside-In ones. Both stories are fantastically cohesive and really exciting because they are so simple, sensible, and practical. And you can do something about them.

Just like achieving your goals.

Achieving Your Goals

Achieving your goals is the first element of the first component. So you can imagine how much it matters to your overall work happiness. The happier you are at work, the more you'll achieve your goals: in fact, 30 percent more. In other words your Contribution will be much higher than many of your colleagues.

Regardless of what you do, work couldn't exist without goals. It's true, they're not sexy and I doubt that a goal-setting session is going to make your heart beat faster. But whatever your job, goals give you structure, focus, and direction. And they encourage you to develop your skills, use your talents, and work productively with others. Not to mention make you feel good. Doing something you set out to achieve gives most people a profound sense of satisfaction because you move from wanting something to having it. Plus you show yourself and others that you can make things happen – which will encourage you to extend yourself when setting your next goal. Achieving what you set out to do is hugely important in shaping your experience of the world.

"We have only three; they're simple and I articulate them ad nauseam. They are to launch and build sales in Europe, to get FDA approval, and to raise our last round of funds. Very, very clear and simple. Nor do they have 95 things underneath them.

You know you're off-piste if you can't make a link back to these goals. It's absolutely plain."

Dianne Blanco, CEO Orteq, London, UK

"When I was editing *The Financial Times* it was very clear what we were doing and I could see the tangible results of what we produced every day. It was a recipe for quite a lot of happiness and extraordinary pride. Then I moved to Lehman's which was a world where you measured success in moving the dial and influencing opinion over six months or a year.

But the most miserable experience of my entire professional life was between June and August 2008. I offered to go to New York because they really needed help managing their communications. What we should have been doing was explaining we had a strategy. But it just wasn't possible to reach Dick Fuld. People would only tell him what he wanted to hear: there was no information flow other than flattery and good news, however manufactured.

The pain of sitting in New York unable to do my job was immense. I realized that despite my knowledge, my contacts, and my experience, I was being prevented from contributing anything at all. My hands were absolutely tied. One day I went back to my apartment and concluded with considerable distress that the job was absolutely not doable. I signed my compromise agreement and the firm went bust the following Monday at 7 a.m."

Andrew Gowers, Head of External Relations, London Business School, ex-Head of Corporate Communications and Marketing, Lehman's, London, UK

That's why we've found goals are so closely connected with overcoming challenges, getting things done, and feeling in control of what you do. It's a truism worth repeating that goals lead to a lot of other practical outcomes. And they are closely connected with Recognition too: that's the reward you have for the achievements you deliver.

Own goals matter, in every sense of the phrase.

Some people set themselves big hairy goals, others are content to go for something smaller: what you want is entirely personal. This makes understanding goals hugely complex yet really interesting. But there is a huge body of research which shows that if this bit of your working life is right, a lot of the rest will fall into place.

But what is it about your goals that lead to the greatest happiness at work? Is it the speed of achievement, the quantity or the quality? Some goals are obviously more compelling than others – think of all those New Year's resolutions that turn to dust, often in a matter of days.

The goals that you'll work hardest to achieve are the ones you set yourself and that match with your interests, talents, and values. Then you'll work harder towards them because you'll want to invest more time and energy trying to get there. If they're yours, they're just more motivating. Lying at the heart of this means ensuring that your goals are aligned with what your organization not only wants but is in a position to offer you: the higher the compatibility between you both, the more you'll deliver. That means thinking through what you want and ensuring that it's possible given your organization's constraints. Otherwise you may find yourself feeling trapped.

Goal traps

Goal traps are like bear traps. You decide to go for it, construct your trap, and then wonder why on earth you went to the trouble. In the same way you can define a goal you want, go for it, and find it doesn't bring you the degree of satisfaction or happiness you were expecting. There are some good reasons why this can happen and they're worth understanding.

The goal's not mine

The first and most common goal trap lies in having a big goal that isn't intrinsically motivating. You just aren't that enthusiastic about it, probably because you've been landed with something that your boss, clients, or customers have dumped on you. If an organizational goal isn't connected to something you want or value, your heart won't be in delivering it.

On the other hand, intrinsic goals are ones which are personally connected to something that matters to you. You'll find them meaningful or satisfying because they allow you to learn. And they're often connected with what you choose to give and do not only for yourself but for others too.

More, more, more

A personal goal that has little genuine and lasting value in and of itself, like striving for more money, praise, or rewards, can cause problems. The big issue with this type of goal is working out when enough is enough because they are not ends in and of themselves. What's worse is that most of these goals depend on other people and what they choose to give to you, so they are much harder to control or influence.

I don't enjoy working towards it

Another goal trap lies in finding that you're good at stuff you don't like doing, so you lose touch with your real interests and values. What you're doing makes you feel like you're going through the motions so you might easily get side-tracked. Then you'll feel guilty about what you "ought to," "should," or "must" do. The more you do things you enjoy, the more you'll invest in the task.

I didn't know what I was getting into

When you chose a goal, you might have chosen it without fully realizing what the consequences of those choices would be. For example, you might have decided you wanted to be a lawyer without realizing just how much administrative work it involves. You find yourself fully qualified and facing mountains of bureaucracy, now depressed by the reality of your choice. Or perhaps you are trapped by a project or job that is much harder than anyone could have anticipated. Or economic circumstances may mean that what should have been an easy challenge has suddenly become very tough. Any of these might then leave you wondering, "What on earth was I thinking when I got into this?" That's a sign that you might have goals you need to readdress – as is feeling exhausted, having headaches, or getting frequent colds.

And I'm just waiting for it to all go wrong
Finally, goals that you work towards positively, like taking on a new initiative or getting a promotion, are much more motivational than goals which involve trying to avoid something or stop it happening.

Here's how this works.

In one organization where I was consulting, I sat in on several management team meetings. The boss was prone to temper tantrums: everyone's key objective was not to be the object of his wrath. He conducted every meeting – literally – from the front right-hand side of the room. That meant his team would rush into meetings to grab the space under his elbow despite the occasional gobbets of spit that landed nearby. Whoever sat right next to him was least likely to draw his fire. At the end of every meeting there were hugs for the demolished and relief from those still standing.

The entire focus of everyone's energy was staying out of the firing line and avoiding something negative. The problem with this was that nothing got done: no-one wanted to take a risk just in case. So the massive problems the team faced simply went unaddressed.

Building good goals and achieving them

"Goals are nothing more than what you want to accomplish. The vision, which should be aspirational, gets everyone pointing at the goals, while the strategy tells you how. The objectives are how you articulate in a simple way what you're trying to achieve."

William Schultz, President and CEO Coca-Cola Bottlers, Makati City, The Philippines

Determining your goals is one of the most important things you and your organization does. If goals are too easy or too difficult, they lead to reduced productivity because they're just not motivational. You might be surprised by this but it's much tougher to have too few goals than too many. Sirota Consulting did a study in 2005 on over 800,000 employees and found that people who say that they are "snowed under" were happier in their jobs than people who didn't have enough to do. It's only difficult goals that increase happiness over time: easy ones just don't make you feel good.

Of course it's true that impossible goals aren't motivating and can easily lead people to do much less than they would otherwise have achieved. That's why the concept of "stretched goals" – when, for example, employees are asked to deliver a "110 percent" target – works better in theory than it does in practice.

What everyone wants is variety. Constantly doing the same thing gets boring, especially if you have to do it over a long period of time. A little boredom goes a long way and you should pay attention to that: it's your brain telling you to change what you're doing. But at the other end of the spectrum, extreme variety is debilitating because you have to keep switching attention. What really matters is calibrating it so that you get the right amount for you. You'll know that it's right when you have a strong sense of personal satisfaction when you reflect on what you're doing or what you've done.

So how else can you make sure that your goals are enjoyable and that you then can break them into achievable objectives? Other than building goals that avoid the traps already mentioned, here are an additional ten things to bear in mind to help you develop and work towards goals that build your happiness at work. All of them are culled from years of coaching and consulting practice.

> "Goals change as you get older. When I was younger my goals were intellectual ones, to understand the way the world worked; to think how things work differently and how things happened in the past.
>
> Now I think more about the community: being an academic is being part of a community and to see the younger generation coming through is really fantastic. I put much more effort into nurturing students and engendering or increasing their enthusiasm; that gives me a lot of satisfaction."
>
> Chris Gosden, Professor of European Archaeology, Oxford University, UK

> "It's not an easy life but the best thing in farming is the spring when you're lambing. Even if you've been up a lot in the night, there's nothing better than going for a stroll around to see the ewes with their lambs out in a field on a Sunday morning. And you think 'I've achieved that.'
>
> In the summer you see them growing up and come autumn time you select lambs to sell and then you keep some on for the following year to breed. Then it's very satisfying to look back at what you've achieved through the last six months."
>
> David Davis, hill farmer, Gwenddwr, Wales

Ten top tips for work goals

1. Make sure your goals are realistic and appropriate for you. Lack of realism about what's possible right now and what you're capable of in the short term is a big predictor of depression.

2. Ensure you have the right personal resources. These can include making the most of your experience, social network, tools, and knowledge. You are most likely to achieve a goal that is linked to your strongest resources; if you don't have those resources, change the goal.

"I've recently been volunteering and that experience has taught me something which I'd never really thought of before.

I was asked to handle this tremendous backlog but the reason things are on the back-burner is because they are not important, no matter how thin resources are. If they'd truly mattered someone would have been assigned to get them done.

Because it's not important to them it's certainly not important to me."

Marilyn Nissenson, author, TV producer, and journalist, New York, NY, USA

3. Develop appropriate strategies for accessing the resources you need. Doing the Lotto as a sure-fire way of funding your new business idea isn't an appropriate strategy.

4. Make your goals concrete rather than abstract. "I want to be better" is a noble thought but won't get you anywhere – it's simply too abstract. Keep asking yourself, "What does that mean?" until you have something that is more concrete and that can be further broken into actionable objectives.

5. Put off other distractions. Your time and energy are finite and you'll only be able to achieve important goals if don't do other things. You need to stop doing some things to achieve what matters most.

"When you do something for yourself and for others, that's what I call a diamond goal.

There are three levels to diamond goal-setting. You get to those by being mindful and first asking 'How can I positively impact all the people I would ordinarily impact?' And then you differentiate between how you can first help, then benefit, and finally truly benefit others on the way. It's in asking these questions, especially at the 'benefitting' and the 'truly benefitting' level, where you'll get the long-lasting satisfaction you won't otherwise find."

Alan Bywaters, founder of the Mindful Capitalist Consultancy, explorer, and author, London, UK

6. Make a consistent effort. Your actions and intentions need to be aligned, so it's no good doing bursts of effort then stopping. The tortoise beats the hare every time.

7. Find the right environment to realize your goals in: planning a high-risk project won't happen in a low-risk culture and will just make you frustrated.

8. Check that you don't have conflicting goals. These can cause huge internal conflict and sometimes lead to becoming totally stuck, stressed, and depressed.

9. Remember that to achieve anything meaningful which results in long-lasting satisfaction and happiness takes time, energy, and effort. Expending any of these may not always feel good in the short term.

10. The journey towards your goal often matters more than achieving the goal itself. I'm sure you'll have experienced a low when you were expecting a high once you'd actually done something you'd worked towards for a long time. That's because what everyone truly values – but forgets – is the struggle you mastered on the way.

Just remember that the harder the goal, the harder will be the next goal you'll strive for. That's how you'll not only develop your potential and increase your levels of happiness in the process, but also contribute greatly to your organization. Although it's cheesy, it's true: success breeds success, so it's worth checking in frequently with what you want to achieve and how you think you're going about it. Which leads into thinking about your objectives.

> "I had one guy in my team who initially drove me crazy. I couldn't find what made him tick. He'd cross his arms and say that he should be promoted. I said this isn't about age it's about performance. If you want promotion let's take action.
>
> I gave him a project to run and I said I wanted a weekly project update and to be copied in on his communications. It really galvanized him and it was weird for me because I was thinking, 'Why did I have to be this task-master and tell you every step of the way?' But he took control of it and was then superb. He worked harder than I could ever have imagined. He had his promotion in mind and everything flowed off the back of that."
>
> Senior executive female banker, London, UK

Having Clear Objectives

Goals and objectives are, of course, closely and inextricably linked. But lots of people get the two confused. Here's the difference. Goals are the big things you set out to achieve in your working life, like landing a promotion, starting a new business venture, changing jobs, or being perceived in a certain light. They are a concrete expression of your purpose, therefore they often represent the internal yardstick by which you judge yourself.

Objectives, on the other hand, are the steps you take on the way to achieving those goals. They tend to be more tangible, measurable, and short term than goals so they usually take less time to achieve. But interestingly, objectives can lead to goals too. Taking on a clear objective then realizing that there's a bigger objective behind what you're doing can push you to adopting different goals and moving in a whole new direction. That means objectives work in two ways: from the top down as steps on your way to something bigger, or from the bottom up as your awareness expands.

"I had 30 grand's worth of debt, our first child on the way, and we were renting from my parents. My wife came home and said, 'I've pledged $5,000 to the Hunger Project.' And she said, 'You should come and see them too.' I was, 'Yeah, I'm going to come and see them alright, don't worry about that.' They were working through empowerment, getting people to share a vision and make everyone completely self-sufficient. Afterwards I was prepared to fulfill the $5,000 pledge. But Lolita, the woman running it, said, 'Bill, I know you're after bigger things than this: I want you to pledge $50,000 – and I know you don't have it.'

I said, 'Lolita, I'd love to but it would be patently insane.' And she said, 'Bill, here's the question. Who would you have to become to make that pledge without pain?' And I rocked back on my heels because I realized I'd have to be completely different to do that. I'd have to be pretty damn cool – and that would be cool. So I went about that and I actually gave $100,000 at the end of that first year and never looked back.

So when I look at anything I want to do, the first question I ask is, 'Is it going to empower someone?' – then I'm interested."

Bill Liao, co-founder Xing, founder Neo, parallel entrepreneur, Winterthur, Switzerland

Objectives may often be things that feel painful at the start because they have clear implications for the amount of effort you'll have to make to achieve them. For example, if your goal was to become a senior executive, your objectives might include doing an Executive MBA, expanding your personal network inside and outside work, getting an international assignment, delivering some highly visible projects, and finding a mentor to help you.

So you can see that an objective involves activities that are solid and measurable. And they can be further broken down into the tasks you have to do to deliver that objective. Those tasks are easily identified because they have clear start and end points. Now here's a difficult issue. Some of those tasks may actively make you unhappy. For example, getting an Executive MBA might involve taking subjects that you aren't at all enthusiastic about: let's say microeconomics is one of them. To pass, you have to devote lots of late nights to understanding your case studies and doing several tough assignments. To persevere, you'll need to keep your overall objective or goal at the front of your mind.

For example, when I started working as a consultant in Belgium 15 years ago, I had to complete quarterly tax returns – in Flemish. Though I'm numerate, numbers don't light any fire for me. But I was determined that after my first quarter, I'd deliver the tax return myself. My goal was to build a successful practice; one of my objectives was to understand that practice from the bottom up.

The task took me two days with my receipts and invoices sorted into piles, a new spreadsheet open, a Flemish–English dictionary, a ministry guide, and a book on double-entry book-keeping. It was hard work and I simply couldn't get my accounts to balance: I kept getting that darn squiggly line on my screen.

Working late into the night I reminded myself why I was doing this. The following day I'd arranged to see an accountant to get everything checked. Sitting over the other side of his desk, waiting in silence for his comments. was nail-biting. When he finally peered over his glasses and said "well done," I had a wonderful feel-good glow of achievement and satisfaction for having done what I'd found to be an excruciating task that took me closer to my objective: understanding the practice I was setting up.

One of the ways you maximize your Contribution is by achieving your goals and objectives. That requires staying focused, getting help, thinking through the consequences of actions, and anticipating road blocks. And you're much more likely to do that when you feel able to raise issues that are important to you.

"I started writing when I was an RAF pilot based in the Falklands. We couldn't fly and I was getting grumpier and grumpier. Finally my navigator said, 'For goodness' sake, Mark, do something useful; write a book, or something.' I said, 'I'll write the opening few pages, if you'll read them and tell me what you think.'

I've now written 11 books: and they've been translated into quite a few languages. I've always had a clear vision in my mind of what I wanted to write and who my readers would be. I write for 6 hours a day and aim for 2,000 words. If I achieve that I stop, if I don't achieve it, I know that I've put in the hours. I've found if you develop a smart target, you can't fail. Provided you look at your screen, you'll achieve it."

Mark Robson, children's author, Banbury, UK

A case study in Contribution: Part 1, Inside-Out

There was a lot at stake. Paul was the new internally appointed CEO of a prestigious global manufacturing business with over 30,000 employees. He'd been appointed with a mandate for change but he knew that the scope of what needed delivering was huge.

Although sales were increasing, the market was growing faster: the business was losing market share. Customers wanted more agile and flexible products but they weren't in development – and reliability was a major issue. Meanwhile, the huge portfolio of products was expensive to service and to maintain. It was clear to Paul that the organization's goals and objectives needed radical overhauling – and that customers needed to really be listened to if they weren't going to defect.

Continued

Paul knew he needed to move quickly so that despite upheaval, people would know what was going to happen, what the business goals were, and how that translated into business unit objectives. The complexity of the job was enormous, but first he had to get his board onside. Business as usual but change as never before. But would his key execs buy into his new strategy? What would they think of his proposal to "reorganize, realign, and resource" around a new vision and all that it entailed?

As he prepared for the all-important board meeting when he'd unveil his new strategy, Paul was keen to signal two issues clearly. Firstly, he wanted to show his respect and appreciation for the previous CEO. Secondly, Paul wanted to indicate that he would listen to the concerns that he knew would be raised. Meeting objectives for redundancies, costs, new targets, facility closures, and unprofitable products would be tough, as would the short-term uncertainty.

D-day came and it was time to present to the board. Paul was delighted when Mike, his COO who'd been a contender for the CEO role, offered him his full support. Paul immediately recognized that this helped bring everyone else onside too. And afterwards Mike came past his office to say how invigorated he was by the new business goals. He volunteered to manage the merger of two business units and make sure all the metrics reflected the new strategy as soon as possible. That way everyone would be clear about the tasks that would ensure they met their new objectives.

Paul knew that while the changes were being implemented people would feel at sea: it was normal. But he also knew that once all employees understood what needed to happen and could see that they were contributing more, a new enthusiasm would take over.

Raising Issues That Are Important to You

Raising issues matters because all the interesting and mentally challenging jobs in our interconnected workplaces involve collaborative project work. Which just can't be delivered by one person but need everyone's thoughts and insights for success. Anyone withholding comments or suggestions will have an impact on overall progress, productivity, and results.

When you raise issues that are important to you, you're improving, not criticizing, the status quo. Because you want to make things better. You want to achieve your goals, meet your objectives, or reorient what you're doing because you see problems ahead. So it's vital in today's project-driven workplace. As well as being an important element of Contribution, it shows that you're going beyond the day-to-day requirements of your job, which in turn indicates that you have strong psychological capital.

Raising issues that matter means that you know it's safe to take a risk, are more confident in what you do, and feel more engaged at work. Plus you'll be much more likely to help your colleagues; our numbers are really clear about all these effects. Finally on the research front, we can see that people who are happiest at work raise 35 percent more issues than those who aren't. Which means problems get sorted, glitches managed, and issues headed off because they are dealt with fast.

So what is raising issues all about? It involves sharing news and views to either encourage something new or discourage something old. You can be fairly sure that if people aren't raising these issues in your organization, their Contribution isn't as great as it could be and it's an indicator that they may not be happy in their jobs. Here is a general list of the types of conversations you ought to be having and hearing at work:

- Suggestions to improve process or practice.
- Ideas for speeding up work flow.
- Challenges to decisions because better choices are available.
- Questions about task allocation.
- Information exchange which may seem peripheral but affects performance.
- New lines of thinking and reasoning.

They can be pretty well characterized by listening out for the "what if …" statements.

"During my last polar expedition I was navigator and head of logistics. Amongst other things the radar that was measuring the depth of the ice went wrong, so we had to hand-drill to collect the data and that took time.

After 35 days I said to Pen, who was leading, 'Look, we're going to have to think about this. We can't do the science, the photography and get to the Pole. If we can't hit every target, something's got to go. We're here first and foremost for the science: the only thing that makes no difference is the Pole.'

I raised the issue when Pen had had a horrendous day because the science was hard and we were behind with the mileage. At lunchtime I said, 'You alright, Pen?' He said, 'No, not really.' So we all set off skiing, which was our way of coping. Pen said, 'I've been thinking about it. You were right. We have to let go of the Pole. I can't do it yet but I know it's right and I'll work it out.'

After the second day he'd decided. That made life so much easier but if I hadn't raised it, I wouldn't have been doing my job correctly."

Ann Daniels, polar explorer, Exeter, UK

"In my organization we deal with lots of unknowns, making judgment calls when we know relatively little. You have to create the conditions where you can have what I call 'hopes and fears' conversations. I make a big thing of that in every business I've gone into; it's no good 12 months down the line when someone who was in that earlier meeting says, 'Yeah, I always thought that might happen.' If you think about that writ large, it's an absolute killer.

If someone can put that thought on the table and get it out, we can all talk about it and assess its implications. It's not personal, it's not your issue because you raised it; it's for all of us to deal with. Doing this has stood me in really good, good stead."

Louise Makin, CEO BTG, London, UK

It's not moaning about hassles, complaining about colleagues, or whistleblowing. In other words, the issues raised will be present- and future-oriented about improving a collective outcome.

As always there's a big but. There are several things that make raising issues potentially tough. First and foremost is fear of the consequences, especially when status, politics, and relationships are involved. And then there's the tension you can create with your peers and not wanting to make a fool of yourself, or feeling that you're stepping out of line with the rest of the group. Finally, there's the time factor. It takes time to develop ideas and manage the consequences, especially if you know what you say will involve a lot of extra effort from many people.

Despite all this, people who do raise issues that matter to them find that they are happier at work because, as our data show, it helps them achieve their goals. That leads to higher status and respect within a group and is an indicator of leadership capability too. And it's connected with the next building block: feeling secure in your job. You clearly won't raise issues that matter to you if you don't feel secure in your role.

Feeling Secure in Your Job

The office was permanently buzzing and we were all keeping half an eye to see who'd come through the doors of the second floor. As a smaller business we'd "merged" with a larger organization. And the only conversations were about who was going to come out on top, who was going to leave, and who'd lose their jobs. I'm not talking about a conversation that lasted days, I'm talking about a conversation that went on for weeks. The time and energy spent on this was completely exhausting. Rumors abounded while work was abandoned.

My lovely colleague Polly, the most senior female director in the business, a woman given to sharp suits and big bows, was the first person to quit. She took me to one side. "Take my advice and start to look for something else."

Then two of the most profitable business units walked out to form a start-up.

Massive layoffs, restructuring, downsizing, right-sizing, and outsourcing are now the order of the day for many people. And will always be associated with a certain amount of dysfunctional behavior, pain, and misery while they're going on. But when no-one knows what functional looks like, workplaces are quickly destabilized. The result is always loss of focus and Contribution.

When we went through our merger, as employees of the smaller business we were totally preoccupied with gossip and worry. Who'd come out top? Who'd lose their job? What might our new boss want? What decisions should we make? Almost nothing got done because we felt so uncertain. The situation I experienced is reflected by our data: when you don't feel secure in your job you won't be on-task or contributing very much. And your levels of psychological capital are likely to be low because you'll be worrying about your future. At its worst, job insecurity can lead to burnout.

The factors that affect how secure we feel at work aren't only externally generated ones. There's a big internal one too: imposter syndrome. I once worked with a very successful finance director who was responsible for huge budgets and global teams. Looking every inch the dapper, bespoke-suited international businessman, he told me that he had a deep-seated fear that he wasn't good enough. He felt he was always on the point of being found out and didn't believe he could trust his judgments. Things were getting to be so bad he was frightened to delegate, and swamped by workload. Every two years he looked for a new job – in case anything he did in his current one caught up with him and that cycle was about to start again.

> "I've interviewed about 2,000 of the most successful people in the world and they have nothing in common except one thing. The one thing all have, every successful man or woman, is that they felt that they are not actually that great – but they got away with it. They hid it from the world. I think that's true of all of them, with the exception of Arnold Schwarzenegger. He didn't feel to me like he was hiding anything."
>
> Yair Lapid, journalist, author, and anchor, Tel Aviv, Israel

You wouldn't be normal if from time to time you didn't question how you dealt with some specific situations. Fear of failure and fear of not living up to what's required of you are common worries. But they are generally tied to one thing – not everything.

There are, however, two concrete elements that can help you feel more secure in your role or find new direction. The first is thinking through everything that your job needs you to deliver. New responsibilities make everyone wobble at the start; the important thing is not to ruminate on any small mistakes you make but to move on.

To make sure things go right, think about the skills, talents, knowledge, attributes, experience, and behaviors that are important for your success. Then look at the goals, objectives, and tasks you're expected to deliver. What's realistically possible and what's not? How will you or anyone else know you're successful? Map everything together and if you want to, discuss it with your boss, mentor, colleague, or friend. Doing this will help you plan and give you something concrete to check success against.

Secondly, no matter how bad things get, everyone wants to work with someone capable, upbeat, and positive. So make sure that this is how you talk about yourself and your work – most people don't want to hang around a doom-merchant, however bad things really are. This isn't about being dishonest or going into denial: it's about understanding the effect you have on others and being mindful of it.

Conclusion to the Four Inside-Out Elements

The inner-driven elements are the primary drivers of Contribution, which is why they are so important. Of course you don't work in a vacuum and you need to be clear that what you're doing is valuable to your organization. But it's important that you think through what you want so that what you do feels sustainable to you in the long term. Otherwise you run the risk of working to make others happy at work before you think about what you need to be happy yourself.

Top take-aways for Chapter 3

- Contribution is the most important component of happiness at work and is made up of two parts: one that operates Inside-Out and the other Outside-In. The elements in the Inside-Out group are: achieving your goals; having clear objectives; raising issues that are important to you; and feeling secure in your job.

- Creating your own goals that suit your personal needs and purposes is vital if you want to maximize Contribution.
- Breaking these goals into practical and concrete objectives will mean they're easier to achieve.
- Raising issues that matter to you will help you stay on track to achieve your goals and objectives. And indicates that there are good team relationships.
- Feeling secure in your job means that you'll be more focused on what you do and contribute more as a result.

4

Contribution from the Outside-In

Introduction

You don't work in a vacuum whatever your profession; other people are always involved in what you do. Even if you're an artist working alone in a studio, this seemingly solitary career will still involve buying materials, shipping exhibits, schmoozing customers, and negotiating with agents or gallery owners. So it's hardly surprising that a large chunk of Contribution consists of elements which depend on the relations and interactions you have with others. And they with you.

You know that the nature and outcome of those interactions can really affect your work. I'm sure a casual throw-away comment has had you steaming at some point in your career, while its opposite, unexpected praise, has left you purring.

When you look at the list of Outside-In elements, you can easily see how they maximize and maintain high psychological capital. And, because they happen in the context of a relationship, they'll build social capital too. They include:

- Being listened to.
- Receiving positive feedback.
- Getting respect from your boss.
- Feeling appreciated at work.

As you can see from this list, the first two are about behavior you want from others as you go about your work. The last two are about positive feelings that flow as a result of that work. Just like the Inside-Out group, they move from the more concrete and identifiable to the more indefinable and abstract.

Now you might look at this list and think that there's little you can do to influence any of these things. But you'd be wrong. Feelings and behaviors are catching and when you consistently model positive behavior, your co-workers and colleagues will gradually start to reflect the same back to you. It's a phenomenon known as the "ripple effect." There's clear research showing that negative behavior has a ripple effect to two degrees. So it's passed on and passed on again. But a *positive* ripple effect spreads even further – by up to three degrees. How much more pleasant would all organizations be if that ripple effect was working in a positive direction. And there'd be a very beneficial side-effect: there'd be a marked difference to everyone's Contribution.

"There's a huge burden of responsibility on leaders simply because people watch their every move, listen to their every word, look at their levels of energy. That gets copied and sets a maximum bar of how people perform. They won't perform better than that."

George Steyn, Managing Director, Pep Stores, Cape Town, South Africa

The thing that would make the biggest difference in this respect would be to listen more to others: and it would mean you get listened to in return.

Being Listened To

When we first looked at the data, we were incredulous. It seemed too mundane, too banal that listening should be so important to Contribution. Because it ranks really highly in the data: in fact, it comes in as the second most important statistic we have. And we're not alone in coming across this finding. On the ground in our consulting and coaching work, "he/she/they don't listen" is one of the most common complaints we hear. When we look at people who feel most and least listened to we can see that there's a 33 percent difference between the two groups. On the other hand, there isn't a gender difference: it's immensely important to both men and women equally. And here's the good news: it's easy to do, it's free, and it's linked to success.

"I was doing a master class playing a piece by Debussy with Ivry Gitlis; we only had an hour to get it together. When we first met we didn't hit it off: our interpretation of the music was so very different. But we were pushed out of our comfort zone into a corner because we had such a short time.

We just had to stop, talk, and listen to each other. Then it started to work and started to unfold. Listening pulled qualities out in both of us so we could do the dance together. It was incredibly exciting – and we gave an electrifying performance."

Charlotte Tomlinson, pianist, Oxford, UK

"When you listen, you signal a lot more than the act itself. You show that you're not arrogant but that you have humility by allowing someone to talk. Everyone wants to speak: by hearing and acknowledging what people say you build up a symbiotic relationship. And trust."

Christophe Cauvy, Director, McCann WorldGroup, London, UK

If you feel listened to, one thing you'll particularly do is raise issues that are important to you. That's something that comes out really strongly in the data. Moreover, it will mean that you'll think your workplace is fair, and you'll feel very engaged with what you do. That all has a knock-on effect on your Contribution, making a lovely virtuous circle.

The hitch is that although there's lots of anecdotal information about the importance of being listened to at work, there's little published psychological evidence about how listening works in practice and what the effects are. In fact, psychologists can't even agree what listening actually is despite more than 50 definitions and models which are all theoretical rather than practical. What everyone agrees is that listening is a fundamental skill at any level and essential to business success. So what's so difficult about it?

The complication with listening is that people use it to mean much more than the simple act that the word implies. From the literally hundreds of workshops we've run investigating what listening at work involves, why it matters, and how you do it, we know that it's much more complex than the mere allocation of air-time.

From a practical perspective, we've found that listening divides into three layers, which become progressively more complicated as you move through them.

Listening: bronze, silver, and gold standard

The first layer of listening is of course being silent, although that doesn't necessarily indicate that you're taking anything on board. But being quiet and hearing the words someone says is just the preliminary step, the bronze medal that you get when you open up to the words coming your way.

The second and more important layer of listening is getting to a shared understanding. Language is a notoriously poor way of doing that because everyone thinks that they are much better communicators than they really are; that they express themselves more clearly than they actually do; and they fail to remember that not everyone shares their knowledge. This layer of listening is not only listening but observing too – to make sure you're getting consistent messages. Interpreting eye contact and facial expression correctly is a big part of arriving at shared meaning because that's the difference between understanding that someone means what they say, or they don't. It's why it can be hard to deal with delicate subjects on the phone: it's harder to gauge whether someone means what they say and what their real intention is. But making the effort to arrive at a shared meaning ensures a silver award.

Gold is reserved for not only understanding the words, arriving at a shared meaning, but validating someone in the process too. It's the deepest layer of listening and is the one that connects you most to others. It involves giving someone 100 percent of your time and focus as you listen because doing that signals worth, appreciation, respect, and value. Doing this means you connect not only on a rational basis, but on an emotional basis too. To do this you have to use all your senses, being aware of the feelings that are evoked in you which arise in response to words that are used. And you need to hear what's unsaid too. When you do this – and it's very hard to do – that's when you are truly hearing someone else.

At this level listening is the shorthand for expressing something much deeper and more complicated than keeping quiet and letting someone else talk. When you're listened to at a gold standard, not only will your Contribution increase, you'll also feel more connected and respected. And this is how you deepen relationships and increase social capital.

So how come deep listening is so rare? Because most people think that they do it when in fact they don't. And that's easy to test. Next time you have a team meeting, while you're waiting for everyone to arrive, ask everyone how good a listener they think they are using any scale you like.

"Though I had contact lenses I normally didn't wear them in Gaza because I always thought I might get kidnapped. But on this particular day I had just been out of Gaza for a brief period and I was wearing these contact lenses. They had to go immediately. So I spent the whole kidnap very short-sighted.

It was grim, especially when they're chaining you up and they're telling you that they're thinking of killing you. You want to be able to look in the guy's eyes and see does he mean this? And I was never able to do that. You wanted to gauge the mood of the captors, what they were thinking, and it was hard to do that without being able to see clearly."
Alan Johnston, BBC reporter, ex-hostage, London, UK

"Hearing what's not said but is implied between people easily adds an additional 20 percent in terms of value. That subtlety has immense importance, especially in the kind of environments in which I work. You just don't get to real quality without it."
Paul House, Managing Director, SGS, Delhi, India

"There are two kinds of listening that are really important. There's listening to recreate, where you put yourself in the emotion of the person you are listening to and really recreate the circumstances they describe. Then there's listening to create, where you listen with a certain intention to have something happen. Both are incredibly powerful."
Bill Liao, co-founder Xing, founder Neo, parallel entrepreneur, Winterthur, Switzerland

Then ask them how listened to they all feel using the same scale. Nine times out of ten this exercise produces very different numbers. Any discrepancy tells you that listening could and should improve.

Here are some techniques and tests to help you.

Listening tools and techniques

Next time you're having a conversation about something that matters at work, simply ask yourself these four questions afterwards:

1. "Out of ten, how much did I truly and deeply listen to this person?"
2. "Out of ten, how much did I plan my answers and wait to jump in?"
3. "What emotional undertow did I detect?"
4. "How did I use that information?"

> "Recently in Washington, DC at 11 o'clock one night a sports surgeon did the classic napkin drawing. He drew something that would greatly improve our product – absolutely breakthrough technology.
>
> Ten minutes into it I said, 'I don't want to talk any more, I am so wowed by your idea that I want to call my chairman in the morning and make sure I haven't gone nuts. We've got to start working on this right away.'
>
> Now he brought this wonderful idea to us – a little start-up. He said, 'I've never seen such a small open company: you understand your product's not perfect but you listen to us. You hear us out.' There's five other places he could have taken this to but he didn't but he brought it to us."
>
> Dianne Blanco, CEO Orteq, London, UK

But the best thing you can do if you genuinely want to learn to listen at a deeper level is to mentally put yourself and your personal thought-stream on hold. That means you can try to tune into what's happening behind the words: doing that will mean you access a much richer seam of meaning.

There is a downside. Doing this requires effort and hard work, so it's very tiring – which leads to another personal test. If you're not tired after a conversation, you just aren't listening hard enough. And there'll be other things you notice the more you truly listen. For example, I become almost physically unaware because of the effort I have to make. To feel more "together" afterwards I need to walk, talk, eat, or drink something.

What's interesting about listening is that the more you do it, the more others will listen to you. If they know you're not a good listener, they'll be in a hurry to get their thoughts in first. Listening therefore begets listening. Which means it's much more than a skill: it's almost a way of being that really affects Contribution. And, of course, it's directly connected to positive feedback too.

Receiving Positive Feedback

Feedback. It's not a good word to use, so at iOpener we talk about feed-forward instead. This implies what's good that you need to keep for the future: feedback suggests something that didn't work in the past. Plus it puts people on the defensive. Doesn't your heart just sink when you hear the phrase, "can I give you a little feedback?" You know you've got it coming. Despite the importance of positive feedforward and its obvious connection to performance, there's a remarkably small body of research about it.

Here's what we know about the elements of positive feedforward. It:

- Is task-specific.
- Outlines both what you do and how you do it.
- Is accurate and upbeat.
- Focuses on things to keep and do more of.

Positive feedforward can really help clarify your role, improve productivity, make you feel good, validate your work, increase your sense of control, reduce negative feelings about organizational politics, increase motivation and the goals you set yourself, encourage more feedback seeking, and strengthen relationships.

And our data show that it's very closely connected to liking your job, feeling engaged in your work, wanting to use your skills, and helping your colleagues – in that order. In short, positive feedforward does almost everything except the washing-up. And you'll get more of it and it will be more positive the higher up the organization you are.

But badly handled and poorly given "feedback" has some really terrible effects. Our research shows that it's demotivating, perceived

"I went out to Pakistan 2–3 weeks after the earthquake to visit our camps where I met a group of women who were having a very difficult time; they'd lived in purdah and had never been exposed to so many people. Walking around was just not what they did.

We were doing water and sanitation and we had done so well because the female engineer had sat down with these women and had worked out what they wanted. We'd built a bathing area that had latrines, cubicles, a washing line, and water tank that were all enclosed. Seeing these women so overjoyed was a powerful and profound personal experience."

Barbara Stocking, CEO Oxfam, Oxford, UK

"My job is very demanding and if I'm having a hard day, I might send out a note to someone I've done some work for saying, 'I need some positive feedback; do you have any to share with me?' It's a technique I call 'going fishing.' That person will often reply with, 'Oh yes, I meant to tell you I thought what you did last week really fantastic.' And I think, 'That's great.'"

Patricia O'Hayer, VP Communications, Unilever, The Netherlands

to be manipulative, and has the opposite effect of that intended: it actually reduces overall performance. Extra investigation that we've done into feedback also shows that when it's neutral or poorly given it increases sick leave by an incredible 100 percent – while other studies have demonstrated that badly managed feedback is strongly associated with burnout and wanting to leave your job.

How does feedback really work? I first got really interested in reward systems doing standard Skinner box experiments with rats. The kind when you put a rat in a maze and, over half an hour, give it different rewards for running through to the end. The aim was to understand which reward system made them scuttle through as fast as possible.

First we taught our rats to run the maze. We did this by giving them a drop of sugared water once they got to the end, and found and pressed a lever. Once they'd got the hang of this, we changed the system so that they had to run the maze ten times before they got their sugar reward. Pretty quickly their efforts tailed off and we had to go back to the one-to-one scheme we'd started with to reinforce their behavior. Finally we tried one last schedule. We only gave them sugared water intermittently but unexpectedly. So they might get it twice in a row, then nothing for four runs, and then get it again on the sixth and then the third time after that.

The effect was astonishing to watch.

Once the rats worked out what was going on they increased their effort phenomenally. It was quite literally staggering to see. What's good becomes meaningless if it's too regular or if it feels too unavailable. Something that's intermittent works best.

Here's how that works at work. If someone doing a presentation gets asked a question and starts their answer with the comment "good question," the first time that statement feels genuine. The second time it's OK, but by the third time you know it's a meaningless utterance being used to buy time. And you've discounted the first two "good question" comments by then too. You'll also like this person less: you know they aren't genuine.

So why is positive feedback so rare when it's an easy tool that brings out the best in someone? Most of the leaders, managers, and employees I've talked to tell me that they rarely get good, clear, constructive, or useful feedforward and they're reluctant to give it too. Mostly because they are unsure how to. In fact, up to 70 percent of managers find talking about performance tough: if they find it hard, imagine how much more difficult it is for colleagues and other stakeholders. Everyone takes their cue from the top, so if they're bottling out, so will everyone else.

But if you get used to doing the good stuff, the harder issues become easier to manage: you'll be used to talking about what excellence looks like. And it's much easier to explore tricky issues like calibrating your feedforward and working out whether it's better to give it face to face, by phone, or in an email when you're talking about what works well.

So what works well? Here are three top tips for feedforward.

"I am a server in an Italian restaurant and the reason I love my job is that I love working with people and getting the tiny details right for them. I love to cook, I love food, and I love the restaurant business. I want to anticipate your needs before you even know what you are going to want: so I give you the same service as if you are in my house. I get a lot of people telling me, 'This is the best service I've ever had – I've never had a server give me this kind of service.' That compensates me for what I do and it gives me fulfillment."

Leah Dipofi, server, Carrabba's Italian Grill, Richmond, VA, USA

Three top tips for positive feedforward

- The best ratio of positive to negative is thought to be 3:1. That is three separate bits of positive feedback to one bit of negative. Ideally they're all given at different times so that the recipient is able to hear each and every message.
- By asking for feedforward yourself, you'll demonstrate that it matters to you too and you'll create a climate where it's easier to give it.
- When things go well, explore the personal factors that led to success, for example the time, effort, and energy that were put into a task. When things go badly, consider what wasn't working in the environment before investigating the individual stuff. The point isn't to offload blame but to open a

"Twenty years ago we started having discussions in our partnership group of peer and upwards feedback from junior staff. Partners would present their colleagues the feedback. It was a way of the group directing itself and what was unusual was the transparent sharing of that information.

It was one of the most powerful things I ever experienced – the degree to which everyone would be supportive and find constructive ways of helping that person deal with their issues. It was an incredibly strong and uniting way for people to improve themselves."

George Pappas, ex-Managing Partner, BCG, Australasia, Melbourne, Australia

"A number of years ago I was crushed by a lift. It was broken and I fell, ending up down the elevator shaft pinned against the concrete wall by the car. I practice a form of Buddhism which probably saved my life because I stayed calm. After the accident everything in my life stalled: the litigation, my career, my health.

One day it dawned on me that I lacked appreciation and I needed to start seeing not what I'd lost but what I had. It was as if one little feather made everything change. It really shifted my perspective and changed my life on so many different levels. I started actively looking for things to appreciate; now it goes to the core of how I see the world.

An important way I practice appreciation is through sending handwritten notes. About six years ago I read a book about their power and although it seemed old-fashioned, I started writing them as an appreciation experiment. I've probably written four to five thousand since then. I've found that there's a double benefit; if I'm in a bad mood and I write some cards, my mood is altered. It feels good to write them and it feels good to receive them. People are starving for appreciation and I see that it's connected to growth, expansion, and gratitude.

Plus it's a mindset; whatever you appreciate, appreciates."

Anita Brick, founder of the Encouragement Institute, Chicago, IL, USA

conversation. You'll find that this approach helps do just that – and it's more likely to get others then to consider their own shortcomings too.

But the main point to remember is that giving and receiving specific and positive feedforward about work is motivational. It feels good to do and good to get. And it increases Contribution: the recipient knows they're doing the right thing. Plus it adds to feeling appreciated at work.

Feeling Appreciated at Work

Feeling appreciated at work means being valued for who you are. The difference between it and positive feedback is that feedback is attached to what you do; Recognition takes place in public and is connected with what you do or who you are; but appreciation is related to what's special about you or your circumstances. And it consists of a comment or small act that signals to you that you are appreciated. Just like at the listening gold standard, it's something that has meaning beyond words and gestures which indicates you connect at a more profound level.

You can recognize appreciation because you'll feel a warm fuzzy afterglow when it's happened. For example, just after I'd written this, a box of smoothie drinks arrived from Innocent, the company that makes them. They were accompanied by a note wishing me good luck writing the rest of the book. Arriving as it did, completely out of the blue, it made me and the team feel terrific: thank you, Paula. When you're appreciated, you'll feel and do a host of additional and positive things in the short and long term. You'll feel more motivated and energized, help others more, set more challenging goals, want to stay longer in your job, and take less time off sick.

But appreciation doesn't just have a feel-good effect. It also increases output because you'll be more likely to repeat whatever it was that led to that appreciation. And the other side of the coin, feeling unappreciated, has effects that aren't merely neutral, they're negative because you actively withdraw your labor.

Appreciation also includes praise, but what exactly do you praise?

Psychologist Carol Dweck showed that when kids were praised for trying hard, they tried harder the next time. They wanted to learn from their mistakes and work out how to do things better. When they were praised for being clever, they tried less hard. Those kids decided that their brains – about which they can do nothing – were to blame, so they just gave up. It's praising the *effort* that matters. Because that enhances the effort that's made the next time round.

Finally, appreciation also includes the simple words "thank you" delivered in a heartfelt and genuine way. It always stuns me that it seems to be so hard to say; it's easy to remember, and has a wonderful impact on others' Contribution. And there are plenty of opportunities to try it in everyday working life.

Like this.

Waiting to interview Adam Parr, CEO of Williams Formula One team, I stood in the huge sunlit hall at their factory in the middle of rural England. Plum in the middle was the car Nigel Mansell had driven to victory in the 1992 World Championship. It looked scarily small to me but

"I really like this store because the managers appreciate us. They say things like, 'We're glad you're here.' You feel you're needed.

When I came to America from Ethiopia as a new immigrant it was hard for me to relate well with everyone. At the start I didn't mentally engage: I wouldn't feel the importance of that. Now I see things differently and I've learned to appreciate everyone and everything. It helps you do your best eight hours a day. So you could say that some good came out of civil war. I would never have thought that."

Habibo Hirsi, server, Au Bon Pain, Boston, MA, USA

"The Duke of Wellington was asked on his death bed, 'What do you wish you'd done more of?' And he said, 'Given more praise.' The iron duke, notorious disciplinarian. Everyone underestimates the effect of praise."

Edward Bonham Carter, CEO Jupiter Asset Management, London, UK

"I get huge appreciation from my team. It's my strongest source of energy and value and until recently I didn't understand how much I need them.

It's been very difficult recently and they have led me sometimes, pulled me up when I needed it, and reminded me that we did a lot of good stuff, that we have a lot to be proud of and that I directed that.

Sometimes we're all very focused on feeling appreciated from above

Continued

I could see it was a really beautiful piece of craftsmanship. Around it were five men making admiring noises. Nearby was an employee who was cleaning the marble floor. Adam came down from the executive suite and as he walked towards me, he stopped briefly and said, "Thank you, Liz, for keeping the floor so clean." She looked at him and gave a big smile. Her work was appreciated. Who wouldn't want to put in their best effort when their work was being so publicly acknowledged? And respected by the boss too. And as a bystander there was a knock-on effect on me too. I immediately liked him for noticing.

"One of the most difficult challenges I had was when I was CEO at Aer Lingus after 9/11. There were about 7,000 employees and we very quickly had to reduce that number by 35 percent: a lot of those people were friends of mine – I'd worked there for over 20 years.

After standing in front of them, telling them that this is what you're doing, the thing that really struck me was people saying to me, 'Why didn't you do something about this earlier? You knew there were issues, you should have done something sooner.' There was no point saying, 'Well, I wasn't CEO,' because I was senior management and they were right. There were issues that needed to be sorted out. And it really hit me that not addressing problems doesn't do anyone any favors. I've never seen a problem go away but I've seen businesses go away. As long as you accept that there are tough things you have to do, the sooner you address them, the easier the solution. People respect you more in the long run."

Willie Walsh, CEO British Airways, Heathrow, UK

Being Respected by Your Boss

In today's ever-changing and uncertain working world, people want something solid to fall back on. Which is why they value their boss's respect more than ever. That's clear from our data. And we can see that there's a 30 percent difference between people who report the least and the most respect. If you feel you have your boss's respect, you'll also know that you're respected by your colleagues too – and you'll respect everyone you work with in return. That is very clear from the data we've collected.

On top of that you'll want to raise issues that matter to you because this is a way to gain respect. In turn this is associated with having a fair ethos at work and relishing your job. Which of course is linked to wanting to stay. On a personal front, respect means that your Contribution is valued by someone who is important to you: after all, your boss is the person who probably has the greatest influence over your working life.

Although being respected by your boss is one of the most important elements for happiness at work, what and who deserves respect is determined by the culture you work in. Whatever is worthy of respect, one thing's sure. You absolutely know when you have it and when you don't because it's very easy to recognize. One of the ways of gauging it is with eye contact. Lots is generally good, none is bad. If you don't believe me, try looking at someone you've recently had a row with.

Meanwhile, if you're looking out for the facial expressions that denote respect, Paul Ekman, who has done decades of research into facial expressions, found that respect is shown with a slightly tilted head and wider eyes. So watch your boss's face as he or she talks to team members: you'll be able to tell who's flavor of the month, even if nothing explicit is said.

Respect matters for building the norms and practices of the team. All good working relationships depend on respect as it provides the glue which binds the team together. That glue will mean that you want to work – and work well – with your team members. No respect means no glue, and no glue means less productivity.

But where does respect start? It always starts with someone's behavior. That thirteenth-century proverb of William of Wykeham, "manners makyth man," is really true. Simple things indicate respect. Like acknowledging people when they arrive by standing up and greeting them appropriately, or saying thank you to the mail person who brings you your post and hello to the receptionists at the entrance.

What else does respect at work consist of? Here's a short list of reasons interviewees have given for respecting the people they work with:

- "She's open with the truth – no bull – absolutely straight. That's respect."
- "He showed me that he has the competence and talent to deserve my respect."
- "He respected me from the off – it was really powerful."
- "He has an amazing amount of connections and is brilliant at spotting future winners a mile off. He just knows who to go to and make things happen."
- "I can challenge my boss and he'll reconsider a decision. I really respect that."
- "He's the CEO. Naturally I respect him for his position."
- "He has an absolute and innate understanding for how people react: that's one of the reasons I respect him so much."
- "Respect isn't about who or what you know. It's about honoring someone for exactly who they are. She does that."

A case study in Contribution: Part 2, Inside-Out and Outside-In

Although the last 12 months had been tough and things were improving, it wasn't quite happening in the way that Paul had envisaged. He'd been diverted by events in China and some big customer issues. But right now Research and Development were bothering him more.

R&D was a merged business unit brought together under his "reorganize, realign, and resource" initiative. But they were floundering to deliver what was expected of them. Consisting of a key group of 7,000 employees around the world, their job was to analyze huge amounts of customer performance data; assess new and radical technologies; design two or three innovative and flexible solutions; and bring them to market within three years. Plus they had to find ways to make older products perform better.

These were some of the issues:

- People didn't feel secure in their jobs. Redundancies, job swaps, new hires, and two more mini-reorganizations had created huge uncertainty. It was all made a lot worse when the head of finance had used an "updated" but incorrect organizational chart, which omitted a key member of the R&D management team.
- The R&D employees were feeling under-appreciated, under-respected, and under pressure in comparison to other business units.
- They didn't know what feedback they should get from within the new organization to know whether they were on track. They knew that they needed to realign their goals and objectives but weren't sure how to go about this.

The R&D management team decided to implement a two-stage process. Firstly, key meetings, coaching, and facilitated sessions started to take place regularly both inside R&D and with important stakeholders. This helped revise internal goals and realign roles and responsibilities.

As direction became clearer, so feelings around job security became stronger. Increased feedback meant more communication, which built respect and feelings of appreciation.

Continued

To ensure this cascaded through R&D, a cross-functional project team co-opted experts; developed an internal outreach program; asked for extra development and mentoring; organized a series of customer and stakeholder visits and workshops; and developed a wiki site which took out layers of reporting complexity and information sharing. All this had a big effect on overall Contribution and within 18 months a new product had been designed, developed, and was ready to go to market.

In short you'll be respected for how you behave, the status you have, and what and who you know. Of course there are big cultural issues too which our findings have clearly thrown up. If you come from a high-respect culture, it will obviously be more important to you.

But what we have noticed is that regardless of where you come from and where you work, respect from your boss creates its own positive virtuous circle. The more you're respected by your boss, the happier you are at work, and the more intercollegiate respect there'll be too. And those findings are significant.

Concluding the Outside-In Elements

Being listened to, getting positive feedforward, being respected by your boss and appreciated by your colleagues all have a big impact on your happiness at work. And it may feel as if a lot of these are beyond your direct control. But you can decide that even if you don't get enough of them, you can give them to others. Because feelings and behaviors are catching: when you model positive behaviors and moods you'd like in return, your co-workers and colleagues should notice and respond similarly. That way you'll decrease conflict, improve cooperation, and increase performance too.

In the same vein, what you don't want to do is lots of bitching and moaning about your ghastly boss or awful colleagues to other people: it will only antagonize others and make you feel worse in the long run.

Finally, think about telling people you work closely with what works best for you in relation to these four elements. That way you'll contribute your best, rather than snap because they hit a nerve and you deliver your worst. Most people would like to know what makes you tick and tick better at work, in short, what makes you happier, because it makes their job easier. And when you position what you want positively, it isn't threatening, it's helpful and respectful. Guesswork is much harder, and it's no fun either.

Concluding Contribution

Contribution is the most important of all the five components. So it's the most complex, consisting of both Outside-In and Inside-Out elements that interact with and affect each other. For example, if you don't feel respected or appreciated your ability to achieve your goals will be affected; if you don't feel listened to, you won't voice issues that matter to you. Self-awareness will help you to recognize what's happening, focus on the elements you'd like to develop, and understand why you might feel the way you do.

Almost every manager and leader I've ever met worries about how to hit targets and do more for less. Whatever your position wherever you work, now you know how to make that happen.

Top take-aways for Chapter 4

- Contribution's Outside-In elements consist of being listened to, getting positive feedback, being respected by your boss, and feeling appreciated at work.
- Being listened to is the most important element in the Outside-In group. It's fundamental to your happiness at work and productivity too. Deep listening involves really connecting with someone.
- Getting positive feedforward really builds Contribution: neutral or negative feedback that's poorly given is seen as manipulative and increases sick leave by 100 percent.
- Feeling appreciated at work means being validated for who you are and what you bring, as well as receiving thanks for what you do.
- Being respected by your boss indicates three-way respect: from your boss to you, from you to your boss, and between your team members as well.

5

Conviction

Introduction to Conviction

Chapters 3 and 4 dealt with Contribution – or what you do and the things that affect your work. Conviction is the engine that means you deliver come what may; it's what keeps your Contribution on course when things are going well and means you stall when they're not. Which explains why, when things are going badly, you might feel you have no oomph. We know Conviction is really important to feeling happy at work because it comes in second place just behind Contribution.

Here's what it's made up of:

* Being motivated at work.
* Believing that you are effective and efficient.
* Feeling resilient when times are tough.
* Perceiving that your work has a positive impact on the world.

You can see that these items seem to have a logical kind of snowball effect, each subsequent idea evolving from the previous one, culminating in something really optimistic. Your impact on the world. And there's an emphasis too on what you feel right here and now. That's another reason why Conviction is such an important factor. It has a big effect on your psychological capital: that's why it's key to know what the elements are and how to manage them.

We can see from our findings that Conviction is strongly related to believing that your job fits your initial expectations and thinking that you are fulfilling your potential. But lying at the heart of Conviction is motivation.

Being Motivated

When I was working in Brussels, my boss at the time asked me to write an urgent White Paper for the European Commission on the state of the venture economy in Europe. Hugely motivated to take on a new task, I looked up other White Papers our organization had written. I outlined the contents, the data, potential interviewees and case studies, we agreed, and off I went. Every couple of days I'd email an update and send him chunks of work to check I was on track. Hearing nothing, I assumed that what I was doing was OK. After two weeks of working long hours to get it done, pleased with the results, I printed it out and gave it to him to read. When I came in the next day expecting to have to make a few changes, William told me that he hadn't gone home that night but had instead rewritten my entire report.

I couldn't bring myself to read beyond the first page. I asked what he hadn't liked but was brushed aside with, "Now's not the right time." I never found out what he didn't like but I don't believe that I ever truly put myself out for him 100 percent again.

Motivation allows you to get on with your job because you feel consistently competent and capable. Looked at from the opposite perspective, the more you're demotivated, the less interest you show in your job, the less value you find in your work, and the less effort you make too. Then you feel less competent and can easily fall into a downward spiral that further reduces your motivation.

Our numbers prove it.

We've found that people who are least happy at work are about 50 percent less motivated and 50 percent less productive than their most happy colleagues. That has an immense effect on Contribution: when you're demotivated you just don't set the bar as high as you could or achieve as much as you can. That's not good for you or your employers. But what exactly is this magic stuff?

> "To be a good lawyer in the kinds of areas I work in you really have to want to win. Winning has to be important. How you play the game isn't important in a lawyer. You have to really want to win to be able to persuade a third party, whether it's a judge or jury, that your client's cause is right. That means it's got to hurt when you lose. I know nobody who's good at anything who has not tasted defeat and more than once.
>
> Something else that spurs me on is reputation. If you've been doing things for a while you don't want people to think, 'Gee, it's all smoke and mirrors.' When you've still got the hunger it makes you work 2–3 hours extra or when you're thinking you'll fall off your feet, you'll rewrite or reread something."
>
> Gary P. Naftalis, Head of Litigation and Co-Chair, Partner, Kramer Levin Naftalis & Frankel LLP, New York, NY, USA

Motivation: the source

The word itself tells you a lot. It comes from the Latin "to move" and there are some key internal concepts in this. If you're going to move you need a reason to move, somewhere you're headed, and the drive to do it. In other words you need inner purpose, direction, and effort, all of which spring from you. To see how this works, just think about being thirsty on a hot summer's day, then remembering you have some cold beer in your kitchen. Purpose, direction, and effort will mean you go to get it. In other words they'll lead you to an action that is rewarding in and of itself. And they're not only important internal components of motivation, they're indicators too. If you can't see them clearly in someone, they are unlikely to be motivated.

But the most important thing to understand about motivation is that it's productive. It leads to things happening.

Depending on your interest, education, or beliefs, motivation is based in your unconscious, your libido, your brain, your neurotransmitters, your glucose levels, your personality, your parents, your DNA, your God, your actual ability, your experience, or your environment. Or maybe your desire for status, money, achievement, and reward. Or more simply an innate need to be competent and do well.

Where do I think it comes from? I think that motivation, like happiness, is part of the experience of being human. When did you last have to learn to be motivated? You just are. Humanistic psychology is based on the supposition that we all want to experience as many fulfilling moments as we can. It's what fundamentally drives us. And that's supported by research on dopamine, the feel-good neurotransmitter that gets us to do things and repeat them because not only is the goal motivating, but the activity itself is too. Think Playstations and Nintendos if you want an easy example.

If motivation is innate and our brains hard-wired to want it, what needs to be present for it to appear?

> "As a young troop commander I was involved in a large narcotics operation off the UK coast; some armed Colombians were bringing quite a large shipment over.
>
> It was very challenging conditions and the plan of the ship had no resemblance to the ship we were actually on, so everything went awry. Normal stuff that you'd expect. But we'd intercepted a very significant haul.
>
> I remember we flew back to a small airfield and got on a coach. Very unglamorous. But I was sitting on that coach looking out and thinking, 'You know, in a small way we have made a difference to the fabric of society.' That's a tremendous feeling – hugely motivating."
>
> Senior officer, Special Forces, UK

"When I was young and after I was recognized as Karmapa, I recognized how much responsibility I had and that became intimidating for me as I understood it.

I compared the responsibilities I had with my own personal aspirations as a human being and I got stuck looking for reconciliation. I struggled for some time during my teenage years. I had no choice – the boat had sailed on my personal aspirations. I wrestled with this so that the happiness and the misery could live within harmony.

We all have similar happiness and suffering which is influenced by others. No-one has these due to themselves alone, as life is a process of depending on and relying on others. And we have to reconcile this within our personal desires. We can all find happiness in the seemingly choiceless situations we find ourselves in."

His Holiness, The 17th Gyalwa Karmapa, Trinlay Thaye Dorje, Sikkim, India

Motivation: the conditions

In all there are about 72 theories of motivation. But the one that's best researched and most validated is Self-Determination Theory. This holds that there are three major parts to motivation that are universal and innate: competence, connection, and choice.

- *Competence* means being capable as you do something, engaging in interesting activities, and being able to reliably predict the outcomes of what you do. When you're competent you know you're good and you can recognize it in others too.
- *Connection* involves building strong relations with others and feeling you have them in return. Our research shows that liking your colleagues is a clear part of motivation and vital to making you feel you belong.
- *Choice* entails actively deciding on experiences and behavior to mindfully select those that are aligned with your values. It's not about control, being selfish, independent, or detached. It's about your freedom to align yourself with things that are important to you.

In other words you want to feel competence but in areas you value; you want to feel connected but to people that you respect; and you want choice but over things that work for you. Any task that has these three features will be fundamentally motivating because it taps into deep human needs. Which will mean that your overall motivation levels will be high – and for longer than the time it takes just to do the task itself.

Telltale signs of motivation

It's easy to assess motivation by asking yourself on a scale of 1–10 how much purpose, direction, and effort are clear for all to see in the major tasks or projects that you have to deliver. How much persistence is there? What causes a flash in the pan or endurance over the long term? Your answers will tell you a huge amount about your overall motivation.

That's how you gauge it. But what can you then *do*?

Here's the bad news. The only person who can ever motivate you over the long term is you. You know that if you've ever tried to get a toddler to eat brussels sprouts, or had to pester a colleague to deliver an answer. Motivation comes from within and is released by making sure you feel you have enough competence, connection, and choice. But you can temperature-test these three features by looking at flow, reciprocity, and attitude. Flow tells you about competence; reciprocity tells you about connection; and attitude tells you about choice.

Three temperature tests

The first temperature test is to assess flow. From our data we can see that flow is closely linked to liking your job and to being productive too. Flow is the time when you find yourself "in the zone." Mihaly Csikszentmihalyi, the psychologist who has done decades of work on flow, said that there are some key attributes to flow. They are:

- Clear goals.
- Continuous and unambiguous feedback about progress.
- Opportunities that fully use personal capacity.

And you'll know when you're in flow because you feel:

- Intense concentration and focus.
- A loss of self-consciousness.
- A distorted sense of time.
- That your activity is rewarding in and of itself.

"Work isn't work for me. The hours I do are fun because I'm really in the present, in the moment, when I cook. Everything goes fuzzy round the edges and I lose track of time as I'm caught in the cooking and the creating. That's when I experience real happiness: I forget about the past and future when I go into my kitchen.

I've understood that I can't teach happiness but I can create it. I can create the atmosphere and conditions for it to flourish."

Marut Sikka, celebrity chef, restauranteur, and food writer, Delhi, India

"When am I in flow? That's remarkably easy for me to answer and it's related to teaching. Everyday my chairman and I do what's called a morning report for an hour. We gather all the physicians who were on call the night before and they present the cases of the actual admissions. We listen, discuss, and we share in a very Socratic method.
Continued

It's really group learning based on the experience of the actual patients.

It's incredible: I learn as much as I teach and there's exceptional morale despite the fact that many residents have been up all night. Every year it's voted their favorite exercise; it's an hour of complete happiness. Attendance is 100 percent so we never check it. Everyone comes. My chair has this incredible sense of humor but we share an enthusiasm for the teaching. It's his favorite part of the day too. The same group of residents meet over three years and we watch them develop these skill-sets. It's a very privileged and rewarding time."

Mark W. Babyatsky, Professor of Medicine, Mount Sinai Hospital, New York, NY, USA

"Soon after the Golden Temple was attacked at Amritsar an Indian Airlines aircraft was hijacked. As soon as the plane took off from Karachi to Dubai I was summoned to the crisis room and told, 'This is your pigeon now, handle it.' Sheikh Makhtoum broke the hijack and just when I thought it was all over I got a call from Indira Gandhi's office, 'Go to Dubai and bring back the hijackers.' I thought, 'This is mission impossible,' but I said, 'Fine.'

I didn't know what the hell I was going to do until I got a flash in my mind. 'Let's close all the doors so they have to come to India.' I had them back in three days, no extradition treaty, just a chartered plane. It had never been done before and it's never been done since.

Continued

About 20 percent of people asked say that this happens to them several times a day and about 15 percent of people say that it never happens at all. But you're more likely to find flow at work than anywhere else. You'll probably experience flow as mood-neutral when you're in it because you'll be so focused and absorbed; when you have finished whatever you're doing, you'll feel happy – as our early data clearly showed. In fact the effect was so strong that we didn't need to keep researching it. What's interesting about flow is that it encourages you to look after and protect the things or resources that enable you to access it. Because it's so amazingly motivational.

The second temperature test is reciprocity – the "one good turn deserves another" rule which is at the root of all relationships and therefore at the root of connection with everyone. You can see how this works on a really simple level when you're in a meeting: if you back up something that someone says, quite soon after they'll do the same for you. When favors are not returned or acknowledged, they get seared into your memory. About five years ago I took the rap for someone senior on a conference call, who hadn't done what she had committed to do: I covered her back. That debt is still outstanding. If my good turn had come back to me, I'm sure I'd never even remember the call.

Developing connection means doing something for someone. Or getting someone to do something for you. And that could include volunteering for a task, offering up something interesting, finding out and passing on some essential information, paying compliments, doing something kind, or just helping out. Even getting someone a cup of coffee can start to create a relationship. Going out of your way is a good test to see how connected other people feel towards you: you'll tell by seeing how quickly your good turn comes back to you.

The third temperature test of motivation is attitude. Bad attitude is bad news. Because it's much more often a cause of downfall than failing to do the job well. All attitude is expressed through behavior, which you're finely attuned to reading in eyeball rolling, sighing, negative comments, sloppy work, poor time-keeping, failure to learn, and lack of effort. Bad attitude can happen because people perceive that they have few choices or because they feel they have made the wrong ones.

The worst kind of bad attitude is from people who've resigned on the job and who do as little as they can to get by. Rather than dealing proactively with their situation, they inflict their unhappiness and misery on others, who'll pick up on their negativity and invest a lot of energy to avoid working with them.

So what does great attitude look like? Here's an illustration.

Melissa is iOpener's Operations Director and one wet and cold Sunday afternoon, our office cleaners called her to say that there was a burst water tank which was pouring straight into the main office fuse box and through the ceiling below. Dropping what she was doing, she immediately rushed in to find foul black water streaming everywhere. For three hours she sorted out the mess, which variously involved the police, plumbers, electricians, cleaners, emergency IT, loss adjusters, and the landlord. She did all this to make sure that the office would function on Monday morning, going out of her way to get it all working. And on top of that she stayed cheerful and helpful throughout.

This clearly demonstrates that someone with great attitude will:

- Step up when things are going down.
- Think ahead what might go wrong and pre-empt it.

> Because of the rapport I had, how I'd built up sentiments, I could do it. The whole result was based on personal relationships."
>
> Romesh Bhandari, ex-Foreign Minister, Delhi, India

> "The biggest turn-off at work is a level of negativity, obstructionism, low energy, and lack of motivation. Often these things are intertwined and you see them as a cynical or bad attitude.
>
> I'd much rather work with a kind of Tigger in a box, bouncing up and down. They don't stop bouncing but in the end they do get somewhere and get a lot further than people sitting on the sidelines laughing at them. They get results because they've got an open and positive attitude, which is 'OK yeah, that's a brick wall, I mustn't run in that direction, run in another one.' That effort, energy, and attitude leads to achieving big and important things."
>
> Martin Chilcott, serial social entrepreneur, CEO Meltwater Ventures, Oxford, UK

- Accept additional responsibility willingly.
- Recognize when colleagues need help without being asked.

The STAR acronym will help you remember it.

Getting more motivated

Although it's hard to motivate anyone, it is possible to manage your own motivation. Here are three easy tools to help you: all of them simply involve being mindful in the situation in which you find yourself.

1. Thinking about a task, project, or job's future ending can enhance your present experience of it. Nothing lasts forever and that includes the good times too. You can try savoring the moment, which requires a high level of self-awareness. Or you can try projecting forward to times when you won't be working with the colleagues you like on the projects you find rewarding. Imagine it all coming to an end; this can heighten your motivation to enjoy what you have right now.
2. Thinking positively about the future is correlated with general happiness, which is of course motivational. That means really digging down to think about the tangible yet realistic good things that your efforts will bring.
3. Working through the precise process that leads to success can increase motivation to get there. So analyze in some detail where you're going and exactly what you need to do to deliver.

And recognize in all of this that money might or might not be that motivating. That will depend on you.

Money: is it motivating?

We wanted to investigate money, its effects on happiness at work and motivation. Our aim was to see if we could find out that if, as popular psychology dictates, money doesn't matter, why do so many people behave as if it does? And why do so many organizations seem to believe it too? Lots of executive boards are adamant that they'll lose talent unless they pay for it to stop walking out the door and they won't get long-term performance unless they splash the cash.

So what's the evidence that money doesn't make us happy?

Richard Easterlin wrote a seminal paper in 1974 in which he suggested that more money didn't bring greater happiness. He showed that as industrialized economies doubled, happiness levels remained static. So money doesn't make whole societies happier. What about individuals?

The blogosphere has it that you only need a very low income to be happy: once you've earned between $10,000 and $15,000 a year, your happiness doesn't significantly increase. I'm suspicious. First of all, any of those figures are simply too round and too convenient. Secondly, they don't make sense: you can live like a king on any of those sums in, say, Niger. But you'd struggle with that in New York.

Our findings showed that pay is not associated with motivation, interest in your work, having an impact on the world, achieving your potential, or Recognition. In fact it's negatively associated with it, meaning you actively *don't* want money as a reward for being motivated or for being interested in your work. Nor, according to our statistics, is it linked to any important outcomes like productivity, time off sick, energy, or intention to quit. We were so surprised by this that we've checked it out twice on two different groups of 1,000 people each, one before the recession started and one during it. And the findings were the same both times.

The only significant link that money has is with learning new skills and thinking that you perform better on most tasks than other people. So there's a hint that money matters at some level to some people. Of course you'll get a temporary hike in happiness levels when you get a pay rise, but that soon drops off. Welcome to what's known as the hedonic treadmill.

"I think starting a business and being a successful entrepreneur isn't about the money. People start businesses because they have great ideas and want to make them happen."

Martha Lane Fox, CEO and co-founder, LastMinute.com; co-founder and chair, Lucky Voice, London, UK

"There were three things that really motivated me to start Octel. I wanted my kids and grandchildren to actually think I did something notable. I was very lucky to have picked something that ultimately ended up being a household word. Voicemail. I had no idea.

Second, I wanted to make a big mark, and I wanted to prove to my family that I was a good guy because I remember what it felt like being treated like an idiot for computerizing my uncle's business.

And I wanted to make money because I wanted the things that money bought. And that was pretty much the order. I think money can't make you happy but you can surround yourself with things and make life so much easier.

One of the biggest regrets that I don't have more money is being able to give it away. You can do remarkable things with it but there's a huge gap between having a bunch of money and having enough to do really substantial things. The kind of remarkable things that Bill Gates or Jeff Skoll do."

Bob Cohn, entrepreneur, founder and CEO Octel Communications, San Francisco, CA, USA

But there's some conflicting evidence too.

Gallup's world survey in 2006 showed an amazingly high correlation between money and happiness (for any statistician, it's an incredible .82 – which is just about as good as it gets). And it also found that in the USA 90 percent of people earning at least $250,000 call themselves very happy, while just 42 percent of those earning under $30,000 say they are. In fact this finding about income and happiness is so clear that German researchers are suggesting that it should be used as an overall happiness measure. And to crown it all, psychologists and economists who've looked at tons of data retrieved over decades conclude that when everything is bundled together then analyzed, there is, after all, a clear association between increasing wealth and increasing happiness.

So why didn't we find much of an effect for money? Well, money doesn't make you happier at work because work isn't where you get to spend it – or enjoy its effects. At work you're more likely to be focusing on what you're there to do. Outside work it's a different story: that's where money starts to matter more because that's where you're using it. And that's backed up by our research, which shows that your overall happiness with life *is* significantly associated with money. Not having enough money is an enormous pressure, while having it enables you to make greater choices in what you do.

But there are some important things that will impact your overall life happiness in relation to money. That includes what your attitude to money is, why you value it, and how you intend to spend it. If you want cash to do good things with it, especially for others, you can increase your happiness. If you want it to bolster your self-image, it probably won't; money doesn't equal self-worth and at some level everyone knows that.

To sum up the money question, it does matter – but not at work.

Concluding motivation

Motivation is crucial, especially for today's mobile and unsupervised knowledge workers. Without it deadlines get missed, innovation disappears, and projects simply aren't delivered. To make sure your motivation is high and your overall Conviction too, temperature-test your levels of flow, reciprocity, and attitude when times are good and bad. It will help you build self-awareness, which will in turn ensure you maintain your momentum and help maximize your motivation.

Believing You're Efficient and Effective

Being efficient and effective are obviously closely related to each other. We already know that Contribution is the most important thing everyone wants from work: being efficient and effective means you're using your talents to make that happen. If you're efficient you deploy your resources well with little wasted effort and this describes your input; if you're effective you bring about good results. In other words, it describes your output.

For instance, you may be very efficient at working through your to-do list and completing a lot of it, but you may not be as effective as you might be if you delegated much more, decided to stop some activities, and focused instead on what might help you achieve your objectives more quickly. But it can be really hard to accept that you could be more effective by becoming more efficient. Because it involves acknowledging that you are not working in the best possible way and admitting you could do better. Achieving that means taking the time to stop, think, and question what you do, why you do it, and how you might do it differently.

And questioning yourself is one of the hardest things you can do. It is, however, something that everyone needs to think about from time to time because of the lazy ways we all tend to process information. Most people are passive thinkers who operate using time-saving assumptions and rules of thumb. Those time-saving shortcuts come with a price: they mean that most of us are unable to think "out of the box" because we can't even see the damn box. I know for certain I can't see mine, however much my colleagues urge me to. The only way I can question what I do and how I do it is by getting input and new ideas from others. And by taking time out to reassess and restructure things that matter. That helps me not only to think about being efficient and effective, but to remain resilient too.

> "As a management consultant one of the things we help our clients to do is become more efficient and effective, which means getting a better job done with fewer resources.
>
> To be efficient and effective in this job, you have to have a clear hypothesis, overall logic, and your analysis has to be rigorous, detailed, and rock solid.
>
> I also believe in being absolutely hands on to make sure that written material is understandable, the English clear, grammar and punctuation rules followed, and typos eliminated as well. Being a stickler for quality says something important about who you are, what you do, and how you do it. It sets a high standard, marking out your own efficiency and effectiveness for everyone to see."
>
> George Pappas, ex-Managing Partner, BCG, Australasia, Melbourne, Australia

Feeling Resilient When Times Are Tough

Resilience is the level of inner grit you have to handle situations that require drive, focus, and resolution. And our research has found that it's most strongly associated with being efficient and effective, getting things done, achieving your goals, and fulfilling your potential. So you can see that it's a vital driving force that needs nurturing if you want to make progress at work.

You need resilience in two different situations: the short and sharp, or the longer term. Take 9/11. A series of momentous events was unfolding. The North Tower was on fire, the South Tower was hit shortly afterwards, and the emergency services were not yet there in large numbers. Yet the evacuation of buildings took place in a calm and orderly way as thousands of people made their way out. There could have been pandemonium and panic: there wasn't. The remarkable resilience shown in the moment is really a striking feature of this catastrophic event. Secondly, relative to the entire population of Manhattan it was incredible how few people suffered from post-traumatic stress disorder (PTSD). Shortly after the attacks, it was estimated that 7.5 percent of residents would suffer severe PTSD: in actual fact the figures were much lower. After 4 months only 1.7 percent of the population reported PTSD symptoms and after 6 months this had dropped to a mere 0.6 percent.

You aren't necessarily damaged by being at the epicenter of something awful and you are much more resilient than you know. Because you're beautifully built to withstand a lot. The neurotransmitters and hormones you release under pressure are designed to protect you so that you can perform your best in any

"The first time I was arrested was in 1990 in the middle of the night. They searched my house, broke into my room, and dragged me out. I was arrested 12 times in all. There were many summary trials.

I'm not going to describe where I was held: it's your basic torture chamber, it's any dungeon. I tried to survive one day, then the next, then you survive the next month and the next year, so in a sense it's like the chocolate commercial; one chunk leads to another.

When I was MP for Malé and banished for two years, the whole trial took less than two hours. Being banished to a remote island gave me the opportunity to be more close to the rural Maldives. Throughout everything I always had hope that it could work out, that we could have democracy in the Maldives, that we could be free.

I'm determined, I don't relent or capitulate. No-one would have guessed that there could have been this much change in the Maldives and so fast. Yes, our problems are very acute, but we will work on it, we have a plan, we have a vision, we have focus. I always have been and always will be very hopeful for the future."

Mohamed Nasheed, President of the Maldives, Malé, Maldives

demanding situation. In fact you wouldn't want your body to react in any other way, or you'd never feel any highs or lows; and you have to understand a low to know a high.

But of course nature plays a role too. Just as some people are tall or short, some people are hardier and more resilient. Your levels of resilience are therefore part of who you are as well as what you experience.

And the only way you develop resilience is by doing difficult things. Promotions, bonuses, interesting projects won't come your way without accepting that – nor will you extend yourself by just making easy choices. You grow through things that challenge you and the earlier in your career the better. Glen Elder, the ground-breaking American sociologist, found that children who'd grown up in the Depression were much more resilient than people who faced their first big test later in life. Moreover, later life experiences didn't contribute as much either to personal development or to a capacity to be resilient.

There's something really important to remember about resilience. Firstly, having a lot of work and doing difficult things doesn't mean that you'll be badly affected by it. Professor Rob Briner, Head of Organizational Psychology at London University's Birkbeck College, said to me, "People who have lots of goals, tasks, and responsibilities do much better in terms of their psychological well-being than those who don't." In fact, boredom affects your levels of resilience more than overwork. According to a study done in 2006 by the consultancy SHL, librarians report that they are more "stressed" and unhappy than people working in hospital emergency rooms.

The golden key to unlocking your gateway to resilience is how you choose to cope with what comes your way. When you are feeling pressured, it's time to pay attention to what you're doing so you can choose how you want to react and deal with your situation. You don't want to "manage" your stress: it's there for a reason, telling you to do things differently and to cope better than you are. So how do you cope, well? Here are three main ways:

"There was a time when I was working every day in mine-affected communities. Then you become very involved because you're constantly aware that someone might step on a mine. You get great respect for doing this and that's a very motivating thing. People are extremely grateful for what you do.

To a degree in my current role I have to be detached to do what I now do well – to think about how we do it better, faster, and more efficiently. Out of 8,500 people doing this work there will be 60 accidents in a year. But there are 40–60 children aged between 12–18 who are injured every month. There are serious consequences to what we don't do, and to what we do. Last year we cleared 63,000 anti-personnel mines and 2.4 million tons of unexploded ordnance; the benefit of that is incalculable."

Alan Macdonald, Chief of Staff, Mine Action Coordination Centre of Afghanistan (MACCA)

- *Problem-focused coping*: When you do this, you take responsibility for the situation you're in. That means getting accurate information about it; finding useful and practical help; developing good action plans; carrying them out; and, most importantly, putting off other activities. You focus on what needs to be done and make sure that it happens. That entails thinking flexibly so you won't close off avenues of action prematurely and maintaining an optimistic outlook about being able to fix the situation you're in. You don't consult your horoscope for general advice but you do talk to people who could help you. There is a caveat here: a "fire, ready, aim" approach isn't useful and it's far better to take the time to do the right things more slowly than do the wrong things immediately.

- *Avoidant coping*: When you are in avoidant mode, you shield yourself from an issue; that can be useful if you want breathing space to get more clarity or gear up to manage your situation. The trick is to use avoidant coping as an active strategy because pausing before acting can often save time and effort. In the business simulation exercises that we run, the leaders and managers who act before they think always do worse; those who take the time to get together before they tackle their task always allow better solutions to appear. So it's fine to say you don't know, that you want to reflect on something or that you'll get back to someone because it buys you time. Of course, you can't let things drift for ever because avoidant coping doesn't make an issue disappear; what you get is short-term relief but not long-term resolution.

- *Emotion-focused coping*: This includes making, maintaining, and relying on supportive relationships so that when things go wrong you have resources to turn to for help. Another emotion-focused response is to reframe what you're experiencing. That allows you to think differently about your situation, as does using humor. Things may not feel funny at the time you experience them, but if you can laugh about them shortly afterwards you'll find it's a good coping mechanism.

There's an important caveat to all of this.

Randomized controlled trials clearly show that immediate post-trauma counseling does not reduce distress or promote resilience. It's popularly thought that if you don't emotionally ventilate after a trauma, you'll be at risk; somehow you'll mentally explode, implode, or worse. But there's more and more evidence to show that this approach might actually reduce your mental well-being and ability to manage. For example, a recent study showed that people who didn't express any thoughts and feelings post-9/11 reported better outcomes than those who did. The people who coped worst of all were those who'd ventilated the most emotionally. And this was true two years later too.

So what's the best way to stay resilient? Is problem-focused coping the best you can hope for? There is another way that seems to be the most effective of all. It's known as proactive coping.

Proactive coping

People who cope proactively successfully manage all kinds of difficult work situations, like delivering big and tricky goals, managing impending layoffs, dealing with change, and handling difficult new circumstances. And they flourish as they do it. How? By building reserves of both physical and mental resources. Like boy scouts, they're prepared. And they're happier as a result because they know they'll manage: they have what they need to deal with whatever turns up. When the proverbial hits the fan, they don't waste time by looking for help because they already have it. Which means that they can devote the time to managing their circumstances instead.

Secondly, proactive copers interpret events in a more upbeat way to intentionally generate more upbeat feelings. And it's clear that these positive emotions are used to purposefully maintain resilience. They're not just a by-product but a tool for successful coping.

Thirdly, they see risks not as threats but as avenues that lead to success. They anticipate road blocks, plan to pre-empt any major negative situations, and think "what if?" well ahead. In summary, proactive copers don't get swept up by the situation they're in, they try to shape their experience of it instead.

Why does this matter? Well, you can be absolutely sure that within your working life there will be some critical times when you are called upon to draw deeply on all your internal and external resources. So what are these resources? Where are they? Who are they? Push yourself further by thinking about how you will show the best of yourself when the time comes. How might you want to be seen? Imagine looking back: how will you want to feel about the way in which you conducted yourself? What would you like others to say about you? Your answers to these questions will contribute to your overall levels of happiness at work whatever you have to face and guide you towards help you need.

"I used to visualize a mental lifeboat, a raft just pulling through the waves on some sort of wind or Zephyr of hope. And though my raft wasn't made of real planks, it was made out of mental strategies – ideas. Ideas that this is Gaza, deals can be made. That would be one plank and it would be lashed to another plank, that other journalists have actually died in these circumstances. I was still going and I still had another chance. That this wasn't the Nazi death camps. These were the different planks that were lashed together that made my mental raft. And at low points I would try to visualize this raft.

Sometimes there'd be a mental storm and the raft would break up and planks would be scattered. And I'd have to swim around and mentally imagine myself getting the planks together, lashing them back, climbing on board, and setting sail again for that moment – that lay beyond the horizon. The moment when freedom might come."

Alan Johnston, BBC journalist and ex-hostage, London, UK

"It was the middle of the shift and all we knew was that one of the World Trade Center towers was on fire. It was enough for my news editor to say, 'You'd better go on air,' even though we had no pictures. Within about 15 minutes we started to see the plane ploughing into the second tower and we realized this wasn't just an accident. It was a huge event, a tragic and shocking attack.

Continued

Finally, when something tough comes along, which requires you to dig deep, remember you'll learn from it however unpleasant it seems at the time. One important thing that will help you manage well is being aware of, tuning into, and using the analogies you'll come up with. These can often act as red flags and supportive tools, so they are important to pay attention to.

Using analogy

Analogies serve two purposes. Firstly they act as signposts, and secondly as mindful mental support. Here's how the former work. Willie Walsh, CEO of British Airways, told me that when the mental image of a juggler comes to mind, he knows he needs to change what he's doing because he's got too much on. I see myself plate-spinning when I'm in the same situation. They may both be hackneyed but they're useful because they're signals to do things differently. You can tell because the outcome can only be that you stop or something will come crashing down.

Or analogies may appear for more positive reasons, indicating that you should take action. For example, Marilyn Nissenson, the writer, told me that she knows she's developing an interesting and important project when it feels like she has a "bug buzzing in her ear." That bug tells her it's time to pay attention.

What about using analogy to develop mental resilience? Curiously, tests of physical endurance often seem to reflect the mental effort that you might be making, especially in a work context. So scaling mountains, running marathons, sculpting statues, riding a bolting horse, trekking through deserts to find oases seem to be common – as well as comforting.

They're comforting because, unlike warning analogies, they usually have a positive end or a goal that will be met. You'll arrive at the top of the mountain, complete the marathon, finish the statue, control the horse, and reach the oasis. Which reflects the fact that at some level you know that whatever you're facing won't endure. Once you've found your analogy, a really useful technique is to ask yourself what you need right now to accelerate to the end. Then you can translate meaning into action.

How do you find analogies? Many people find that they spring to mind, especially when they're used to working with them. If this isn't the case for you, just ask yourself, "what's this situation or event like?" Starting your answer with "it's like …" will help you find your analogy. Make sure you keep going until you've got something useful and push yourself because chances are it will take more than one or two answers to get there.

Finding positive meaning in tough circumstances

Finding positive meaning isn't about becoming delusional in a Pollyanna-ish kind of way. If you're very resilient, you'll experience anxiety, frustration, and worry as anyone does in a difficult situation. But you'll also experience positive emotions at the same time. And you can make things better or worse for yourself by chewing events over in a negative – or positive – light. The important thing about finding positive meaning is that you'll recover faster physiologically, improve your mood, and decrease your chances of depression too.

As a human being it affected me very deeply but I had to maintain my composure because I was broadcasting. I couldn't say what I was really thinking. The proverbial swan, poised, elegant, always struck me as a rather banal cliché but I was conscious of a voice telling me, 'Nisha, you've got to be like a swan.' I had to dig very, very deep to stay calm and focused because I knew people were dying as I was talking and I couldn't express my fellow feeling. I was thinking, 'How many people are jumping off the towers? How many people are in that building, how many people are in those planes?' I came off air shattered, wiped out, physically shaking.

It affected me immensely.

There happened to be a church on the corner of our street and I just used to go and sit there. It was an Anglo-Catholic church, very soothing, the smell of the incense and the dim light. A warm enveloping space. I needed to reflect and find peace and although I'm not Christian it felt like an honest, safe place to be.

As a result of the whole experience I feel I can do anything as a broadcaster. I simply don't worry about my work. Even though I was a victim of 9/11 it also gave me a gift. It's allowed me to live in the moment and to trust myself. It's given me a different way of looking at what I do."

Nisha Pillai, BBC anchor and journalist, London, UK

So how do you change how you feel? Sounds like a tall order, but it needn't be. You can start to feel differently just by reappraising your situation and asking yourself:

- How have I grown or developed as a result of this experience?
- What personal skills, attributes, or strengths have I developed as a result?
- What have the positive consequences been so far?
- And what other benefits can I foresee?
- What am I thankful for in all of this?

Doing this has been shown to help bring closure – and bring increased happiness too. Because what you're doing is showing yourself that you are in fact resilient.

Case study in Conviction: losing motivation and finding it again

Robert was a clinical psychologist working at senior level in a well-known hospital. He'd been in his role for seven years and he was exhausted. He knew he was really good at his job and could run his clinic with one hand tied behind his back. But he no longer felt he had a positive impact on his world. "All I get to do is diagnose chronic terminal illness or brain damage, then break bad news to their families. I went into medicine to make people better; that seems to have got lost on the way."

With four young children he didn't want to change careers and he couldn't see a way forward either.

It was clear that Robert:

- Had lost his motivation: his sense of direction was low.
- Was worried that he might drop the ball, questioning how effective he was.
- Felt very despondent about his inability to find anything positive in his working life.
- Couldn't recall when he'd last felt in flow.

Continued

Robert realized that he needed to find something else. Most of all, he needed to be doing something that would allow him to reconnect with making people better in some way.

Eight months later Robert found himself in Latin America with his family. By getting in touch with a colleague with whom he'd written a paper five years before, he'd heard of and got a two-year secondment. His mission was to set up a clinical psychology department in a very under-resourced provincial hospital. And he had to launch specialized training of local clinical psychologists too. He'd found that not only was he really good at this, but he got huge satisfaction from it too.

Six months after that Robert said, "I can't believe I let things slide so badly back at home. It just seemed to happen but I can't imagine feeling that now – I really was asleep on the job. I'm working crazy hours but I love what I do. We are really under-resourced here but the effect I'm having is so much more profound. The big unblocker for me was allowing myself to think as widely as possible around what 'making people better' actually meant. But I've understood what that means in such a new and profound way."

Perceiving That Your Work Has a Positive Impact on the World

This element originally came from our focus group work: lots of people were very enthusiastic and passionate about the impact their work had on the world. Although they found it hard to articulate exactly what this meant, they just knew that it was important to them. Incidentally, I haven't ever come across anyone who *wouldn't* like to have this effect. Because having this feeling gives you the sense that life is purposeful, comprehensible, and somehow you've made sense of the chaos that work is.

Feeling that you have a positive impact on the world shows that you're getting to a much deeper

"I ask myself the question whether I'm having a positive impact on the world a lot. I was studying zoology and I discovered that 30 percent of the world's food was destroyed by insects every year. I liked agriculture and I thought maybe I'll become an entomologist because it's obviously a big problem and that it was something positive to work on.

But bit by bit the world changed and the most unpopular thing became pesticides. There I am doing research to develop pesticides, killing the most wonderful things on the

Continued

earth: insects. And society's constantly saying that we're poisoning the planet, so it would be very easy to get into a negative spiral.

But I honestly couldn't go to work and think that I'm not doing something which has a positive impact. Even though it's hard and you're dealing with difficult issues. Very little in this life is black and white, but if you can make it a bit better, and I do think we make it better, then that's a privilege."

P. L., entomologist, Brussels, Belgium

meaning that goes way beyond the effort and hours you put in. You've accessed what's important about what you do and integrated it into a bigger view of who you are. By making this connection you know that your career choices, lucky breaks, goals, effort, and energy have been fruitful. Of course, this is a lot easier to do after years of experience and much harder if you're near the start of your career journey.

From our data we can see that people who score most highly in this area believe that they have an amazing 40 percent more impact on the world than those in the lowest-scoring category. And this is not related to being at the top of the hierarchy. Moreover, perceiving that your work has a positive impact is strongly connected to liking your job, being interested in what you do, and experiencing positive emotions at work too. So you can see that the linking theme is upbeat emotion – or simply finding pleasure in what you do. These positive emotions obviously serve a purpose: they tell you you're on the right track and to keep doing more of what you're already doing because it feels good. They're there to boost the Conviction you have about your work.

But sometimes it's easy to miss the wood for the trees. That may simply be because you haven't had enough experience or you just can't see the links because you haven't joined up the dots. Of course it's easier if you're in the caring professions, have a vocationally based career, or work in a support role. The red thread between what you do and the impact you have may be easier to see.

If you want to think more about this for yourself, imagine sitting opposite me and start to describe your career history by answering the following questions. Write your thoughts down if you like.

- Who does your work affect positively and how?
- Who in turn does that impact?
- What images, words, and anecdotes would you use?
- How do you weave all the bits together? And then interpret them?
- What themes emerge?

Sharing all this with someone who knows you well will help you work out how your job has a positive impact on the world. What's interesting about sharing your thoughts with someone else is that it not only validates you, but allows them to validate you too. Which is very reaffirming. And it allows you to maximize your Conviction at work.

Concluding Conviction

Conviction is composed of elements that tell you how you feel about what you do. Overall these elements give you important clues about the level of inner drive that helps power your Contribution at work. But because each piece involves self-awareness and sense-making, they are easy to ignore until things go awry. So Conviction acts as a warning too: a lack of any one of its elements will indicate that you're probably not happy at work and that you might need to make some changes.

"I was the front person for all the visitors and their relatives on the 7/7 London bombings. It happened on a Thursday: I don't think I went home until the Monday or Tuesday. I made sure that every friend, relative, and visitor who came was met and supported throughout the whole time; and I did a lot of the liaising with the Red Cross.

When you've been in an event like that it's important to know that you took stress away and that people didn't have to worry. I felt that I used everything I had, all the skills I'd ever learned over the years in order to make that difference. It made me feel I'd really done something, that I'd contributed at a very difficult time."

Eileen Sills, Chief Nurse/Chief Operating Officer, Guy's & St. Thomas's Hospital, London, UK

Top take-aways for Chapter 5

Conviction is about knowing you're doing the right things and they're right for you too. The key elements of Conviction are:

- Being motivated. This involves purpose, direction, and effort which you're hard-wired to have. And it's enhanced when you have choice, competence, and connectedness.
- Being efficient and effective are closely linked but being effective matters most. Both require energy to stay at the top of your game.

- Being resilient is something that happens in the moment and the longer term too. Proactive coping is the most effective way of building resilience as you resource yourself for what might come.
- Perceiving that your work has a positive impact on the world is about making sense of your working life in the broadest context. Linking what you do to the effect you have on as wide a group a people as possible will show you the breadth and depth of that impact.

6

Culture

Introduction to Culture

Culture is the third of the 5Cs. And the first and most important thing to state about it is that this is not about working in a place where hugs 'r' us or where "happiness angels" – I kid you not – leave little treats on your desk. If that suits you, I'm very happy for you. As a cynical Brit I'd want to quit in a trice. In general terms Culture when looked at through a happiness lens means working in a place where your preferences for *how* you like to work are matched.

Culture is very different from Contribution and Conviction: these two are about what you do at work and how you feel about it, while Culture is the environment in which you do it. The consequence is that you'll have much more control over Contribution and Conviction, whereas if you work in a large organization, you'll probably have much less impact on Culture. Quite the opposite; it will have a big effect upon you. That's because every workplace has its own Culture which, by and large, governs how people behave.

Like this.

Take two organizations. One is an old-style manufacturing business in what used to be the British industrial heartlands. I walk in at 7.30 in

"Culture is made of the norms that are acceptable. At Appex we had a flat structure, completely open offices, no titles or dress code, which actually became a big deal over time. The question arose, what are the limits of 'no dress code'? An engineer had come in wearing really, really short shorts and a really skimpy top and we had a Dutch banker in looking for a robust system that had security for their worldwide deployment. And I could see him glancing at her and it just didn't fit. So I said that anything that could be mistaken for underwear couldn't be worn.

Anyway, one of the senior engineers said dress had nothing to do with performance and that he'd prove me wrong. He showed up in his bathrobe and nothing else. His tattered old bathrobe didn't have a belt so the HR person was going crazy. Then he had an interview; someone shows up in a suit, there he is in his bathrobe ... so we compromised. One day a month we'd have bathrobe day and anyone could come in dressed in anything.

Continued

People know through those interactions that I am willing to listen even to something I think completely wrong, so they start to know it's okay to question anything. It signals the kind of place that it is and greatly influences motivation. When people feel that there are all these rules and constraints they try and game the system; they take their most creative energy elsewhere."

Shikhar Ghosh, CEO Appex, entrepreneur, Senior Lecturer Harvard Business School, Boston, MA, USA

"I remember long after Octel had been sold someone told me that they came to work there and stayed for many years because of something I did. I said, 'Really, what did I do?'

He said, 'Well, I was interviewing for a job and you walked by and they said, "That's our founder." And you bent over and picked up a piece of popcorn that somebody had dropped on the floor. "The CEO picks up popcorn?" I said. And my interviewer said, "Sure, why not?" And I thought, "Any CEO that leads by example like that I want to go work for." That's why he came to work at Octel.'

I didn't create a culture, it was my personality gathered from my parents and all the things that happened to me in life. It all came together in the way I thought it ought to."

Bob Cohn, founder and CEO Octel Communications, San Francisco, CA, USA

the morning and the receptionist looks up, asks me if I've come far, and gets me a cup of tea even though it's not really her job; she lets me in to use the bathroom even though she shouldn't. In fact she goes out of her way to help me before anyone's arrived. Later on people passing in the corridor catch my eye, smile, and say "hello," "good morning," and "good evening." The team I'm working with volunteer information that they think will be useful and three times in one morning I'm offered a tour of the factory. At lunch time two of them guide me round with passion and pride, explaining how it all works.

The other is a luxury brands business located at an upmarket address in central London. No-one says anything in the elevator: there's no eye contact. One of the heads of department working there told me, "Even if you're working on the same floor and pass them every morning on the way to your desk, you simply don't acknowledge them. It creates a sense that no-one here really belongs or cares." I learned that there wasn't an organizational chart, so knowing who was who was almost impossible. Yet if you sent an email to a group of people and got the order of seniority somehow "wrong," those who felt slighted would simply not read or respond to it.

Culture makes a big difference, right or wrong.

When it's right you almost don't notice it. But when it's wrong, it's really wrong because you'll feel that you simply don't fit. Like wearing casual clothes to a formal party, it's really uncomfortable. And that can easily lead you to doubting yourself rather than the place you're working in.

At the same time, Culture can be a convenient scapegoat too. After all, it's much easier to dump all your issues at the door of the place you work rather than accept that you might be part of the problem.

So it's worth understanding what kind of Culture you value working in.

Identifying Culture

Culture anywhere is made up of the norms, values, and behavior that are particular to any organization, large or small. You definitely won't find Culture represented in mission or value statements. But you do find it just by asking, "What does it take to get ahead in this place?" And "What would be a show-stopper here?" The answers to those questions will tell you a lot about what you might want to know. Then take a look at the pictures on the walls; what icons are important to the organization you're in? What does the office furniture say about who they are? Finally, pay close attention to the language and metaphors someone uses as they talk to you. They'll tell you an immense amount.

Here's what I mean.

Let's assume that Harvard Business School, ranked number one in the world, writes the best business educational material there is. It's easy, accessible, and often thought-provoking. Of course the editorial and advertising teams need to reflect their readership's reality, and that reality is immensely warlike and military. Articles refer to "killing," "front lines," "battles," "fight," "firing," and "arsenal" for starters. Recently there's been a lot about surviving – and even "defusing land mines." All this language seems to crop up almost regardless of the subject matter; the last phrase is taken from an article about coaching.

In our work inside large multinationals we often hear references to the "front line," "staff," "campaigns," "strategy," "mission," "opera-tions," "divisions," "silos," "maneuvers," "company headquarters," "morale," "must-win battles," or that someone is "out of action." And more creepily, comments on people "spear-heading" or "executing." How helpful is it to always be on a war footing? How does it build partnerships, enhance working relationships, or create a service culture? Why should any employee fight a permanent battle? And who exactly is the enemy?

I want to be fair. There's a lot of sporting vocabulary about too. Look once more at *Harvard Business Review* and you'll find articles that refer to boxing, Olympian experience, "racing," "baseball," and so on. As one article asserts, "Winning is everything." Again, this type of metaphor is

> "Culture is absolutely important and people never analyze it enough because you can't put it into numbers.
>
> For example, in a takeover you look at revenues, cost, overlapping losses, then you and I look at each other over the table. When you think, 'What an a-hole,' there's a huge loss of value because one of us is going to leave. The reason that happens is that no-one's bothered to analyze the culture and if they'd done it, they haven't taken the two accounts seriously."
>
> Edward Bonham Carter, CEO Jupiter Asset Management, London, UK

typical of large organizations – but is it helpful? Does it make anyone make that extra effort over the long term? Does it genuinely motivate all employees regardless of gender, creed, and race? What about courage and sustainability given the recent economic past and its fallout?

Then there all those burning platforms so beloved of many corporations. The origin of this phrase is the North Sea Piper Alpha tragedy in 1988 which killed 167 workers, most of whom were under 30 years old.

It's not a motivational expression, it's a tragedy.

Language reflects Culture. Positively or negatively, and there are reinforcing consequences as a result. Here's a great example. At CERN on the French–Swiss border, 7,000 particle physicists are building the largest atom smasher in the world to find out about "Big Bang." When you meet anyone there, they don't talk about "work" or "experiments." They talk about the "collaborations" that they're working on. It's no surprise that the World Wide Web was born here. It grew out of work that can only be done by sharing a huge amount of data and information. And sharing is clearly implied in the word collaborating. Now CERN is pioneering grid computing, which is also all about sharing: this time it's power and storage.

Most people are not running marathons or fighting serious life-or-death battles at work; they are doing things which are far more humdrum and prosaic. Interestingly, I noticed that none of the servicemen I interviewed for this book used any military metaphors. They are aware of what these terms really mean and therefore do not use them lightly. Yet the constant use of sporting or military language reinforces norms and behaviors that become part of a workplace and get reflected in its values. Because when you use a term all the time, the context in which you use it contributes to its meaning: that's what

"I like to compare how a collaboration functions with a symphony orchestra. Everyone is technically perfect because even with untrained ears you can hear the one wrong note.

Individually, you'll never have anything beautiful. You have to understand that you perform together and depend on everyone else for a beautiful and successful concert and a fantastic experience for the audience. A collaboration is just the same."

Felicitas Pauss, Professor for Experimental Particle Physics, ETH Zurich; External Relations Coordinator, CERN, France/Switzerland

"Pep Stores is 1,500 stores, trading in 10 African countries, selling 500 million items per annum. That's about 60 items a second.

We don't have this 'boss' mentality. We hardly ever use the word. You won't hear the word 'employee' either. You will hear 'dynamos,' 'leaders,' and 'teams.' These three words you will hear more than any others. And we work on a first-name basis always. We realize that if we want our sales force to treat the customers well, we must treat them well. You cannot expect anyone to treat a customer better than you treat that person."

George Steyn, Managing Director, Pep Stores, Cape Town, South Africa

pragmatics, a huge chunk of psycholinguistics, is all about. There's no doubt about it: words affect behavior as well as the way you and your colleagues work.

If your business or organization uses military language or sporting vocabulary as a way of reinforcing messages, you can bet your bottom dollar that it will impact employees' approach as well as their psychological and social capital. If we want to build sustainable cultures and sustainable working practices, we need to find a different language, and one that seems much more appropriate is that of farming. Which says much more about continuity, stability, and harmony than war or sport.

> "The fund management business is like farming: it's inherently cyclical. Part of the stress of farming as I understand it is dealing with the changing and challenging environment all the time, working in difficult or uncertain conditions. One of the faults of the City and working in this sector is that it's very, very short term. Overly so in my opinion."
>
> Edward Bonham Carter, CEO Jupiter Asset Management , London, UK

Understanding Cultural Preference

There's plenty of research showing how important it is to culturally fit within the place you work. And feeling out of sync with everyone else is absolutely exhausting. Now here I want to clarify something important. When I'm talking about Culture, I'm referring to our research and its impact on levels of happiness and productivity at work. That means you might think that certain things which you might have read about organizational culture are missing. And you'd be right. We've isolated the concepts and elements that we've found specifically impact these two important areas: happiness and productivity.

When we started thinking about happiness at work, from our consulting work we theorized that cultural preferences would be divided into two continuums along what was fixed–fluid and enabling–restrictive. Furthermore, we thought that this would apply not only to people but to teams and organizations too.

Here's how this works in practice. A bureaucracy would be at the more fixed end of the continuum with more rules, processes, and procedures; a successful IT start-up lies at the more fluid end as employees have to adapt and change rapidly as the business grows.

When you're in the right Culture, you'll feel you're more enabled in your work. That's because the fixed–fluid continuum is operating well for you. For example, if you are someone who loves systems and processes which tend to be more fixed, and you have that in your work, you'll feel enabled in your job and you'll be in the systematic quadrant. If you're someone who hates process yet that's what's valued in your working Culture, you'll feel that your work is more fixed and more restrictive: overall you'll fall into the static quadrant. What you'll want is a workplace where you can do things by making them up to a certain extent because you find this fluid approach is more enabling. And you'll be in the organic quadrant. This type of Culture would feel chaotic to those who prefer clear guidelines. They'll feel restricted in such a Culture because "the way things get done" may be opaque or invented on the hoof.

Here's what this looks like.

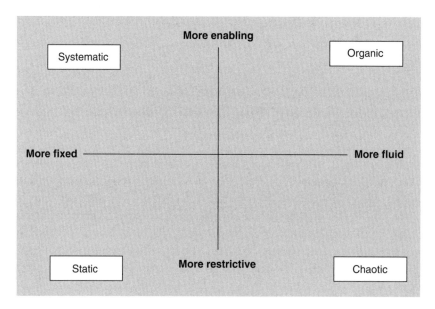

Figure 6.1 The cultural fit matrix.

But whatever your preference is, it's likely to be governed by whatever you see as most enabling and whatever you believe will lead to the greatest fulfillment of your potential. This matters because it plays out in some detail when getting to grips with Culture.

Understanding the Elements of Culture

As we hypothesized, the elements that comprise Culture cluster into two groups: things that are more fluid and those that are more fixed.

More fluid elements

These include:

1. Relishing your job.
2. Liking your colleagues.

Both of them are affected by the day-to-day minutiae of your work, which means you can feel really positive about them one week and much less so the following. But the most important thing about them is your ability to influence them. It's much greater than the elements that fall into the more fixed category.

More fixed elements

These elements are more static: they change slowly and you'll have less impact on them than you have on the fluid elements. They consist of:

1. Appreciating the values your workplace stands for.
2. Having a fair ethos at work.
3. Being in control of your daily activities.

Having the right amount of each of them for you tells you that you really fit your Culture well. All of them are important but the most important of them is the first one, relishing your job.

Relishing Your Job

If you relish your job, you love what you do. You've stepped beyond the logical and rational boundaries of your role and have an emotional attachment to your work. This isn't just about fitting within your role or your organization and liking your daily activities: it's about much more than that because of the strong feelings you have. That's evidenced in our numbers: people who relish their job most show a 68 percent difference when compared to those who don't like their jobs at all. If you relish your job, you'll also be motivated, get things done, have high energy, raise issues that are important, and want to stay in your current role. You'll know you deliver at work and you'll feel that you're fulfilling your potential.

"I've always retained that sense of utter excitement walking into a television studio. The idea that you can share events immediately in real time with millions and millions of people is still magical.

When the tragic events of 9/11 happened and I was Director of Television at the BBC, I realized I had to get back from network control to my office. I needed to make a call to change what was on in 90 seconds. And I started running: I was 44, 45, and I was still doing a job where sometimes you have to run. Even now I can feel like a 22-year-old kid with a script in my hand running down a corridor and that's very exhilarating."

Mark Thompson, Director General, BBC, London, UK

"I think that one of the things Frank [Williams] has in common with our drivers is that he loves what he does so much. Sometimes I'll say when we've had a really tough day or tough meeting, 'That was hard work.' And he'll say. 'Yes, it was fantastic wasn't it?' And we were in the same meeting. He loves the bad bits when you have to get down and dirty just as much as he loves the good bits.

In the same way, a driver who can get out of a car when he's spun off or been hit and it's all gone horribly wrong and still say that he loves it – well, that takes you to another level."

Adam Parr, CEO Williams Formula 1, Wantage, UK

And assessing this is easy. All you have to do is ask someone how much they relish their job on a 0–10 scale. A high number will tell you that lots of positive things are in place.

Yet here's the rub.

Everyone interprets "relishing your job" differently. What you specifically relish will depend on activities, tasks, people, personality, processes, experience, colleagues, goals, and a whole host of tangible and intangible factors that are personal to you. But one thing we have noticed, regardless of what you relish, is that the fixed/fluid dynamic must work well for you. In other words, you'll relish your job because the Culture you operate in meshes with your personal preference.

Here are some statements which show how people actually experience the fixed/fluid dichotomy.

Fluid examples

- "I love my job because it has such a huge variety and the constant change is exhilarating and energizing. From one week to the next I don't know exactly what I'll be doing or even where I'll be."
- "Getting into the office on time is something I'm just not interested in. If I decide I want to go to the gym first then work to midnight, that's how I do it."
- "No-one tells me how to do my job: I get some big targets then I work out how to deliver them."
- "It is up to me to decide some quite difficult things. From time to time I would like more input on decisions I make because it can feel like I might be hanging out to dry. But that's not how it works round here."

Fixed examples

- "The Asian culture I work in rewards loyalty as well as performance. If people are loyal but don't perform well, they're supported, but performance without loyalty isn't tolerated. Exactly the opposite of the US business I worked for."
- "I have to report every decision, every action to head office. The email traffic is huge as a consequence and it's suffocating for me to work like this – even though I think I come from a highly consensual working culture."
- "In my job it's problem, hypothesis, analysis, solution. The inputs, outputs, process, and application are clear."
- "My work is about managing a process and constraining everything within it. It's logical and it works, so although others see it as pure analysis, I see it as almost chemistry it's so structured.

As usual this fixed–fluid dynamic isn't an all-or-nothing event. For example, a loose process for claiming expenses might be infuriating, just like an unclear project briefing. But generally speaking you'll have a preferred location on the continuum which will be governed by certain tolerances: you'll be able to accommodate movement so far, then you'll go no further.

If you want to know what works best for you, ask yourself, "In an ideal day, what would the split between fixed and fluid activities be?" Then compare your actual working day with those two figures. With luck they should be more or less aligned. If they aren't, start to think about what you need to be doing and where to help you identify the right Culture for you.

"Every day we report some aspect of our operation upwards. We've got fixed structures in our roles and I like it, knowing what we have to report. It means we constantly have our fingers on the pulse of some aspect of performance so we end up driving it. It helps everyone stay focused and it's predictable: free-floating anxiety stays in control to some degree.

Nursing is fixed, there are routines and processes that have to be done. But humans are fluid: we're looking for that order in the chaos."

Betsy Blair, COO, CJW Medical Center, Richmond, VA, USA

"To be honest I hate my job and it has been a big sacrifice for me to do it. I am a New York cab driver and I came here from Algeria in 1973. I would like to have been an artist, a sculptor.

The traffic, the people, other drivers all wear me down. The worst thing about doing something you hate is how tiring it is. When I get home at 8 p.m. in the evening I am exhausted. Completely drained to the point where sometimes I cannot speak.

I have done this for my children and I have big satisfaction in giving them what they want. My son is a banker with an MBA, my daughter a dentist. My sacrifice is worth the satisfaction of their achievement."

Mohammad Das, cab driver, New York, NY, USA

Whatever your preference is, you'll know what suits you most because working with it will make you feel more enabled and more energized. And working against it will make you feel more restricted and exhausted. If you have to do a job which doesn't suit your preferences at all, the best way to manage this is to connect to the reason why you're doing it. That can help provide you with the motivation you need to persevere. As will finding colleagues whose company you enjoy.

Liking Your Colleagues

It's simple. If you don't like your colleagues you won't like your job. Since ancient times tracts have been written about why comradeship mattered because everyone recognizes that you'll hardly go out of your way for someone you don't like. The more you like someone, the more you'll look out for them – and they for you. That's why liking your colleagues is such a cornerstone of psychological and social capital.

Put the other way, I've never met someone who *didn't* want to like the people they work with. When you dislike your colleagues the day goes very slowly indeed. Being part of a group you gel with is a fundamental human need, as well as central to making a concerted effort. You know you like your colleagues when you can identify with them, anticipate how they react and what they might feel. And the benefit of that is less conflict, more cooperation, and better teamwork.

Liking your colleagues has an effect on your health in the short term: if you like your co-workers, you'll take about 1.5 days off sick a year. If you don't you'll average 6. Nor will you improve those relationships by being absent: adding to someone else's workload will not win friends or influence people.

It matters in the long term too: research over time has found that lack of support has a worse impact on your health than smoking or obesity. People with better social networks and close relationships live longer, have better mental health, are better teamworkers, and achieve wider and deeper goals.

"I always go where I like the people; that's hugely, hugely important to me. I like people I respect because with that comes trust.

I like and look for people I can have a bit of a laugh with, who don't take themselves too seriously. They have to take what they do amazingly seriously, but they have to be able to have a laugh at themselves, the situation, and rejoice in all of it. It shows you are a part, a custodian, an actor in this whole thing.

If you can laugh at yourself you recognize that you're very important – and at the same time you're nobody."

Louise Makin CEO BTG, London, UK

There's a quick caveat here. There are of course cultural differences associated with liking your colleagues and the extent to which you want to develop relationships with them. For example, it's evident from American data that people want to make friends at work; it's even an item in Gallup's Q12 questionnaire, designed to assess employee engagement. But outside the USA friendship at work doesn't always translate as a concept. Take France. Or the UK. Or India. We know because our numbers haven't built a really solid case for the fact that friendships make you happy at work.

What most people look for is social support because that helps you cope. You'll find that support by being friendly, helpful, and going out of your way for others. By making sure that others like you.

To foster liking, look for the things you share rather than the gaps between you. Focusing on similarities bridges differences rather than expanding them into a chasm. Once you've done that, then you can start to deepen a relationship by starting to disclose certain information and feelings. People who disclose more tend to be liked more and they get more help as a result.

In summary, the more you like your colleagues, the better you'll work together and the more you'll like the Culture of your workplace – probably because you share the values that it stands for.

> "When I started working in Papua New Guinea, if someone did something unacceptable, then things would turn nasty because the community is all anyone had.
>
> When that happened, then the head man would give the person a stone and say, 'You're dead.' That was all they'd do. What it really meant is that you are no longer part of this community: they could have gone to live in the bush and stay alive in terms of food but people didn't. Once they were told they were dead, they were dead."
>
> Chris Gosden, Professor of European Archaeology, Oxford University, UK

Appreciating the Values Your Organization Stands For

There's a ton of research to show how important it is that your personal values are aligned with those of your organization. So what exactly are they? Broadly speaking, values are important guiding principles which lead to certain decisions, behaviors, and actions. In organizations they provide the norms for how people should behave and where resources should be allocated. They definitely aren't those statements you find printed on badges, trumpeted on websites, or published in corporate annual reports. And in

"I've got 20 years of senior business development experience in B2B and I've worked all over the world, but the worst experience I had was setting up a global sales force for a Chinese company. I'd had a job for a multinational in China, so I thought I knew the culture. But when you're working for a multinational you're protected and it's different.

My background and experience is very different: it's open and we discuss things, we can talk about what matters and disagree. I learned I couldn't challenge anything or they thought I wasn't being loyal. So there was a big breakdown of trust. Imagine, they sent two people to sit in my office to watch me and just report back on what I was doing. The stress was huge.

It started to affect my judgment and confidence. And once your confidence is affected it impacts your self-belief too. I'm still feeling the consequences."

M.L., Business Development, Denmark

many workplaces you find that the official corporate values are very different from employees' actual practice.

But if you appreciate the values of your workplace, we've found you'll be happier, help your colleagues more, have higher trust and pride in your organization, and intend to stay longer in your role.

Having this appreciation goes beyond just feeling that you're in the right organization. It boosts your psychological capital because fundamental beliefs that you hold precious are being confirmed and mirrored back to you by something much bigger than you. So you get active endorsement of your self-image and identity. Work is always tied up with your identity because it goes such a long way to answer those tough questions, "Who am I?" and "What matters to me?"

Identity also explains why it's so devastating to lose a job or to work in a place which is going through a fraught time. Because who you are is so tightly wrapped up in what you do. For example, at a conference in early 2009 I met a woman who introduced herself in the standard way, with her name, job, and employer. Then she closed her eyes and vehemently exclaimed, "Don't say anything." Her identity had been damaged by the lousy and extensive PR her bank was getting: what she was hearing wasn't consistent with her personal values or the values she expected from any major financial institution.

If you don't like the values of your organization, you just won't feel good about working there and you won't put in 100 percent effort. You won't like your colleagues or communicate well with them and, as our research has found, this will be a big drain on your energy and performance. When you don't connect with the values of a group, you'll disconnect with the individuals in it, who will ignore and ostracize you in return. That will impact your happiness levels which, predictably, will plummet. That means it's really important to find out what the values of any organization are before you take a job there: in today's working world, it's much more likely that you'll have to flex to meet their values than they'll flex to meet yours.

Liking the values of your organization has other important effects. It results in reduced misunderstanding because you have better formal and informal exchange of information. People just do communicate better when their values are aligned with their colleagues and their workplace. A shared way of understanding means interpreting and reacting to events similarly. And that results in better team performance as well as better relations with your colleagues and with your boss.

On a wider canvas, values can pull disparate groups of people together to make sure they achieve the same goals. And these commonalities bridge the gaps between separate teams, divisions, functions, and business units. Shared values mean you have a way of naturally understanding what's expected of you and how to work well with others. That's how you build Trust and it is the very basis of social capital. So if you find yourself at loggerheads with another person or team, it might be worth getting together and asking:

> "At the end of 2005 I handed the business over to a banker, the biggest mistake I ever made. The new model was corporate with a huge plush office, cars, all the fountains, a dining room ... It wasn't sustainable and it lost its core.
>
> Now I'm restoring what the business is all about and the energy is coming back. One of the first symbolic things I did was to sell the fancy head office."
>
> Dr. Iqbal Surve, doctor, social entrepreneur, Chairman and CEO Sekunjalo Investments Ltd, Cape Town, South Africa

- What are we trying to achieve together?
- What do we share?
- What lies at the root of the things we share?
- How can we galvanize ourselves around what we've found?

Answering these questions together will ensure that you maintain fusion rather than build fission into what you're all delivering.

But there's another reason to connect personal and organizational values too. Relating to your organization's values can help you go that extra mile.

Using values to increase persistence

Appreciating the values your organization stands for can help you in another way too. It can help you to keep tackling tough tasks. Actively working with values can have a big impact on your persistence levels.

"Running Friends of the Earth was a huge job. It's not like running a normal business because we work with volunteers, people who come not because they want money but because they want to change things in a certain way: they are values-driven and everything needs to resonate with those values. The only way to do that is by being participatory, giving individuals lots of autonomy.

For example, delivering the work is complicated so we took quite a bit of time to step out and think about things. We'd spend a day or so camping and about 150 people would go off with tents and sit in a field to debate what needed to be done. But this was all organized by self-selected groups.

There's a lot of leadership outside those with management jobs, so people are encouraged to show initiative. When you do that people get to feel that they are bigger stakeholders than their job might suggest. They build their skills and it elevates their profile as people get to know each other better. And we all showed we lived our values in the process."

Tony Juniper, environmentalist, activist, and author, Cambridge, UK

Of course you know you only have so much gas in the persistence tank. And that gas gets used up especially when the daily grind is tough and seems to be unending. One way of filling the tank is by eating: I'm sure you've snacked to keep going at work. But actively thinking about and expressing values has been shown to have a big impact on effort and self-control. So try the following:

- Write down the precise values you think a difficult task fulfills for both you and your organization.
- Rank-order those values.
- Look at the top value and think through why this one is so important for you and your organization.
- Write down any thoughts that come to mind and what you might be feeling as a result.

Now go and talk it all through with a colleague, boss, mentor, partner, or friend.

By intentionally tapping into your guiding principles you will keep yourself going longer and push yourself further. After all, your ability to reflect on your existence, your values, your role, and your activities is a major mental activity that separates you from your primate cousins.

However, you are similar to those cousins in one major respect – because your evolutionary past would have demanded it. You are super-aware of and super-sensitive to what's fair and what's unfair at work.

Having a Fair Ethos at Work

Although happiness at work is generally pretty stable, one of the things that can cause it to fluctuate greatly is fairness. Or to be more precise, something that's unfair. The fairness with which you are treated is something that everyone wants regardless of nationality or context. Being treated unfairly has a huge and negative impact on how you feel and therefore how you think and behave. For example, our findings show that people who find their Culture most unfair also report that they are disengaged for 32 percent of their working day, while people who find it fairest are disengaged only 6 percent of their day. That's an astonishing difference.

And fairness ultimately affects your health. The well-known Whitehall study of public sector employees undertaken over a ten-year time period showed that lack of fairness was associated with poorer thinking, sleeplessness, and a significantly increased risk of heart attack.

Fairness and the perception that things are done fairly touch virtually every aspect of your working life. Like being allocated money, resources, and interesting projects; understanding decision-making; being hired or promoted; having access to information; and knowing that behavior is reliable. In all of these areas, fairness is the topic that crops up most and has the biggest effect on happiness, especially when it concerns your boss or your pay. If the wages you receive are not the same as those of other people doing the same job as you, you will feel very resentful of that fact.

In short, being fairly treated is particularly strongly associated with wanting to stay in your job: if you think you are unfairly treated you won't be there for the long term, and in our data this is particularly true for Americans.

All you have to do is look at unfair behavior to know how damaging it can be. Unfairness leads to favoritism, office politics, and factions as people look to find personal benefits that they can't get any other way. It creates lots of uncertainty because people are thrown by what seem to be arbitrary decisions or occurrences; then it's a big drain on psychological capital because it increases worry.

When something unfair takes place, you'll probably be shocked that it's happened and have an immediate emotional response to it. You'll feel anything from annoyance and irritation to

"I work in financial services and although I lead a small team of six people, we have big responsibilities. Last year I found out by doing a chance audit that the man who had done the job before me earned considerably more than I do. I was so angry that I walked out; first I marched around the block, then I left for the rest of the day.

I don't want to earn a reputation as a troublemaker or I'll never work in this sector again, but it makes me seethe with anger. Did my boss think that he could simply get away with it? That I'd never find out? Fair play is a big thing to me and this isn't it."

K.L., financial services sector, London, UK

anger and boiling rage. The immediate effect is likely to be increased con-flict, decreased focus, reduced productivity, and less happiness at work. But worst-case scenarios result in outright sabotage as people try to restore some psychological balance.

The major cause of this intense emotional reaction is generally because the do-as-you-would-be-done-by rule has been broken. You believe that you've put in effort and Commitment and it's deliberately been ignored. That's why unequal pay causes such strong reactions. As do appointments that ignore the best candidate. The worst thing about these decisions is not the decisions themselves, but the long-lasting ripple effect that they have. An unfair event seeps into the very bones of an organization.

For example, I once went to do a consulting project in an organization where the CEO had said that anyone not directly involved in selling the company's product would have to watch out for their jobs. This was still hot gossip two years later as marketing, accounts, HR, and purchasing were wondering when the axe would fall on them and what exactly their CEO had meant. To all those employees that statement felt deeply unfair and was very destabilizing: the implication was they were somehow wasting company time and resources.

The hardest thing about fairness is how little you can do to manage it. Either you leave because it has such a negative effect on your working life, or you decide to manage your response to it. Which can range from doing nothing to doing something small or large. But feeling that the ethos of your workplace is fair is really important for your psychological well-being: just as being in control of your daily activities is too.

Being in Control of Your Daily Activities

When I first started work, the equivalent of instant messaging was the office telex machine. To send a telex, I'd write my message out by hand and give it to my secretary. She'd type it up and wait for the office messengers, who in turn would deliver it to the telex operators. And twice a day I'd get my incoming and outgoing typed-up telexes back in triplicate. Sending any-thing quickly required a lot of begging and was very frustrating. The way we work today is unimaginably different from the office I started in 25 years ago.

Today's workplace expects that you use your brain in a self-sufficient way to meet the flexible demands of your job. With that flexibility comes an explosion of choice and opportunity. You can work from home, when you're traveling, at the weekend, when you're with your kids, or even in bed at night. Your email, your boss, colleagues, and customers are always just an iPhone or BlackBerry away. Working boundaries are now limitless, so does that mean more control or less control over your working life?

Before I tackle that question, it's worth remembering that a central idea in psychological research over the past 30 years holds that the more control you feel you have, the better your overall well-being. Because you can make decisions about what to do. The more control – real or otherwise – you perceive you have in your job, the more you can deal with its daily pressures. And we've found that people who are most happy at work experience 33 percent more control than their unhappiest peers.

Control is divided into two parts: what you actually have as well as what you think you have. Of course it's not always the case that you have as much control as you might believe. A quick examination of some tumbled heads of large institutions will tell you that. By the way, control isn't the same as self-control: one you have over what you do, the other is over what you think and how you behave.

For people who don't feel that they have enough control, there are some serious conse-

> "Whatever you do you have to learn the process and then it gives you complete freedom to work within it. For example, I used to design kilims and once I understood about curves and circles within the weaving, I was free to design what I wanted. It's liberating to understand your constraints."
>
> Nelly Munthe, philanthropist and social entrepreneur, London, UK

quences. Feelings of low control have been shown to be connected to lethargy, burnout, time off sick, conflict at home, and, amazingly, heart disease too. And we've found that it's strongly related to performance, taking on challenges, being energized at work, and raising issues that matter to you.

Some parts of your job are more fixed, for example the demands of your role and the deliverables your boss wants. But a good boss will allow you to decide how you manage all of that. Interestingly, quite often you don't need huge amounts of control to feel you have it. For example, something as simple as just deciding the order in which you do a list of tasks can increase your sense of control and significantly reduce anxiety.

Culture: a case study

The marketing team of an American multinational based in Europe was in disarray. A range of strategic products was about to be launched in Europe and it had to go well: the pressure to deliver was intense.

But all was not well with the team. Employee turnover was high, running at the rate of double the rest of the organization. Spaces in the team were open and rumors of a head-count freeze had started to circulate. Meanwhile, expectations for the new product range were huge.

Marsha, the team leader, had only been in her position for two months. She'd come over from the USA to "sort the team out" and launch the product range. "They just don't get it," she exclaimed with frustration. "We need to stop everything to start again. This feeling that somehow it's not in our control won't get us anywhere. The team has to grab this with both hands if we're going to launch successfully."

Her problems were made worse by the fact that three key people had only been in their jobs for less than a year and one of them was new to the organization. And one team member, Axel, was causing trouble: half the team couldn't stand him and the other half supported him because they didn't want to risk his unpredictability.

Marsha needed to take action fast.

She decided to get everyone together to tackle their needs from an upbeat standpoint. Having consulted everyone, they decided to deal with:

1. What everyone relished about their jobs and what they could do to build that feeling.
2. What values they wanted to work by and how they would recognize them.
3. What actions the team and individuals needed to take to ensure they felt in control of the European product launch.

At the team session, everything started well. But it was clear that Axel was unhappy. Halfway through the day he said he had to go because he had an "urgent" customer meeting. Marsha had to act. It was a Culture-forming moment. Her authority and the team were being challenged and if she wanted to take the team in a new direction, it was now or never.

In a one-to-one session she explained how important Axel's presence was, and how personally she'd take it if he left. She told him that she would see his behavior as clearly challenging her leadership and actively sabotaging the team too. That was unacceptable and moreover didn't sit well with the values he and the team had just adopted.

He left anyway.

Marsha emailed HR: one person was going and it wasn't her. A clear signal about Culture was vital for building a successful team and launching a successful product. That was what she'd deliver.

One key issue is the effect that your personality has on your perceptions of control. Research over the past 50 years has shown that either you'll be a person who thinks that you have high control and that your efforts make a difference (an "internal"), or you'll believe that chance, fate, or other people determine what happens in your life (an "external"). And this is applicable whatever culture you come from.

The downside in being someone who is a high "internal" and who likes lots of control is that working life can seem very uncertain. Especially when handling tasks that are unclear, complex, and difficult – that need someone to adopt a more organic approach. When people are pressurized in this way they tend to react in one of the following three classic ways:

- Wanting more data, reports, and information to defer decision-making.
- Becoming over-controlling and wanting to decide every tiny detail.
- Doing an ostrich act and hoping it will all just go away.

All three reactions arise because everyone wants to make the "right" decision and to feel a sense of control in what they do. Curiously, you can sometimes achieve the greatest sense of control by simply making a decision and moving on. Even when you're not sure it's the right one.

"The minute you understand that you have to think business on a 24-hour basis then you are relieved of the pressure.

It's much better for me to be on my BlackBerry, receiving emails and voicemails 24 hours a day because then I can manage the way I want to. Saying that it's between 8 a.m. and 8 p.m. is much more restrictive. The whole way of looking at the world has changed because you can mix your life, day and night, work and play, in a more harmonious fashion which you choose. It gives you much more control."

Sylvain Hefes, Chairman, Paris-Orleans Bank S.A., holding company of N.M. Rothschild, France

"You need to set limits and stick to them. Sticking to limits reinforces you for subsequent events; it's not so much the current event that matters when you change your mind but future ones. Setting personal limits trains you psychologically never to cave in. From then on you know what's non-negotiable for you.

That way you increase your sense of control because you do things right for yourself time and time again. Your colleagues can read your determination in the whites of your eyes and from that judge if they can push you."

Malcolm Smith, Chairman, GT Tools Ltd and consultant, Derby, UK

The secret to understanding how you feel about control is correctly assessing what causes you to feel pressured and where you think agency actually lies: with you or elsewhere. Which brings me back to the BlackBerry question. If you see this as something that's managing you, it may increase feelings of pressure. If you see it as something that makes your life easier and gives you more choice, you'll think it increases your sense of control: you've put yourself, not it, in the driving seat.

Getting a greater sense of control

You can develop your sense of control in three major ways. Firstly, by deciding what you're not going to do. Choosing to say no to one thing is much harder than choosing to say yes to another: after all, you probably regret what you didn't do rather than what you do. But saying no is vital in building your sense of control. That means thinking through what you won't do in any specific context, then not crossing that line. Otherwise you'll start challenging yourself and everyone else around you will immediately pick up on it. At which point you've reduced, not increased, your control.

A second really helpful way of developing your sense of control is by finding a mentor. Mentors help you build career success by explaining what to do and how to do it. These two things greatly increase a sense of control because you have someone experienced supporting you. A good mentor is someone who is similar to you, works in your area of expertise, and, most crucially, wants to see you succeed. The best mentors do that by balancing challenge with support to get you to deliver your best.

A third way of enhancing your sense of control is to get more involved in decision-making. Getting involved shows that you care and you're committed and you're likely to get responsibility – and more control – as a result. It's what all organizations under pressure should encourage because, as our data show, it builds Commitment. Unfortunately, the pendulum often swings in the opposite direction and just when senior executives should let go of control, they grab it back because they're scared to let go when the going gets tough.

Finally, it's important to know that you probably have more control than you realize. And much more control in your working life than was possible in the very hierarchical organizations of 25 years ago. Then we did what we were told when we were told, and had fewer choices and far less control. In today's working world, what you don't control you may easily influence because information and access are so much easier to get.

Once you truly realize this it will free you to take actions, however small, to make your job or your situation better. So actively seek out what you can do rather than ruminate on what you can't. It will show you that you are the creator of your responses and author of your happiness at work.

Concluding Culture

Culture differs everywhere. From person to person, job to job, organization to organization, and country to country. So it's hardly surprising that we've found significant geographic differences. For example, in India and Pakistan people like their working Culture much more than employees in China say they do, while Americans are just ahead of the Chinese.

Culture in terms of happiness at work is made up of fixed and fluid items, some of which are prone to fluctuate more than others. For example, if you have an argument with a colleague, "liking" may take a dip: if that person then goes out of their way for you, that liking will then be boosted. It's the hardest of all the 5Cs to affect because it's the one that you may think lies least within your control. But because Culture is so influenced by tiny details and little signals you shouldn't roll over: instead think

"The ideology of building Galileo was not to make another company. It was to make something different. For example, the meeting zones were outside in nature, there were wonderful views. Later when we grew we were distributed all over the country like little start-ups. They were next to people's houses so they didn't have to travel.

Now I'm involved in philanthropic activity, which means we're trying to build models that can be duplicated and that are economically sound. When we get into a program our commitment is for 30 years. It takes many little details, philosophies, and values to make something different, but culture is everything always."

Avigdor Willenz, ex CEO Galileo, philanthropist, and social entrepreneur, Herzliya, Israel

about what you can grab, influence, and change around you because that will affect something that matters to you. Being happy at work.

Top take-aways for Chapter 6

- Culture is governed by a fixed–fluid continuum. Under this it consists of relishing your job, liking your colleagues, appreciating the values your workplace stands for, having a fair ethos at work, and being in control of your daily activities.
- Pay attention to the language that is common in your organization because it reflects Culture; if you don't like what you hear, change the terminology you use.
- Relishing your job means that the systematic vs. organic mix in your job is right for you.
- Liking your colleagues indicates strong social support.
- Appreciating your organizational values is something you can use to increase persistence.
- Having a fair ethos and control of your daily activities are really important for psychological well-being; you probably have more control and influence than you realize.

7
Commitment

Introduction to Commitment

You can't be really committed to your job unless you're happy at work – because you'll always be holding back some bit of yourself. It's that easy. Lower happiness at work results in lower Commitment, and that's abundantly clear from our research. And it explains a huge amount of your attitude, behavior, and motivation, which in turn affect your overall Contribution. When you are committed, you know why you do something, what you're aiming for, and you'll keep going until you've got there.

Commitment is what every organization wants from every employee because it has such a big impact on the bottom line. While everyone is aware of what it looks like, not many people understand how to make it happen. You'll know how hard it is to generate Commitment if you've ever been asked to do something that you disagree with. Or dislike. Or feel too exhausted to contemplate. Your lack of Commitment means you just can't deliver or perform at the levels you can when you have it. But there are some things you can do to purposefully increase it – if, of course, you want to. And that's worth considering because Commitment is such a big part of being happy at work.

"I was asked by GE to defend them and Rudy Giuliani was the US attorney. I was dealing with the senior people who were extraordinarily impressive: Jack Welch the chairman, Larry Bossidy the vice-chairman. And I said what would be a great idea if one of you guys went down with me. No knock on me but the CEO or chairman going to the US attorney's office doesn't happen. Me, they see me all the time, so it would send a different message.

So Larry Bossidy went down and we did the presentation together and it did enormous things in terms of showing that GE was serious and committed to cleaning up the mess at Kidder Peabody.

Fast forward a few years when we were doing the Salomon Brothers case and I said Warren Buffett should come down with me to do the presentation. Warren Buffett's Warren Buffett: he doesn't need much presentation, he's just good. And again it worked really well: it was all about commitment."

Gary P. Naftalis, Head of Litigation and Co-Chair, Partner, Kramer Levin Naftalis & Frankel LLP, New York, NY, USA

The Elements of Commitment

So what is Commitment made up of in relation to happiness at work? Here are the elements and how they work.

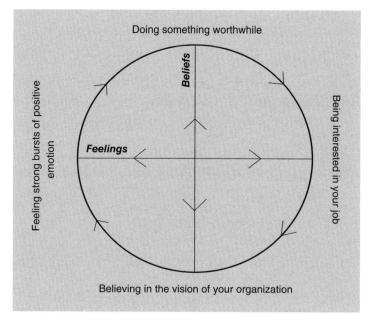

Figure 7.1   The elements of Commitment.

You can see that Commitment is made up of feelings and beliefs – in other words, it consists of a "head and a heart" approach with all the elements working to reinforce and impact one another. The starting point is the belief that you're doing something worthwhile. That generates feelings of interest in your job which in turn enable you to connect to the vision of your organization. All of these elements are then boosted by strong bursts of positive emotion. In other words, positive beliefs interact with positive feelings, creating a virtuous circle that builds your Commitment both now and in the future.

And here's how they stack up in numerical terms. Compared to those who are least happy, people who are most happy:

- Find their job 30 percent more worthwhile.
- Are 36 percent more interested in what they do.

- Believe 50 percent more in the vision of their organization.
- Feel 50 percent more bursts of positive emotion.

In other words, Commitment is much higher when you're happy.

Once these four elements are in place as well as interacting with one another, they have a kind of ripple effect impacting other things around them. Specifically, we've found that Commitment is also strongly related to loving your job, and being energized and motivated at work – as you might expect. It's also really well correlated with wanting to stay in your role and knowing that you're having a positive impact on the world.

And you'll be really clear that you have a positive impact on the world when you're doing something worthwhile.

Doing Something Worthwhile

Everyone wants to feel that they're doing something worthwhile at work. Doing "make-work" is really depressing because it's a waste of time and energy. Writing reports, making recommendations, developing plans, analyzing data, or creating budgets that you know are going to get sucked into the vortex, going unnoticed and unread, will affect your Commitment badly. Your heart won't be in it because you know what you're doing simply isn't worthwhile and your effort is meaningless. The effort you put in won't be balanced by any real kind of reward.

There's a really important issue to highlight about getting involved with things that are worthwhile. Big projects and goals which create a lasting sense of happiness and fulfillment may clash with short-term happiness highs. That's because doing something worthwhile often requires effort, discipline, and grit,

"I have this passion to save the world and to do something about it now, not tomorrow. What is more worthwhile than that?

I can't just sit by and watch because I know what I'm doing is right. Maybe it's my sense from having been a journalist; I know what I need to do and I can't stop: I want to right the wrong, correct the injustice, and to turn the world into something that is clean, green, and blue. Like it was.

No-one said it would be easy but what motivates me is that it is difficult to accomplish. I can't do it alone but if what I do touches the life of one person, influences one person, that's good enough."

Senator Loren Legarda, Manila, The Philippines

"We rescued 20,000 people so far this year and save the lives of two people a day; we're an emergency service of quite remarkable proportions. I came across a saying from the northeast of England, 'Drown we may but go we must': people are saving others' lives while putting their own at risk. They go out in huge seas and sit alongside other ships – it's genuinely dangerous – but ordinary men and women regularly go out and do extraordinary deeds which make everyone's eyes light up. There's a huge sense of belief in what we do and that it's all enormously worthwhile."

Paul Boissier, CEO RNLI, Poole, UK

"I always look for something where there's a real job to be done, something important and worthwhile where I'll face and deal with difficult issues.

For example, when I came in as CEO it was a turnaround situation. I knew I had to get breathing space from the City while we worked out what next, so I announced cost savings. And the only real costs we had were jobs.

Because we are a public company I had to announce that to the City before I announced it here. I remember walking back from the conference room after we'd done a live webcast for the analysts at half past nine in the morning. Everybody in the open-plan was listening and as I walked back through nobody caught my eye, nobody. The chairman popped his head in and said, 'It's tough sometimes, isn't it?'"

Louise Makin, CEO BTG, London, UK

"It's not possible to have all the experiences in the world. You have to take it step by step to find something which attracts you, then bring that forward into your life. Because you have the whole world in your hands, you need to find your inner voice, your inner sense, and you don't need to go to a machine or to Google for that.

You're there to do something in the world, not to consume it; to do that you need to think about what that is. Just take 15 minutes a day for meditation alone. To contemplate and to discover meanings, not to

Continued

none of which are popularly believed to be conducive to happiness. When you say no to a night out because you want to finish something important, that means something to you, any passing moment of regret will be more than compensated by making progress in that meaningful activity. Which is why we've found that people who were happiest also work hardest and score highest in the worthwhile stakes. Hard work and happiness go hand in hand, especially when you believe you're doing something worthwhile.

And knowing that you're doing something worthwhile means that you're prepared to make that effort over the longer term, ready to make difficult decisions and stick by them. That's clear from the numbers.

On the flip side of the coin, it's impossible to stretch yourself and achieve your potential if you don't think you're doing something valuable. Our findings tell us that too and of course it makes sense; why would you waste your time and effort if you didn't believe in what you were doing? Work has to mean something to you if you're going to make your best Contribution. And it has to provide you with some kind of sense of purpose.

Finding meaningful work

Desire for meaning is quite simply a basic human motivation. It's always thought to be something positive even if theorists disagree about what it is and how you get it. Finding meaning and knowing you have it are key contributors to your psychological capital and indicate that you enjoy your relationship with the world at large. And there are health benefits, which include less depression, reduced cortisol levels (indicators of pressure), and less heart disease later in life.

So what provides meaning? That's a question that philosophers have tackled for centuries; from Plato, Aristotle, Kant, Bentham, Stuart Mill, and Karl Marx (who in 1844 wrote that meaning was important if workers weren't to be alienated from what they did) through to Camus and Russell, to name just a few.

Meanwhile, psychologists have provided answers that range from the mundane, which include making daily decisions and taking action, finding the right goals, creating the right relationships, self-improvement, and meeting personal needs, to the sublime, which include finding coherence and transcending oneself.

In 1943 Abraham Maslow, whose hierarchy of needs is in almost every development or leadership book you'll ever open, wrote that meaning is acquired through "self-actualization" or maximizing your skills and talents. As a humanistic psychologist he emphasized the importance of experiencing the best of yourself. Not a million miles from the flourishing or self-fulfillment frame that positive psychology takes today.

But do all these answers really apply to today's working world? Today's workplace and practices change at lightning speed in a way that other societies and groups never did. Right now you need agility, flexibility, and resilience as never before. Boundaries are unbelievably opaque as real work is done by networks of people in fluid project teams. Because tight-knit, long-lasting working teams are rare, the new hot issue is how you find what's meaningful to you when you're part of a fast-moving, possibly peer-led group.

I think everyone finds meaning in a very pragmatic way. From all the coaching and consulting work that I've done, I believe that you start to create meaning by making decisions – as Frankl proposed. Almost everything you do – or don't do – both large and small, is a decision whether or not you're aware of it. And

make them. To hear them with your heart.

It's like the old Jesuit Father, the paleontologist who was asked why he was hammering stones. He replied, 'I am looking for the heart of the world.' Everyone has to find the heart of their world to find out what their calling is and what they have to do."

Brother Paulus Terwitte, Capuchin friar, Würzburg, Germany

"I think that you have to hold onto the very small signs of interest and follow them. You're much more likely to have interests but not know what they plug into. The idea that you would know what to do and the answer would come as a career-shaped thing is very modern.

There's a weird way in which, without quite knowing for sure what we can do, we feel the outlines. We feel, 'I could give that a shot,' even if we've never tried it. It's an affinity for some people and some things. If I see a lawyer I think, 'That just rings absolutely no bells.' Whereas if I see an architect I think, 'There is a potential me wandering around.'

I think that there's a connection between what you're good at, your intrinsic capacities, and what you're interested in."

Alain de Botton, philosopher, writer, and founder of the School of Life, London, UK

"I've always had a sense that what I'm doing is what I'm meant to be doing. Bit by bit I discovered my way into it. You take little steps and it all eventually becomes clearer.

Knowing who you are and where you are in the world is quite an important thing, and believing in something helps too. I'm a dissenter so I like taking on impossible problems and battling with them. I also like taking on things when civil servants say 'you can't'. I think it's a sign you're onto something when you see the same thing popping up in different places that you've nothing to do with."

Lord Andrew Mawson, President of Community Action Network, social entrepreneur, London, UK

as particular decisions are built up and repeated, meaning starts to emerge.

The reason that you repeat those decisions and choices is that you are drawn to and then drawn into certain activities, tasks, and relationships. These are the things you want to pay attention to. Notice the word "pay" here. What you're doing is investing yourself. You might do that because you've fallen in love with something, but I think that's rare. It's more likely that by continuously investing in something, by increasing your knowledge of it, your connection with it, you deepen your relationship and the intrinsic meaning you find in that activity.

This process is how seemingly trivial activities can become meaningful. The more you care, concentrate, and invest your time and energy, the more you'll build an extended and extensive relationship with it, whatever that "it" is. From this you derive value and meaning. As my good friend Lucy Studholme said to me when she was managing a holiday rental homes business, "there's beauty and meaning in a well-made bed." That's because as a nurse she had been taught bed-making in a specific and very detailed way, with the pillow-case opening turned away from the first sight of the bed and with beautiful "hospital" corners. Perfecting the detail and doing the job to the best of her ability is what created beauty for her; she found her work meaningful because she was not only doing this for herself but for the person who'd sleep in that bed. And, as she said, a bed is a place of intimacy – a place of birth, death, solace, and refuge. What could be more meaningful than that?

Identifying what you find meaningful

Unfortunately this won't come down like some divine inspiration. It's a realization that takes place in fits and starts and continues to grow over time. To arrive at meaning takes consideration and thought. Here are some questions to help you.

1. What am I consistently drawn to and why? Look back as far as you can remember to answer this question, then try to draw the threads together.

2. What truly matters to me and how does my job enable me to fulfill this? This question isn't about a short- or long-term goal but it's about something that lies beyond or behind that goal. For example, important personal values or a big life ambition.

3. What do both I and my organization gain from what I'm doing? This is important: one of the underlying causes of burnout is when you don't find meaning for yourself in what you do.

4. Who am I working with and what larger task am I doing in a collective sense? You are more likely to find meaningful work when connecting with others than when working alone, something that is very counterintuitive. Most people think that because what you find meaningful applies to an individual, you don't look for it in a group. That's a false assumption.

Answering these questions takes heightened awareness and effort but will help you identify what you find meaningful. And that in turn will help you clarify your sense of purpose.

Recognizing your purpose at work

Once you know what gives you meaning, you know which direction to go in. In other words, you know what your purpose is. Meaningful work is the direction: purpose is the road you take.

Purpose in life is important because it helps manage anxiety, while lack of it has been linked to depression. So according to Carol Ryff's research, it's pretty fundamental for your psychological well-being. But your overall purpose in life may – or may not – be exactly the same as your purpose at work.

It's clear from our data collection and analysis that the ultimate reason everyone works is to achieve happiness in some way. That's the end game, pure and simple. Even if you're only there for the wages you earn and you hate your daily working routine. You'll want those wages to pay your bills because that's what makes you happy.

"Everyone should realize that they have a purpose. While you don't know what your purpose is, you must at least try to add value and make this world a better place, not only for yourself but mostly for others.

The people who inspire me the most are those who do everything for others and not themselves: the purely unselfish. Like the cleaners in my office this morning. I know the hardships in their community, how they fear for the safety of their children … and they work particularly hard. But it's all smiles and 'are you satisfied with the office?' It's a wonderful attitude. Nothing I ask of them is too much: that keeps me going.

Through them you realize that you have a purpose to add value and make the lives of others better by using the talents you have."

George Steyn, Managing Director, Pep Stores, Cape Town, South Africa

Being able to pay those bills makes a difference to you or you would find another way to live.

Most people at work want to make a difference by doing their job. I haven't met a single person who *hasn't* wanted to achieve that end. Just to give you an idea, every single interviewee for this book told me that they want their work to make a difference. What defines your unique purpose is the route you take to do that. Here's how some of the interviewees for this book have answered my question, "How do you want to make a difference at work?"

- "By sustaining nature to keep the planet intact." Tony Juniper, environmentalist, UK.
- "By doing what's right for humanity." Senator Loren Legarda, The Philippines.
- "By meeting the needs of our teachers and partners to meet the whole needs of the child." Kate Scott, assistant headmaster, USA.
- "By upholding Britain and all she stands for." Senior officer, Special Forces, UK.
- "By making a lovely environment for our guests to be in." Hotel cleaner, USA.
- "By doing something that fully transforms a particular area of inequity in a way that means it can't turn back." Olivia Leland, Gates Foundation, USA.
- "By helping people wake up." Henry Shukman, poet and author, USA.
- "By contributing to the advance of science." Professor Felicitas Pauss, particle physicist, CERN, France/Switzerland.
- "By making something happen in the world through wisdom and beauty." Alain de Botton, philosopher and author, UK.
- "By addressing a wrong and righting an injustice on a playing field that isn't level." Gary P. Naftalis, lawyer, USA.

There are two things to note here. Firstly, all these answers go beyond the practical day-to-day stuff of any job or career. There's something almost noble in all the statements, a connection to a higher and harder-to-realize concept: that's an indicator of purpose. Secondly, when you look at all these statements, embedded in them is an idea of service to others.

There can be challenges to your sense of purpose too.

If you've gone through massive downsizing, are unemployed, or are having to do a job you don't like, you might be seriously questioning the very notion of purpose or happiness at work. Perhaps you can't see how you can make a difference, or to whom. Big life events by their very nature will require you to rethink what the route to happiness in a work context means for you and then how you achieve it. Your changed circumstances will necessarily give you pause for thought.

If this is you, I recommend that you start thinking about who would be negatively affected if you weren't who you are or doing what you do in or outside work. Who – friends, family, colleagues past or present, and people in your community – are you now making a positive difference to? Then work out how you deliver that difference in or out of work. If purpose is too much to think about, at least think how these positive differences quicken an interest in what you do.

Being Interested in Your Job

Interest is the stuff that engages your energy with a task. So it was no surprise to look at the numbers and see that it's strongly associated with both energy and engagement. The more interested you are in what you do, the more engagement you'll experience. In fact the numbers reveal that people who are most interested in their jobs are literally 110 percent more engaged in what they're doing than the least interested and engaged groups.

If you're not interested in what you do, the hours really drag. A day seems like a week and a week like a nightmare. So what makes you really interested in your job, other than believing that you're doing something worthwhile? According to psychologist Amy Wrzesniewski, work divides into three categories: what she calls jobs, careers, and callings.

A job you do for the money – it's simply the means to an end because you find purpose elsewhere. Maybe you volunteer, something which is well known for increasing happiness, are caring for others, or pursuing educational aims

"I was going around the office and I asked this guy, 'Where does what you process go next?' 'Don't know,' he said. 'Do you want to know?' 'I suppose so.' His boss just happened to be there and he started asking around. It turned out for 18 months he'd been sending stuff on to the bloke who was sitting next to him. It was just the way the office was configured.

I said, 'Would you like to talk to each other? Does he do a good job? Are there things you think you know that could be better?' It's the thought and interest that people have in all the small things which create a lot of value when you add them all up."

Matt Idle, Head of Operations, British Gas, Delhi, India

instead. You're not attached to the job you do and will stop if any aspect of it becomes inconvenient or wrong for you.

A career you do for money and status, so when these run out you'll start to look for a new job. A career only has a certain level of interest attached to it, which is why the material benefits associated with it matter so much. It partly explains why so many people who were in finance are now looking at radically different career options – the money ran out. And they want to try to find their calling.

A calling involves intense interest in the work for its own sake. When you have a calling, you'll see what you do as fulfilling in and of itself. Because it has meaning and gives you a sense of purpose. So even if the money or status cease, you'll continue with the work. The time you put in is immaterial because it doesn't feel like *work*. That's why some people choose to work such long hours: because they truly find that there's no more fun than work.

Whether you see yourself as having a job, a career, or a calling doesn't depend on seniority or the kind of work you do. According to Wrzesniewski, about one third of the people in each and every job will be working at their calling. In fact her original study was done with 28 hospital cleaners who fell into all three categories. But there's no doubt about it: if you see what you do as a calling, you'll be working additional tasks into your job because that increases your interest in it. That is, you'll be crafting and customizing your role.

Job crafting implies that there are tasks and relationships which can be expanded, reduced or changed, or done differently to make your job more interesting and meaningful to you. The first step is to ensure that those tasks and relationships fit your needs and preferences over a period of time.

The second step is to reframe what you do to perceive it differently, so you can see the job as a whole rather than as a set of separate tasks.

> "Since foot-and-mouth disease in 2001 there's not the same interest as there was. A lot of people spent three generations breeding a flock of sheep or a herd of cows and then they were all slaughtered. They had to start up again and you know, there's nothing there; the interest and enthusiasm for it's gone when you've lost 100 years of breeding. Everyone carries on as best they can and farmers go to market now, but we don't congregate and talk and discuss things like we used to."
>
> David Davis, hill farmer, Gwenddwr, Wales

> "In order for me to get up in the morning and feel excited about what I do, I have to think that more funds will be going to issues that I care very deeply about. That's why I'm doing it, why I work the hours I work. How do you live in a world where people have such tremendous differences in opportunity? If you could actually do something about these issues, why wouldn't you?"
>
> Olivia Leland, Senior Program Officer, Bill and Melinda Gates Foundation

There's the famous story of John Kennedy bumping into the janitor at NASA and asking him what he did. And the man replied, "Helping to put a man on the moon." That's how you see a job as part of a whole endeavor.

Of course some jobs are much easier to craft than others, especially if you're in a management role. But all jobs can be crafted by taking on additional tasks, building close relationships, and thinking about your work differently. Doing this actively not only creates strong intrinsic interest in your job but also adds to your overall Commitment because you get what's interesting for you.

If you take job crafting to the next stage you'll arrive at something a level deeper than interest. You'll get to vital engagement.

Understanding vital engagement

Vital engagement is something that Jeanne Nakamura and Mihaly Csikszentmihalyi have been investigating. Built on moments of flow (see Chapter 5), it reflects a powerful experience of doing something worthwhile that takes you beyond interest into something much deeper. When you're vitally engaged, you're doing something which is profoundly important to you, which links your past, present, and future, and which connects you to a community of others who share your passion.

When you are vitally engaged with something, you'll find it so compelling that you want to invest more of yourself and deepen your relationship with it. That relationship will then feel as if it's much greater than the sum of its parts; there'll be a value to you way beyond the activity itself.

That means you'll be so drawn to and interested in whatever you're doing that you wouldn't want to do anything else; it's intense, positive, and compelling. And over time it forms a strong part of your identity.

If you've never experienced vital engagement, the place to start is by identifying flow moments

"I remember the first time I wrote a poem. I was about fourteen and it was the most surprising and exciting thing I've ever done. I was trembling afterwards with an energy which was wild, vital, exhilarating: I'd never felt so alive. All my senses were heightened and so acute. Something that was deeply in love with the world seemed to wake up in a way that I'd never experienced before. And to continue to experience that kind of love and wakefulness seemed more important to me than everything else.

Poetry is a form of connection with another order of reality, which is a deeper, truer one. You're pulling on things that don't yet exist by following this current of energy which throws words up and you grab them. It's an amazing thing to do. The best analogy is that famous Michelangelo one, where he says that he's looking for the sculpture in the stone that's looking for him."

Henry Shukman, poet and author, Santa Fe, NM, USA

and connecting to others with similar interests. Vital engagement is boosted when you're part of a group of people doing the same as you do, so finding others and making those links is important.

When you are vitally engaged, it's easy for you to relate to the vision of your organization; after all, your workplace is enabling you to do what you love. But if that ever changes, you'll work intensely and passionately to preserve what's imperative to you.

Believing in the Vision of Your Organization

One of the best vision statements ever written is the American Declaration of Independence. Like all enduring visions, it doesn't need updating or rewriting. It's unique and aspirational, painting a bright and better future for everyone. Best of all, it's inspirational while simple to understand: there's nothing difficult about "Life, Liberty, and the Pursuit of Happiness." And just in case you don't get the message, or you want more detail, there's a lengthy explanation why the current state of affairs won't do.

In essence all great vision statements are brief motivational outlines of a specific future that applies to a specific group. In other words, they reflect a broad-brush outline of long-term direction. It's interesting to bear in mind that the very word "vision" implies something sacred. After all, a vision is an experience associated with a seer or religious mystic. Yet while it's absurd to think that any organization should be aiming for the same effect, there are some important reasons why you should connect with your workplace's vision.

For example, there's good evidence that clear and appropriate vision statements can help you up your game. Because you know where you're headed you know what you should do. Additionally, our research shows that if you

"I've got a number of non-traditional business influences from being a doctor and social activist in the time of apartheid.

My vision is to change society by using different business models and working with communities. For example, we decided not to go into gambling when we had the opportunity because we would not exploit people; instead we built partnerships.

We got our workers on boards, making decisions and participating, engaging them as partners in the business, and sending people on development programs.

Business is a great platform to do things differently, to shift the focus to poverty reduction, to develop a skills-base, to be patriotic to your country and your continent. It's an ideal which is very difficult to achieve but we shaped a lot of the good you see today."

Dr. Iqbal Surve, doctor, social entrepreneur, Chairman and CEO Sekunjalo Investments Ltd, Cape Town, South Africa

believe in the vision of your organization, you'll be more productive and have a higher overall level of Commitment and Contribution, which you'll intend to maintain.

We know that because if you have high levels of Commitment, showing maximum belief in the vision of your organization, you'll intend to stay in your job for 75 percent longer than your colleagues or peers who do not think or feel the same way. This matters not just for you, because you know you're currently on the right track. It also matters for your employers because of the high costs of replacing you wherever you are in your organization.

Unfortunately, there are simply hundreds of thousands of really poor vision statements which are simply screeds of meaningless drivel that, like the old Martini advertisement, could fit anytime, anyplace, anywhere. Which means that it's highly unlikely that anyone will be inspired by them, believe in them, or even start to make them happen. Because this is what a great vision does. It unites and commits a disparate group of people to achieve a long-term and often opaque future.

So what makes a great vision which everyone can easily connect with and commit to? According to Kouzes and Posner, just like the American Declaration of Independence the best organizational visions imply an excellence yet to be achieved. In addition our work with teams and businesses has found that really good vision statements:

> "When the company's vision and strategies are understood and articulated at staff level that feels good. We've shared what's important, they get it, seem excited, and talk it back. The messages have started to resonate back up the organization.
>
> That's a positive sign. It tells you there's a lot of pride in the environment and that they believe in what we want to do."
>
> Betsy Blair, COO, CJW Medical Center, Richmond, VA, USA

- Indicate where a bigger, better, and brighter future lies.
- Set you apart from others.
- Help people move from the abstract to the concrete.
- Indicate clearly where priorities lie.
- Imply certain values and behavior.

Because a compelling vision clarifies direction, you'll know where best to commit your effort and energy. When everyone can articulate that vision you know that a huge amount of personal effort will flow in the same direction. That means a vision should be a useful checking mechanism: when everyone's agreed to the same thing and talks positively about it, you

"At the UN in September Gordon Brown spoke about user fees for health care and said that they were killing poor people – and then the head of the WHO said it. That was a moment when I thought, 'Fantastic, it's been said,' because we've been advocating it for years and we're starting to see it happen: Malawi has stopped having user fees.

You're never on your own working these big policy issues but you have to keep articulating them to keep everything moving along."

Barbara Stocking, CEO Oxfam, Oxford, UK

"Today I felt a high like I hadn't felt in years. I was picking up my voicemail and I got a call to tell me that a huge donor was interested in taking my charity national. It would be immense for all the kids in the UK and for us too.

What I felt was a whole body experience and I had to let out a shout because I thought I'd otherwise implode. It was absolutely amazing."

Juli Beattie, Director and founder, The Art Room, UK

know you'll all be working together to make things happen.

You know that when leaders get this right and articulate the vision in a clear and compelling way that actually means something and isn't expressed in tortuous "management-speak," then followers listening to them feel inspired, motivated, and connected. In other words, the result is a strong burst of positive emotion.

Feeling Strong Bursts of Positive Emotion

What I'm talking about here are the highs you experience at work. Those marvelous moments when all's right with the world. You experience yourself at your best and your mojo's doing magic for you: your ideas were fabulous, the praise was public, the problem was solved, and the customer or client was delighted. All because of you.

Isn't a happiness high amazing? Isn't it sad how short-lived the effect is? This is another one of the few areas where we've noticed a gender difference: women report that they are not only happier at work but that they experience significantly more positive emotions than men do.

These highs are important, and not only for how you feel in the moment. They are a huge great signpost that tells you to keep on going. How you feel affects what you do and the effort you put in, and the better you feel, the harder you try both now and in the immediate future. In addition you're building a store of moments to use as boosters for when the lows come along: those peaks can create resilience when you're faced with a trough at a later date. This is exactly the stuff that psychological capital is made of.

There's another benefit to generating positive emotions. They create what Barbara Fredrickson calls a broaden-and-build model, which suggests that when you're feeling good, you're more likely to have wider thoughts and this will translate into broader actions. For example, if you're feeling good you might make time to explore a problem with someone and light upon a solution. By broadening, you build. When you're feeling overwhelmed by hassles, you might skip a conversation that is actually helpful and productive. Having this broader approach has a benefit over the longer term: it means you'll increase your skills, resources, and development. So pursuing positive emotions has a benefit over and beyond the immediate feel-good factor.

Given the benefits of positive emotions, it's good to work out how you get more of them. Is it by breaking a big goal down into manageable objectives? Nurturing important relationships? Pushing until you make a breakthrough? Taking time for a coffee? Doing something courageous? Persisting when no-one else would? If you keep track of what leads to your highs at work, you'll start to see patterns emerging. And you can then use those patterns to help generate new and additional highs by seeking similar circumstances. Or by looking for new contexts to do similar things in.

Case study: Commitment

Beth had a background in the government sector. After her MBA at a prestigious business school, she'd decided to accept a position working for an international charity whose aims she passionately believed in. She had been strongly drawn to the vision that this NGO had and the advocacy work it did. And she knew her aspirations and beliefs would be completely aligned with the organization's aims and ambitions.

Recently, however, she'd started to ask herself where her job was going. Beth was aware that she'd lost interest in what she was doing and her working days had started to feel like a grind. She'd had some big goals to deliver, liaising internationally with ministries in developing nations. And although she only had the support of a small team, over the past two years she had more than delivered what had been expected of her. Exceeding expectations was her forte and her political savvy had led to some astute handling of difficult government officials and some big wins for her NGO.

Continued

But when she thought about her immediate future, all she could see was more of the same. Was it just going to be an eternal round of flights, egos, meetings, and minutes? There'd been a time when she'd lost herself in her work because she found it so compelling, when the highs had really been that. Now she felt little excitement or positive emotion about what she had to do.

Realizing that her levels of Commitment had dropped off dramatically, Beth took some time to think about where the issue really lay and what she could do about it. She realized that it wasn't the travel that she minded. What she felt was a disconnection from the people whose lives her NGO's work most touched. Each flight somehow reinforced a lack of attachment to the wider community within which she worked.

Beth understood that while she had been delivering great things for her organization, her work wasn't meaningful enough for her. She knew she didn't want to leave, but she wondered if moving outside the organization's corporate structure and working out in the field was what she wanted. But was that what she had done an MBA for? What would her business school peers think?

Having thought about this for a couple of weeks to see how she felt, she knew that, MBA or not, this was the direction she wanted to go in. In that time she'd started looking at projects she'd like to support and had found two she thought particularly worthwhile. Now was the time to talk to her boss.

Six months later, ensconced in a new assignment, she emailed to say that the hardest part had been admitting to herself that her Commitment waned as much as it had. But once she'd done that, everything else had just seemed to fall into place. And she'd been delighted to find how much support she'd received from her peers for following her real interests.

This is all very well and good when things are going well. What about when times are tougher? Or you're under pressure being bawled at by a tricky customer? How do you access positive emotions at those times? One instant fix-it is to ask yourself, "What am I hopeful of in this situation?" In the above example, you could be hopeful that that customer will eventually stop, that you'll handle the situation professionally and with dignity, and that he or she will apologize to you later. By thinking about what you're hopeful of, you turn your mind to a positive future. Which is where hope always takes you. That's why it's so useful when you want to access more upbeat emotions.

Hope

Like lots of psychological concepts, hope is both a trait (your personality) and a state (your mindset). Whatever it comes from, it's valuable because it's a kicker to action and it's clearly associated with higher job performance and happiness. In fact some psychologists call it a "Velcro" concept as it seems to enable you to stick to your commitments regardless of your other attributes. For example, pessimists achieve incredible goals when they have high levels of hope.

So what is hope made up of? According to positive psychologist Rick Snyder, it has two important elements: the way to success (pathways) and the will to do it (willways). He found that when you have a big goal that you want to achieve, any one pathway is likely to be only about 20 percent successful. So to ensure success you need at least five or six pathways. These pathways are not options that you evaluate but different ways of getting to the same thing.

For example, the pathways to getting this book published meant finding out how to write a proposal by talking to two people about what it should contain; writing that proposal and bouncing it off several others to get their feedback; talking informally and formally to a couple of agents; meeting with three publishers to find out what they were currently looking for; and getting advice from people who'd done what I was trying to do. And I was pursuing all those actions at the same time hoping that everything would come together in a contract. That's how pathways work.

"To lose hope is to die. As long as I'm still breathing and as long as people are still listening, we shouldn't lose hope.

Hope is what I owe the millions who voted for me. I owe them the inspiration and hope to change things: these emotions have to propel me and I must keep that flame burning. Hope pushes me to fight."

Senator Loren Legarda, Manila, The Philippines

"For those who are hopeless I give hope. I tell people you'll never succeed if you undermine yourself. You'll never succeed if you worry and tell yourself, 'I'm not educated, I can't do this.' God gave you brains and hands to do things. All my life I worked for the ANC and I don't have a pension. I don't blame them because they gave me strength to do my thing, to organize myself. The more you go through fire, the more you can do and the more hope you can have and bring to others."

Monwabisi Maqogi, ex-freedom fighter, entrepreneur, Khyalitsha, South Africa

You know that you are developing pathways if there's a follow-on action to achieve the ultimate goal – and one action alone won't lead to the goal itself. But developing these alternatives means that you are building a more robust success strategy.

Willways refer to your level of motivation and dedication to each pathway. You can check that by asking yourself, "0–10 how much do I want to pursue this particular pathway?" and "0–10 how much am I prepared to invest in it?" Anything 5 or under means you're highly unlikely to take action.

Snyder also found that hopeful employees have some interesting characteristics. They:

- Engage in positive self-talk.
- Focus on success, not failure, thereby motivating themselves and others.
- Tend to be future-oriented in their conversations and thinking.
- Use positive language around goals and objectives.
- Experience fewer negative feelings when they experience failure.

What you'll notice about these is that, with the possible exception of the last point, they are all behaviors which are under your control. Hope, which seems so intangible when you first think about it, can actually have some very solid and tangible effects on your overall motivation and Commitment.

Concluding Commitment

One thing is certain. Commitment can either snowball because you become so connected to and involved in what you're doing. Or it can melt and evaporate. Then you'll definitely find it hard to be interested in your job, let alone relate to the vision of your organization. As for strong bursts of positive emotion, they'll probably turn up regularly but only as you leave on a Friday afternoon.

Commitment is a concept that's harder to get to the core of than Contribution, Conviction, and Culture for two reasons. Firstly, it's rare that you get to talk about Commitment. How would you ever be able to own up to your boss that you have a Commitment issue? And on top of that it's very tough to talk about subjects like meaning and purpose at work.

Because it's a largely unaddressed subject, most people will judge your Commitment and make assumptions about it by looking at your Contribution levels. If you don't deliver in the way they want or expect, one automatic conclusion will be that you're not happy, engaged, or committed. So it's worth thinking through what others might see in you from this perspective. Put yourself in their shoes and run through a couple of interactions. How might they interpret what you say and do?

What else would you like them to think and what will you have to do to make that happen? Actions may speak louder than words, but sometimes it's the thought that determines the quality of those very actions.

Finally, Commitment is one of the most interesting of the 5Cs because it's something that's so hard to get to grips with. Our research and practice have not only done this but shown the effect it has and what it takes to build it too.

Top take-aways for Chapter 7

- Commitment consists of doing something worthwhile, being interested in your job, believing in the vision of your organization, and having strong bursts of positive emotion. All these feelings and beliefs interact and reinforce one another.
- Doing something worthwhile breaks into two parts: finding meaningful work and identifying your overall purpose. Fundamental to this is making a difference to yourself and others.
- Being interested in your job is more likely if you have a calling: job crafting will help take you there. Vital engagement is what you'll experience when you have it.
- Believing in the vision of your organization is affected by a strong vision statement and leaders who can communicate it effectively.
- Feeling strong bursts of positive emotion tells you you're on the right track. And hope helps you access positive emotions when the going gets tough.

8

Confidence

"Most big jobs carry a level of complexity which means no individual can be fully across all of it. Confidence is essential for trusting your judgment to the point when you know to make the call.

Take the Barings debacle. The bank went bust over the weekend and over the course of the next three days I was responsible for 1,500 people in Asia. On Monday everyone was saying, 'What do we do next?' I honestly didn't know what to do next. HQ had blown up and theoretically the administrators were in charge. I just had the approach that I'd take responsibility because no-one else seemed to want to do it and I had the confidence. That meant getting everybody involved in keeping things going.

We decided we'd deal with our customers as we always had but start a conversation with, 'I'm not going to be charging you for this.' Because we could still show we valued our relationships and our work.

Confidence and risk are closely linked: you won't take a risk unless you have that right combination of a rational basis and emotional commitment. It affects everyone

Continued

Introduction to Confidence

Confidence is the last of the 5Cs in terms of statistical importance. But it's one on which all the others depend: you can't have Contribution, Conviction, or Commitment without it; that's why having Confidence and being aware of it is vitally important in your working life. With it, today's hopes turn into tomorrow's reality; without it, motivation is never converted into action. If you're in the category of people who have the highest levels of happiness at work, you'll have a whopping 40 percent more Confidence than your least happy colleagues. That Confidence affects what you do and how you manage in your working environment because it tells you that you are making the right choices and doing the right things.

Most of us take Confidence for granted when it's there and become beset by doubt and indecision when it's not. So you can easily see that it's essential for psychological capital. And Confidence gives you the knowledge you can handle not only tasks, but relationships too. That shows how important it is for social capital too.

What about lack of Confidence? When you lack Confidence you'll know how tough it is to make a decision or to do difficult things. Your self-belief, ability to deliver, and energy all take a knock as we can see from our data. People who have more Confidence also have 25 percent more self-belief, get 35 percent more done, and have 180 percent more energy than their least Confident colleagues. So it's essential for delivering a sustained effort in the short and long term.

around you, which is why I always look for it in others. But crucially, humility must be there too. You need confidence to prioritize and use your judgment to make decisions, but at the same time arrogance is a big business risk. We've all learned that to our cost in recent times."

Jeremy Palmer, senior financier, Oxford, UK

What Does Confidence Consist Of?

If you're like most people, you'll experience Confidence as something that has a hard center surrounded by softer and flakier edges. The hard center is made up of getting things done, the solid evidence which tells you "yes I can." The softer, flakier, and more fragile edge is made up of self-belief and your understanding of your role. These three are the key elements of Confidence in a happiness framework.

That harder center is more difficult to dislodge but the flaky and fragile edge is much more vulnerable: it's what you'll notice most when your Confidence takes a knock. All it takes is a gut-churning split second to turn from certainty to hesitation and action to inaction.

The most vivid experience I ever had of that was leading a strategy team event with a colleague in Switzerland ten years ago. We'd just finished most of the serious indoors stuff so it was time for a climb in the Alps. As someone dropped out at the last minute, the professional mountain guides we were working with offered me the place. Not wanting to be a wimp, I found myself in a harness and hard-hat standing around in an unprepossessing car park about to do a "Via Ferrata" or iron way. That's mountain climbing attached to ropes, cables, and harnesses and involves a lot of clipping then unclipping of karabiners with one hand to attach them to bars embedded in the rock face. Although I'd watched the safety briefing the night before, I'd not actually practiced using all the kit.

Stephan was climbing behind me. Just before we set off he mentions that he's nervous and gets vertigo. Now I'm not great with heights but cope by always looking out, not down. We chat about it as we start to clamber across the rocks, distracting ourselves with talk about handholds and footholds as we climb steadily higher. Then he asks me if I have the time. I glance back as I tell him. Fatal mistake. My anxiety, already heightened by his and our situation, spins out of control as I look down into the valley. I feel and taste a massive rush of heart-pumping adrenalin and cortisol.

I can't breathe properly and, hyperventilating, I start to shake. Now I can't reach for the next foothold: I'm bathed in sweat and pinioned to the rock face unable to move. Nor can I hear what the mountain guide is yelling at me, which is to let go, relax, and rely on the harness. I'm only 10 feet from him but he can't get my attention. Finally I hear Stephan telling me to breathe in through my nose and out through my mouth. I calm down and he talks me out of the only full-blown panic attack I've ever had. Three minutes later we've reached the lip, which I hadn't been able to see. My complete lack of perspective and total breakdown in Confidence meant I was unable to trust what I was being told.

That's how the flakier and more fragile part of Confidence can grab you unexpectedly. And it's particularly affected when you don't have the skill to cope, will to take action, or a good understanding of the environment you're in.

Other things that affect it include your personality and your previous experiences. For example, you might be a typically confident person, but could feel really apprehensive and uncertain just before presenting to 500 people for the first time, even though you're comfortable talking to your team of 20. What matters, though, is not your level of Confidence per se: it's how you cope with the physiological effects.

The Effects of Lack of Confidence …

When you find you're short on Confidence, you'll have doubts about your ability. The more you dwell on those doubts, the more anxious you'll become about your performance and worried about what others will think of you. This anxiety reduces your mental capacity to handle the task and the attention you have: you're flooded with worry instead. That lack of space further reduces your Confidence. You'll feel unable to take a risk, you pull back, and the result is a negative downwards spiral.

... and Excessive Confidence

If lack of confidence is difficult to deal with, over-confidence can be much worse. Especially when it appears as arrogance. But here's a fact. Most of us over-estimate our abilities from time to time and think that we're much better than we are, especially when the task at hand is a tough one. And actually that's a psychologically healthy thing to do. If you had accurate thoughts about what you could do, you'd never set the bar any higher nor make an extra effort to jump over it. The world's innovators, leaders, and reformers take a highly optimistic view of their capabilities, which, as long as they aren't unduly exaggerated or over-blown, builds Confidence.

But this over-estimation also explains why projects, deadlines, and schedules are so often late. And although both the experienced and inexperienced do this, it's particularly true of people who don't know their personal limitations or can't do anything about them. Ignorance is bliss – except if you're affected by its impact. And can't get your work done.

Getting Things Done

When we looked at the data and saw that "getting things done" was part of Confidence, not Contribution, we were really surprised. But on reflection we saw it made sense. It's the only outer measure you have to judge your inner Confidence. And the more you get done, the more Confidence you feel: that real-world validation creates an internal positive feedback loop which then reinforces your ability to plan, manage, and deliver.

"Over-confidence can result in a weird accelerator effect; in 2007 I was in a room with a very senior person from Lehman who went to great lengths to tell me how investment banks should be on twelve times earnings not seven times earnings because the whole world misunderstood their intellectual depth and quality, and their ability to trade successfully through any economic cycle.

And you know he wasn't a stupid person but he really believed it. Twelve months later Lehman had disappeared."

Jeremy Palmer, senior financier, Oxford, UK

"By asking, 'What must we do to achieve our goal?' you fundamentally change the answers and your focus.

For example, when I was at Procter & Gamble something we really focused on were 'unspoken' consumer needs. Take washing powder. If you asked people at that time, 'Is there a problem opening your soap boxes?' they'd say no.

But when we watched them in their houses, we saw people using scissors, knives, and even saws to get the boxes open. It's what led us to the zip-open top. It was a game-changing initiative which we got to by focusing on those 'unspoken' needs."

William Schultz, President and CEO, Coca-Cola Bottlers, Makati City, The Philippines

Planning is a really important part of getting things done and it implies two important things: being able to put some things off to focus right now on some future moment when you will have delivered. By the way, it's not only humans who do this: chimps, orangutans, and even bees do it too. But the hardest part in maintaining focus is not getting involved with competing activities. That can only be delivered with high levels of self-control, which, just like hope, has a big impact on motivation.

Exercising self-control: the route to breakthrough

Self-control is hard. You'll know that perfectly well if you've ever been on a diet, tried to adopt an exercise regime, do professional exams, or simply drunk too much alcohol on a week night. It's an area that challenges many of us much of the time, which is why it takes "exercising." If you never use it, your self-control will certainly be flabby. But if you ever want to do anything difficult, the only way you'll get there is by sticking with it – by persevering – because that's how you achieve breakthroughs and get things done.

What you may not realize is that self-control is tough because it's a limited and therefore precious resource. You'll have noticed that when you've done a 12-hour day. But even a single act of self-control appears to reduce what's available to you.

When you're exercising self-control you're involved in three important mental processes: thinking things through to imagine the consequences of doing or not doing a task; delaying doing what you really want to; and managing procrastination. The first one is easy, the last two much tougher.

> "I've got two, three big ideas not counting the things I'm currently doing; but I know one day they're going to happen and I'm not letting them go.
>
> Breakthroughs come with absolute determination and visioning. When I get an idea and I can see it, then I know it's going to happen.
>
> I don't let things go and I bring them up with the right people to find the right partners to work with; I know how to have influence. That's how I make things happen."
>
> Lynne Franks, PR guru, visionary, and author, London, UK

Delaying what you want, also known as delayed gratification, is a huge part of self-control. Walter Mischel did a series of famous experiments in the 1960s offering marshmallows to 4-year-olds but doubling the amount if they could sit alone and wait 15 minutes before eating them. Amazingly, some kids could wait for more than an hour while others simply couldn't resist at all. Even for 30 seconds. Fourteen years later, these teenagers were revisited. Those who'd managed to wait the 15 minutes could plan better, were more socially competent, paid greater attention, and could handle life's frustrations more skillfully than the kids who had been unable to sit it out.

So how do you work to put off the pleasure? Mischel discovered that thinking more about "cool" or informational qualities (the shape of a sweet) made it easier to wait than thinking about "hot" qualities (the taste). It's no surprise that dwelling on hot stuff is more arousing, frustrating, and leads to quitting faster. In the same vein at work you don't have to focus on the "hot" qualities of annoying colleagues, irritating tasks, or difficult interactions if you're working to a tight deadline. Thinking about the "cool" qualities of a task or process will make it easier to complete what you're doing.

Another approach is purposeful self-distraction. The kids that waited longest would often distract themselves by singing, covering their eyes, turning round, kicking the desk, and even stroking the marshmallow. They took their minds off the task by doing other things. In a work context you can reduce distraction by turning off your emails or cell phone for short periods and hiding out in meeting rooms to finish important things. Actively controlling your attention or directing your thoughts to create conditions in which you can focus is how you increase will power.

Exactly the same process but working in a negative direction results in procrastination.

Understanding procrastination

Procrastination takes place when you don't like doing something because it's too tough, too boring, doesn't feel important, and you get less feedback for it. Which is why my backyard looks like a jungle. In one study more than 90 percent of students reported that they procrastinated – a number that holds true outside student life too. Just in case you thought you were different, note that:

- Professional workers are more likely to procrastinate than unskilled workers.
- The cleverer you are, the more you procrastinate.
- Age, gender, and education don't affect time spent procrastinating.
- The average employee spends a staggering 80 minutes a day doing personal activities as a way of avoiding the tough stuff.

Procrastination isn't good for your employer – or you. When you procrastinate, you:

- Teach yourself to avoid things instead of doing them.
- Strengthen and reinforce your avoidance habit every time you do it.
- Create self-fulfilling prophecies about the difficulty of a task.
- Waste energy and time on thinking rather than doing.
- Pile stuff up.

You're more likely to take action when your choices are limited, you're working to externally imposed deadlines, and you have routines and systems to help you. As unglamorous as it is, people who are organized tend not to procrastinate.

But here's the good news for the procrastinators out there: it may not be all bad.

Some people are what's called "active procrastinators." If that's you, you'll intentionally put things off because doing that gives you a big buzz. You're the kind of person that finds pulling a rabbit out of a hat three minutes before a deadline a wonderful self-challenge. And active procrastinators believe that they incubate ideas better, maximize time, are more efficient, and create more flow experiences as a result. If this is you, just let your colleagues know so that you manage their expectations.

Meanwhile, you can build focus by using some of the tried and tested mind tools that are common currency amongst sports professionals. What's important about these tools is that they have been empirically shown to help athletes minimize procrastination and – literally – stay on track.

"Once there was a monk who left the monastery to look for herbs. He climbed and as he was climbing he came across a tiger which was incredibly frightening to behold. The monk was terrified; he didn't know what to do. He wanted to run away but it was too steep and he knew he'd fall.

Then he remembered that he had packed a rope which he tied around a tree; he descended down it to try and escape the tiger. But he only had bad luck. He looked up and saw a rat gnawing away at the rope and the
Continued

Using mind tools to help you deliver

There are now thousands of research papers that clearly show how mental techniques can boost Confidence and performance. But it's hardly new news that what you think or say to yourself has a big effect on how you feel and behave.

Positive tools that sports men and women adopt include *thinking techniques, using self-talk, centering,* and *working with imagery,* all of which fast-track learning, preparing, focusing, and performing in the moment. And most importantly have been shown to increase Confidence.

Thinking techniques

If I ask you, "What are the positive benefits of being a parent and having a demanding job?," you're primed for positivity. You'll think about the upside and what you have, not what you lack. Feeling swamped and acting out of a pressurized negative place is not a good way of getting things done because anxiety narrows your attention, reducing your ability to think creatively or to problem solve. If I ask you, "Are you stressed?," what are you likely to reply? You've been primed to think negatively.

It might surprise you to learn that I'm not into stopping thinking negatively. That's because "not thinking" is an impossible act. Try not thinking about food when you're on a diet. Or not thinking about cigarettes when you want to give up smoking. "Not thinking" causes more thinking, so the process backfires. Somehow suppressing a thought makes it permanently at the front of your mind, which means that you think about it all the more.

Dan Wegner has done decades of experiments asking people not to think about a white bear. The major problem with this task is the only way to be certain that you're on task and not thinking about a white bear is to check into – yup, you've got it – that white bear. The consequences of doing a task like this is often a big mental block as you struggle with what you can or can't think about.

In the same way pressure to avoid a pitfall or pratfall can be so intense and at the forefront of your mind that it's exactly the outcome you achieve – and you fail. Golfers whose smooth movements suddenly disappear when putting call this the "yips," and darts players who suddenly can't throw or release darts smoothly know

tiger looking down on him too. The monk lost hope rapidly as he thought he was doomed. Then he saw that there were berries growing and he paused. Even in the middle of that pressure-filled situation, he found it was possible to discover something else.

When we look at the world full of psychological and mental suffering, we don't have to be obsessed by the past or focus on the future. We can focus our attention on the present and allow that to support our calmness and well-being. The precious circumstances of human existence can bring well-being to our minds and it's important to reflect on that."

His Holiness, The 17th Gyalwa Karmapa, Trinlay Thaye Dorje, Sikkim, India

"Sometimes when it's minus 78 degrees the pain of the cold is all consuming and you can't focus. Or you decide to put it in a box. You say, 'Yeah it hurts, but I can't deal with you right now.' I did that especially when I was out front looking for the route north.

Sometimes it was so cold that when I fell I'd think, 'I can't bear this anymore.' Or when I was getting up in the morning and it was snowing inside the tent because of the condensation. I'd just sob. But I didn't want the others to see me crying. It wasn't that I couldn't deal with it, it was a mechanism to help me get through. It was my last luxury."

Ann Daniels, polar explorer, Exeter, UK

it as "dartitis." This is what you might have experienced if you've ever really rehearsed what you wanted to say then forgotten to deliver your message; spilt your drink publicly and humiliatingly even if you were telling yourself not to; or struggled to retain a vital concept or name despite being frequently reminded. In all of these situations, and the countless others that exist beside, you're wrestling with another mental white bear.

There are two ways round this. The first is to think about what you can do, not what you can't. To refocus and redirect your attention, so that for example if you're scared of someone or their reactions, instead of telling yourself "don't be scared," which you know won't work, you tell yourself to "be confident." The second is to get to the root of the issue by challenging your negative thinking, which is what cognitive behavioral therapy (CBT) is all about. What's exciting is that over the past 20 years CBT has been shown to be an incredibly successful collection of techniques that teach people to identify and monitor their thoughts or beliefs about negative emotions, and then to work out which are inaccurate or unhelpful. And to replace them with something more realistic and useful.

But if you want something immediate, think about your self-talk.

Using self-talk

Self-talk is about the internal messages you give yourself. It's a technique that sports psychologists have been working with for a couple of decades because it's been shown to help improve performance in a variety of sports. It works because it helps you:

- Enhance attention and focus ("Focus").
- Trigger automatic performance ("Run with it").
- Control thoughts and emotions by creating upbeat moods ("Relax").
- Determine your effort ("Try hard," "Let's go").
- Build confidence ("I'm confident," "I can").

What you'll notice about the accompanying phrases is that they are short and snappy. When

"I do a lot of programming and we do evaluations for all of it on a scale of 1–5. I used to focus on receiving 5s in the evaluations and then I thought, 'That's kind of sad because it's almost like begging,' even though I wasn't asking anyone.

But then I shifted my focus on being a 5 rather than receiving a 5. I can't control what someone else does but it means I feel comfortable and confident enough and appreciate the value in myself."

Anita Brick, founder of the Encouragement Institute, Chicago, IL, USA

"A great driver is able to do a number of discrete tasks simultaneously and calmly. They have to drive the car at pretty frightening speeds, with incredible accuracy, and *Continued*

you're under time pressure you don't have time for long fancy personal messages. And it's what your inner gremlin does when it's delivering Confidence-reducing schtick. Short and sweet is less complex and helps you focus.

Looking at the above list in more detail, you can see it boils down to two types of message: instructions you give yourself and the motivation to succeed. Interestingly, athletes and psychologists say that of all the different types of self-talk, it looks like motivational self-talk has the greatest impact on performance. So when in doubt, try "I can" to boost your Confidence. Because self-talk isn't only for athletes: it's useful for anyone who has to perform anywhere.

Centering

Centering has two aspects. The first aspect is physical and involves taking a deep breath, being aware of muscle tension, and exhaling strongly to relax your muscles and achieve physical balance. Counting to five while breathing in and out is a technique that lots of sports coaches teach. The second aspect is to connect this to self-control; that's most easily achieved when combined with self-talk. By giving yourself a short and positive message, you're shutting up and shutting out your internal gremlin. Doing that means you focus wholly on your physical and mental state in order to maximize Confidence and perform your best.

Working with imagery

Mental imagery involves seeing yourself in your desired and attainable state. It absolutely isn't fantasizing but it is thinking about what's possible and probable that you can deliver. And there's lots of evidence showing that mental images can increase effort and performance. Possibly because the very act of imagining makes it seem more likely and you therefore work harder to bring it about. For example, while writing this book, I've thought literally hundreds of times about standing at my desk and holding a printed copy of it in my hands. That's been my way of keeping myself going, especially when I've become bogged down or completely stuck.

think what's going on mechanically and physically because that's how you improve. They have to be spatially aware all the time and communicating with the pit some of the time.

The best example I've seen was Nico Rosberg in Monza. It was pouring with rain, absolutely pouring. Listening to him on the radio he was talking about the brakes, the traffic, driving with one part of his brain and optimizing everything with the other part. He was so in control, relaxed, and confident. That was a glimpse to me of what a really good driver can do. The challenge is to do that all the time."

Adam Parr, CEO Williams Formula 1, Wantage, UK

"We had these suits so we could cross open water. In the Arctic you can die if you're swimming and you get wet. The first time we used them they leaked. I was in first and my suit was leaking; I was thinking, 'I'm in terrible danger here, what the hell am I going to do?' I kept going but I felt rising panic as I was getting more and more cold, more and more in danger. I was saying, 'Stay calm, stay calm.' The energy that took was huge. I got out and water gushed out of the suit. I was so cold, so wet, I thought, 'You could die here, Ann.'

I curled up in a ball and lay down in the sun. I used my mind to drag warmth from the sun into my body. I'd done it before in 2002 when I'd been out in a horrendous storm and got hypothermic – deathly cold. At that time we hadn't eaten for three days and couldn't put the tent up. I crawled back under the covering and thought, 'All you have is your mind. Just think of a fire inside you.' And I thought of tiny little flames. 'Build it, build it,' I told myself. Eventually I felt a bit of warmth and instinctively I knew I was out of danger.

When you're on the real edge, the last and only thing you have is the power and energy of your mind."

Ann Daniels, polar explorer, Exeter, UK

Mental imagery can be really useful in reliving and overcoming previous situations in which you were less than successful. Imagining that situation turning out well seems to help people avoid repeating the same mistake.

There is no ideal or correct way to use mental imagery so you'll have to use trial and error to find out what suits you best. You can either play out a scene in detail through your own eyes, using the first person, or you might see yourself as an observer in a wider context. For example, if you wanted to imagine yourself giving a really successful speech, you could either visualize yourself facing the audience, or you could be a member of the audience watching you. There are advantages to both. Research suggests that people who do the former feel more intense emotions, while those who do the latter find broader meaning, significance, and increased motivation. By trying both you'll discover what works best for you.

Using imagery is of course directly connected to mental rehearsal. To mentally rehearse you ideally have some experience of what you're trying to do. You simply take a few seconds or minutes wherever you like and see yourself doing that activity. Sports psychologists encourage athletes to do this at least a few times a week and to engage in mental rehearsal as they practice in order to embed the thoughts and mental and physical feelings as they play. Which makes the mental rehearsal later much easier. There's amazing evidence that doing this triggers the same connections in your brain as actually doing the activity itself so it helps you learn faster. And increases your Confidence.

Not all these techniques will work for you and some you'll practice already. Mindfully using them will not only strengthen your feelings of control and therefore what you get done, but boost the second element of Confidence. Your self-belief.

Having High Self-Belief

Before delving into self-belief it's important to understand what this and other self-issues are; they can be pretty confusing and they're often wrongly used. For example, people say that they have Confidence issues when what they are really talking about is self-worth. So here are some definitions:

- Self-esteem is based on others' judgments of you; you assess it by comparing how you are with how you aspire to be, using other people's evaluations. So although it originates from external sources, it comes to affect your self-worth.
- Self-worth is how you feel about yourself given your accumulated experiences; it may vary depending on context but it springs from an internal source.
- Self-belief is what you think about your personal capabilities to perform certain tasks and achieve certain goals. It comes from internal and external sources.

Self-belief, known in psychology circles as self-efficacy, is the second most important Confidence element. And according to our data, it has a big impact on performance. That's not to say the other self-concepts don't affect Confidence at work: they just don't come into the picture statistically and self-belief does. Self-belief is one of the most studied topics in psychology because it has such an immense impact not only on Confidence, but also on behavior, motivation, ambition, goals, and achievement.

Albert Bandura, the foremost researcher in the field, found that when you have high self-belief amongst other things you'll:

"Back in the '90s this young American, maybe 25 or 26, came into my office. He'd graduated from Harvard and spent two years at Goldman Sachs in New York where he worked out all the restructuring of the real estate in the US. He said to me, 'I've studied the French market, it's very much like the US five years ago and all these institutions will have to sell or die. And they'll have to sell at big discounts; we can make a tremendous amount of money.' I thought this was daring, this guy from California, he'd never set foot in France and didn't speak a word of French. He wanted me to support him for a year to see if we could make an impact.

Fast forward three years and Goldman bought most of the real estate loan portfolio in the French market and made the most money out of a principal investment ever done.

Goldman allows you the confidence to dare, to have a big idea, and to take it forward. That's the kind of confidence and risk they encourage and it allows you to be as successful as you want to be. No French institution at the time would allow you to do that kind of thing at such a young age."

Sylvain Hefes, Chairman, Paris-Orleans Bank S.A., holding company of N.M. Rothschild, France

- Set challenging personal goals.
- Focus on opportunities rather than risks.
- Visualize successful results and use these as a problem-solving guide.
- Break larger tasks down into smaller, more manageable ones.
- Find helpful role models.
- Think that failure is due to lack of effort rather than lack of ability.

Where does this self-belief come from? From four main sources.

Experiencing success
Success is the first and foremost thing that builds your self-belief. Which means the corollary, failure, undermines it. But that success has to be obtained by working your way through setbacks, overcoming obstacles, and dealing with difficulties. These teach you that success comes only through making a sustained and concerted effort. When people only experience easy wins, they come to expect quick results and are easily discouraged when they hit setbacks. You have to exert yourself to achieve success because persistent effort builds self-belief.

Observing others
Observing other people and what they do is the fastest way everyone learns. The most powerful way of growing self-belief is seeing people like you succeed; it gives you the impetus to think that you can succeed at the same thing too. The greater your similarity to someone, the more strongly influenced you'll be. That's why it's good to compare up: you'll become more aspirational as a result. The only downside with learning by watching is that if you see someone like you failing, you won't be super-keen to have a go yourself.

Being persuaded
Other people, especially those you respect, can often talk you into having a go: it's one of the reasons receiving positive feedback matters so much. It boosts self-belief. Some bosses are really good at this and seem to be able to get incredible stuff out of their team members, probably because they set the bar really high in terms of expectations while ensuring that challenges remain manageable.

An important caveat here is that it's much easier to undermine someone than to boost them into action.

Interpreting mind and body responses

Everyone relies on internal signals when judging their capabilities. But it's easy to misinterpret what you feel and destabilize yourself as a result. Your physical and mental state, including tension, tiredness, or negative moods, diminish self-belief. And it's easy to fall into the trap that because you're under pressure, you must be failing in some way. That's just not the case. For example, starting to sweat or noticing your legs tremble before a really important meeting actually tells you nothing about your level of competence. It tells you about the situation you find yourself in. That's why managing your mind and maintaining self-control are so important: so that you correctly interpret what's happening.

Generalizing self-belief

What lots of people are not aware of is that self-belief is both specific to a situation and can be generalized too. For example, you might feel comfortable about presenting to an audience of 15 people and your self-belief would be fine in this respect. But presenting to 500 people might make you feel altogether different. The way forward is to think through the elements that mean you have high self-belief in one situation and apply them to another.

And then use your intuition to help you too. Because that can be really useful in building your self-belief.

> "I can make myself pretty miserable when I lose perspective because I've got stuck with a book. I can fall into a dismal frame of mind and think that this will never work out, it's unbearable, horrible, and I'm no good. Sometimes I don't catch it quick enough and I fall into an abyss.
>
> One strategy I have to deal with this is to have several projects on the go at once. Right now I've got three prose books and one book of poems which are all live projects. I think of it a bit like those painters who have many unfinished canvasses around their studio turned to the wall. The one turned out is the one you're working on. If I get stuck, I'll pull out another one and put what's stuck back to the wall. Sooner or later something's ready and out it goes."
>
> Henry Shukman, writer and poet, Santa Fe, NM, USA

Looking internally to develop self-belief: working with your intuition

Your intuition – or inner tuition – is something that grows with experience, judgment, and testing. There's a lot of tacit knowledge involved in it, which is why it's harder to be intuitive when you're young. This kind of knowing divides into two groups: intuitions, which are more often physical sensations, and insights, which are generally clear-cut solutions or answers.

"I can tell really, really quickly what's going on because I've got a nose for it and I've got nous. I use my intuition, which is tuning in your senses to what's happening around you and allowing them to work like radar. If you don't follow your instincts you lose what it means to be a human being.

When you've spent years and years doing something you know about it. You don't need systems, processes, frameworks, strategy, and partnerships to tell you. They fail and fail profoundly. You need antennae and instincts to survive in a difficult world. Then you can be responsible, take the wheel, and grow in possibility."

Lord Andrew Mawson, President of Community Action Network, social entrepreneur, London, UK

"I've woken up and gone to the bridge because I felt that something wasn't right. Once it happened when I was in command of a submarine and I had an inexperienced officer of the watch who was driving right into the middle of a fishing fleet because he didn't know how to avoid it. He hadn't told me because he'd got in so deep he didn't want to be embarrassed.

I don't know what it was, but something woke me, I went up and we sorted it out. I think you have to understand something at another layer beyond the norm if you're going to drive a ship really well."

Paul Boissier, CEO RNLI, Poole, UK

Classic intuitions and insights are both spontaneous and involuntary, which means that you can't control them by making them come or go, they simply appear.

When you get them you'll probably feel that you "know" but you may not be able to articulate how you know. For example, when you're at a traffic light you can sometimes feel that someone in the car next door is watching you. But it's hard to say *how* you have that knowledge.

And it's not unusual to have this kind of knowledge in a work setting. For example, one study found that nurses in a neonatal intensive care unit could detect life-threatening infections before blood tests showed up a problem. Another looked at diagnoses made by psychiatrists and found a strong role for intuition in a clinical setting. The same goes for intuition in education, management consulting, and leadership. In short, it may play a much larger role in effective decision-making than most of us are aware of.

To learn to use both intuition and insight, you need to distinguish them from normal inner doubt or wishful thinking. You should also be aware that intuition and insight tend to kick in when conscious thought is disengaged. Which means that cudgeling your brain doesn't work. If you really want an answer, go for a walk, listen to music, or stare out of the window. Because these kind of thoughts often come in your mental downtime. Noticing when they appear means you'll better be able to set up the circumstances that allow them to occur. And by asking yourself, "When do I know that I know?" and "What do I know that I know?" you'll track the times they appear and understand what they bring you – always recognizing that intuition is a human activity and may therefore occasionally be fallible.

There is a caveat here. When I'm talking about intuition, I'm not talking about excuses that you might hear in the working world. "I just know that it's not the case" is often an example of lazy thinking or stubbornness; it's highly unlikely to be the genuine article.

By the way, there is no evidence that women are "better" than men at using their intuition. On the contrary, we appear to use it similarly but talk about it differently. But the one thing that everyone does is to rarely talk about how they arrived at answers obtained through intuition or insight. Appearing flaky isn't going to build your own Confidence or anyone else's in you.

Understanding Your Role Backwards and Forwards

When you have high levels of Confidence our data tell us you'll know the following. You:

- Think that your job matches your initial expectations of it.
- Can see how your job fits your overall career plan.
- Want to stay in your role.
- Would recommend your organization to a close friend.

What's interesting about these four items is that they align the past, present, and future: there's a clear red time thread which comes about when overall Confidence is high. And it's all about the biggest and broadest perspective you can have when reflecting about your job. This element and all its pieces operate rather like a balance sheet, providing you with an overall personal statement of your Confidence over a period of time.

"I put a hell of a lot of how I commanded down to intuition. For example, at staff college I'd know what the answer was within minutes and I'd have to backtrack to work out how I'd got there. Or sometimes work would come in and I'd know straight away we could do this easily, it was right.

But a few years ago I spent a very difficult time where I made some decisions and the results hadn't been good. I got into a position where I started questioning every decision I made and every time I thought of doing something I second-guessed it. It was awful. I started not to trust my judgment and beating your own demons is the hardest thing.

You have to believe you can do things and know you can too."

Senior officer, Special Forces, UK

"I'm a High Court judge in the family division. I like listening to people give evidence, discovering how they work and what makes them who they are. And also trying to decide whether they are telling the truth. That's a mixture of intuition and experience. Just a simple analysis of what they're saying against what you know – the old-fashioned advocacy tricks. But it's also about watching the way people tell you things. Do they tell you in a way that stacks up with what you know about life or are they telling you something that simply makes no sense?

Sometimes the evidence all points in one direction but then actually you decide that there's an exception. You weigh everything against your experience, judgment, and intuition."

Sir Paul Coleridge, High Court judge, Exeter, UK

And, unlike some of the other elements, these are more anchored and unlikely to change that much over time. That means they're useful to turn to when you are feeling buffeted by the storms of your day-to-day working life. Recognizing you're there for the duration will mean you can turn your attention elsewhere without wasting energy on what's probably peripheral stuff. Like job hunting when you don't really mean it.

Thinking that your job matches your initial expectations

Think about landing your last job. Bursting with enthusiasm and high expectations you discover after a couple of days that it's nothing like you'd thought it would be. When your imagination runs riot you're bound to be at best surprised and at worst disappointed; I've never found that fantasy matches reality.

Role clarity is something that contributes to your overall happiness at work because it gives you granularity about what you need to do to deliver success. But that's less important in this context. Instead of going down a level, try going up a level and aim to think in headlines instead. For example, don't picture cosy chats over beer with your boss, decide that you'll be having lots of interesting conversations with many different kinds of people. Don't conjure up precisely the many different projects you want to be doing, expect variety at work instead.

The only thing you can guarantee about your working life is that it is never exactly what you thought it would be. But taking your expectations up from the narrow to the broad means it's much easier to decide whether you're doing what you want and not getting sidetracked by what may be irrelevant minutiae.

Another technique that helps here is to make a realistic estimate of how much of the time you expect to feel happy at work, feel neutral, or feel unhappy at work. Our data show that the average person spends 55 percent of their time feeling happy at work, 19 percent of their day feeling neutral, and 27 percent feeling unhappy. For the happiest group these figures are 77 percent, 9 percent, and 14 percent; and for the unhappiest they are 30 percent, 35 percent, and 35 percent respectively.

I think those figures are pretty amazing. Even if you are really unhappy at work, you're still enjoying a third of your working day. I think this says a lot about the positivity and optimism of the human race. But calibrating your initial expectations against what you actually get will help you think about anything you want to rebalance or craft within the framework of your job – and the overall perspective of your career.

Seeing how your job fits your overall career plan

Retrospect is a wonderful way of looking at your working life and joining the dots up forwards is almost impossible. Some people, and I think they are rare, do plan out their lives. They know what they want and how they'll achieve it. But for lots of us our careers are outcomes of sheer good luck and happenstance. My own career, entirely unplanned to date, has spanned teaching, finance, and working for a venture capital trade association before starting a consultancy. The most important piece of work I ever got was through a chance meeting in a café.

Although each move didn't add up at the time, it's clear how that journey got me to where I am now and taught me invaluable stuff on the way. If you're worrying that you have a disjointed career, hold fast. Everything you're doing builds on your previous knowledge or adds something new – you may just not see it yet. The more helpful question is, "Does what I'm doing serve me right now?" If the answer is yes, that's all that matters.

So what does that mean for the standard exercise beloved of so many business schools which asks, "What's the legacy I want to leave?" It's often used as a quasi-guide to help people discover their long-term choices. But when times are uncertain I'm not sure how useful a legacy mindset is. What it does is narrow your thinking

"One of the illusions of success is that you caused it. So much of success, particularly entrepreneurial success, is luck and just being at the right place at the right time.

There are certain pivotal breaks that you get – for us it was early customers, where somebody we knew happened to be in the right position to make a decision at that time.

The ability to jump on that opportunity is something that you do. But having it show up in front of you is something that might or might not happen. It's just luck."

Shikhar Ghosh, Senior Lecturer Harvard Business School, CEO Appex, and serial entrepreneur, Boston, MA, USA

"What psychological health there is in someone who can accept the passing of things in lightness; who can say, 'Well, I know it's not going to be there in 20 years, but that's alright, I'm enjoying today.'

There's wisdom in accepting, like Buddhists, the passing of life, the flowing waters. It frees you not to worry about the end product but to involve yourself in the process. Life is chaos; freeing yourself allows you to live through the chaos and not get upset by it."

Alain de Botton, writer, philosopher, and founder of the School of Life, London, UK

when you may want to go broad and wide to keep your options open. Right now flexibility and adaptability are the name of the game and that requires a lot more lateral thinking than you may be used to. Just think hard if you want to be hampered by a preordained legacy that you conjured up.

If, on the other hand, you're doing a job which you have taken because you must, and it doesn't fit your overall career plan, the most useful question to give you some perspective might be, "Given thisjob, what else can I do to be happier at work?" Then think about how to craft your job to get more of what you like. If that's impossible, make sure that you keep your mind and social circle as active and wide as possible by developing a strong "hinterland." Your hinterland involves activities that:

- Give you meaning and pleasure that go beyond taking part in the activity itself.
- Require active participation and personal investment.
- Create flow moments for you or make you feel vitally engaged.
- Broaden who you are because of the knowledge you develop and people you meet.

The activities that make up your hinterland are the things you can't do just by sitting on the Internet. They involve time, effort, and interactions with others. If you're not happy at work, an active hinterland is critical to ensure that there is an area in which you experience the 5Cs in a non-work context. It will give you the mental wherewithal to stay in your role even if you don't enjoy it.

Wanting to stay in your role

Staying in the job you're in is a really important indicator of happiness at work. In fact it's so important that psychologists use it all the time as a way of measuring well-being, job satisfaction, engagement, and happiness at work. We've found that it's most closely associated with Confidence in yourself and your organization. Our numbers are really clear that the happier you are, the longer you'll stay in your role. In fact if you're really happy you'll be there for two years or more; if you're really unhappy you'll be planning on leaving within 9 months.

Nor will you be a great colleague as your mind will be elsewhere, so you'll be unlikely to go out of your way to help your co-workers. In fact our statistics show that you'll be 20 percent less helpful than others who have the highest happiness and Confidence levels.

If this is you, you'll need to really think how to connect with what you do to remember why you're doing it. Like keeping a picture of your family visible at all times, or something else that will help you get through the day. You might find journaling helpful or possibly enrolling in further learning: the former will help you manage the present and the latter your future. So that when your circumstances change, you'll be ready and able to make a move because your Confidence will be high. Whatever situation you find yourself in, actively think about how you maintain your Confidence because this will affect your Contribution too.

Recommending your organization to a friend

This really matters. Because it's so strongly connected to all the 5Cs and the elements they contain. What's clear from our data is that if you would wholeheartedly and unreservedly recommend your organization to a friend, you are truly happy at work. And you'll have amazingly high levels of Pride, Trust, and Recognition. In fact the numbers are simply incredible in statistical terms. If you are prepared to recommend your organization to a friend, we know you are very motivated, relish your job, feel you fit your Culture, believe in the vision of the organization, and think you're doing something worthwhile. And you'll score highly on all the 5Cs too.

In more concrete terms you're likely to want to stay for at least three years, have probably taken about two days off sick in the past year, and are on task three quarters of your working day. Not to mention the fact that you'll be hardier and happier too.

In other words, recommending your organization to a friend acts as a proxy question because it tells you so much about someone's job and how they find their work or their organization. And it tells you a massive amount about their Confidence levels too.

Confidence: a case study

Will was the founder and CEO of a medium-sized IT business that operated internationally. Downturn, that looked like possible recession, was starting to affect revenues. This, coupled with customer feedback, suggested that the organization needed to adopt a more flexible sales and service approach. Services had previously been outsourced but Will and the board had decided to bring this in-house to capitalize on potential new revenues.

Sales had been something that the business prided itself on: year-on-year the global team had always outperformed themselves. Developing new products and educating the sales force was an area which the organization excelled in and took very seriously. So Will thought that wrapping services into sales would be a challenge that everyone would manage relatively well, especially if guided by a well-honed and process-led approach. He expected he'd see results within about 6–9 months and that key indicators would show things were getting done according to plan.

But it was proving really tough: Will and the board needed to understand why. The analysts were getting antsy and that was causing more pressure. They needed to get to grips with this fast. Will decided to start by talking to the key players informally. During his third conversation it dawned on him: this wasn't a process or personality issue, this was all about Confidence. For the following reasons:

- The business hadn't had single-figure growth since after the dot com bubble burst and back then it had been a much smaller organization. None of the key players had experience of managing a downturn and constant customer uncertainty was really affecting everyone.
- Lots of small things that ought to have fallen into place weren't happening. The excuses and delays weren't due to lack of talent but they sent strong signals further down the organization. That was making everyone question Commitment to this implementation.
- The niggles about the new service side of the business were just that. But some of them had been blown out of proportion; irrel-

evant difficulties were taking up way too much management time. Voicing issues wasn't the problem: focus was.

Replacing a huge number of key players was not an option: they needed to work this out now. Will decided to get everyone together; he'd keep quiet about his own diagnosis but he'd push them all to find their own way forward. That would be the best Confidence boost of all. And he'd bring someone in to talk to everyone: someone on the ground who had made real customer in-roads with the new approach. He knew renewed enthusiasm and self-belief were the only way to make this happen and catalyze new momentum.

Six weeks after the event the energy around the team was much better. The project was getting back on track, customer calls and commitments were starting to happen. Exactly what Will had hoped for.

Concluding Confidence

Confidence is the last but not least of the 5Cs. It's made up of elements, some of which fluctuate more, some of which fluctuate less, because they are rooted in a harder center. Interestingly, too much or too little Confidence results in the same thing: lack of performance. That means finding a middle way that works for you and you can do that best if you:

- Choose jobs, goals, and challenges that push the boundaries of your comfort zone so that you grow your Confidence. If you always look for the easiest option, you'll become less and less confident in your capabilities. Start by thinking about what you're good at and build on that; then you know you'll be able to tackle more difficult things. That will mean you can take bigger and bolder steps because you know you can succeed.
- Make sure you have the right safety mechanisms and support when you're doing new and difficult things. Setting yourself up for failure by hoping that "you'll be alright on the night" is not a way to actively build your self-belief or your Confidence. You'll need planning and practice so that you get things done without any nasty surprises because everything unfolds in the way you want it to.

- Check how you might be coming over to your colleagues because you don't want them to think you are overly arrogant or a wet blanket. Just imagine what you think they might be seeing in you and saying about you too.
- Chart your progress by mindfully tracking the steps you make and the Confidence you feel. Think through all the different and new things you've done over the past 5–10 years; what successes and experiences have built your Confidence? There are bound to be things that you could transfer to any new situation you face.

The most exciting thing about Confidence is that when you break it down, there's an enormous amount that you can do to nurture and build it so that its center stays solid and its edges far less fragile. That's important if you're going to deploy your talents and abilities to your best advantage – and ensure you're happy at work.

Top take-aways for Chapter 8

- Confidence consists of three key elements: getting things done; having high levels of self-belief; and understanding your role backwards and forwards.
- Getting things done is influenced by self-control, understanding procrastination, and using mind tools that work for you. These include understanding your beliefs, using self-talk, centering, and working with imagery.
- Having high levels of self-belief happens when you experience success; observe others like you succeed; are persuaded to take on challenges; and correctly interpret your mental and physical state.
- Understanding your role backwards and forwards is crucial for Confidence: it's made up of knowing that your job fits your initial expectations, seeing how it meshes with your overall career plan, wanting to stay, and recommending your organization to a friend.
- Asking if someone would recommend their organization to a close friend acts as a proxy question for how happy someone is at work: that's because it's so closely linked to many of the elements contained within all the 5Cs.

9

Pride, Trust, and Recognition

Introduction to Pride, Trust, and Recognition

Once we started to analyze our first big data set, Laurel (our head of research) and I had a major wow moment. That happened when we saw just how important Pride, Trust, and Recognition were. Or to be more precise, Pride and Trust in your organization and Recognition for your achievements. They matter enormously because they attach themselves not only to all the 5Cs, but to each and every single element as well. That means everything outlined in this book is strongly connected to Pride, Trust, and Recognition.

They are so crucially linked with happiness at work that we've found they are also proxies for assessing it – just like the question "Would you recommend your organization to a friend?" So another oblique way of gauging whether someone is happy at work is by asking: Are you proud of your organization? Do you trust it? And do you feel you get enough recognition for what you do? The answers will not only give you a very clear general indicator of how happy someone is in their role, but will also tell you that the 5Cs are working for them – though of course you won't have any specifics – and you'll know a lot about their levels of energy and achievement.

In other words, Pride, Trust, and Recognition act like signposts, confirming that you're on the right road, in the right vehicle, and heading in the right direction. And not having them is strongly associated with less productivity, more sick leave, and a greater intention to quit.

And though Pride and Trust work similarly while Recognition is different, you'll need all three in place if you're going to feel really happy at work. Pride and Trust without Recognition will make you ask, "Why do I bother, no-one notices what I'm doing?" Then your Contribution will drop off as

"We were typically known for being a risk-averse, boring, and conservative bank. To discover we were so exposed to the US mortgage market was absolutely shocking. People are in mourning for what they thought would have been, disappointed in choices that were made, and wishing they were elsewhere.

I believe in this organization, I just don't trust it as I did. It was such a mantra here: talk respectfully about the past, realistically about the present, and optimistically about the future. Now we're an organization where people tear each other down. We're consuming ourselves from the inside because trust in who we are and pride in what we do isn't there."

Senior female executive banker, London, UK

"We are in the business of ensuring quality. I've got 4,000 people in 70 locations and 10 business segments: there's a lot to be proud of. Pride is what holds us together and ensures we really deliver in all we do. I talk about pride without power: we don't need empire builders in our business.

Organizations come to us because they trust SGS, our standards, and our integrity. I talk about integrity every single day because it's critical in our market. Forty percent of our competitors operate what I call a 'brief-case option'. At some point that unravels.

If I were to find anything untrustworthy I'd flush it out and take decisive action. You have to be able to walk away from a person or a
Continued

Pride and Trust implode. And lots of Recognition without Pride and Trust will feel fraudulent.

How Pride and Trust Work Together But Recognition is Separate

Back in the 1980s I worked in an organization called Stewart Wrightson. Just before I joined, the Brinks Mat bullion heist took place. Six armed men broke into a warehouse at Heathrow airport and stole 6,800 gold bars, worth £26 million at the time. It was major news in the UK and the story ran and ran for years afterwards.

In my new job I happened to sit in an open plan office at the desk right next to the surety team who were handling the aftermath. Just being an employee of the organization who had simply brokered the Brinks Mat insurance policy made me proud. And sitting next to the team handling that claim made me even prouder.

Of course from time to time I'd chat to my colleagues or take messages for them – these were the days before voicemail. And that would make me feel like a totally trusted quasi team member. Chris, the very calm and composed director in charge, told us that anything we learned was privileged information and not to be repeated. And it never was. The Pride and Trust we all felt were huge.

Pride and Trust work in a very similar way. We can see this in our data because they map very closely onto all the same items in the same amounts. That means that they work almost like a pair of facing mirrors. While one mirror shows your front and the other your back, together they reveal multiple aspects of the same thing: your happiness at work.

Because they work together, Pride and Trust have a knock-on impact on each other. Take, for example, a low-Pride environment. There'll be lack of motivation, shoddy work, mistakes, missed deadlines, bad attitudes, and missing or stolen stuff. Little Pride will automatically snow-ball into little Trust. And that means less cooperation, poor working relationships, and wasted time. Productivity goes down while costs go up. And of course you wind up with a disastrous and unsustainable vicious circle.

> deal if you are unable to do the right thing as you understand it. That's very, very important in maintaining trust."
>
> Paul House, Managing Director, SGS, Delhi, India

When you feel Pride and Trust in your organization, what you're doing is connecting to the bigger picture in which you are a player. Pride and Trust serve to remind you that it's good to be associated with your workplace. And they focus you on the fact that you want to stay part of it and commit to it. That's why they matter so much in underpinning psychological and social capital.

Recognition works differently.

Pride and Trust are what you give to your organization: Recognition is what you get back from it. And it is more tied to a specific context, time, and place: too early or late and the effect is spoilt. Plus it needs to feel genuine and it has to come from people you respect.

So if this trio are so important, what exactly are they and how do they work?

What is Pride?

Pride has a very mixed reputation. On the one hand lots of people think it's really good and something that should be fostered, especially in children. On the other, many think it will lead you to the gates of hell. Dante named and shamed it as one of the seven deadly sins; and many religions, Christianity and Buddhism included, believe it's harmful, selfish, and immoral. So what does psychology have to add to the picture?

Recent studies show that pride in any sense, not just as it applies to organizations, seems to be something that everyone feels in the same way everywhere. And one that others like to see in you. People who are proud are seen as more likeable and their chances of landing a leadership role are higher too.

"Goldman is about being number one, the best, the most successful at what you do. That's the driving force. And there's an immense pride in it. That means the greatest pressure is seeing yourself through the eyes of your partners; the real test is being able to go to the table on Monday morning and not be ashamed of yourself.

The worst moment I had was not getting a big privatization that we'd worked very hard for. It was the transaction of the year, the ultimate prize. There'd been so much hope and expectation attached to it.

I called the chairman with the news and he said, 'Okay, okay.' Then he put the phone down. Two okays. You can imagine it. You arrive at the point when you know intimately how others – your close colleagues and partners – feel and react because you feel and react the same way."

Sylvain Hefes, Chairman, Paris-Orleans Bank S.A., the holding company of N.M. Rothschild, France

"There's one view that pride can only come from the serious goal to which your end product is directed. But there's another view which is that it doesn't matter what you do, it's how you do it – the qualities you bring to your job. That's a very lovely releasing idea which says that a lot of jobs are quite alike. It may seem that there's a difference between brain surgery and a warehouse manager, but doing it well is going to involve many of the same things. I think that's true from many of the jobs I've seen close up."

Alain de Botton, writer, philosopher, and founder of the School of Life, London, UK

But there is a caveat here.

Pride seems to divide neatly into two distinct kinds when it applies to an individual. In simple terms there is helpful or genuine pride, which is encapsulated by the thought, "I'm proud of what I achieved or did"; and unhelpful or hubristic pride, which is summarized by the statement, "I'm proud of who I am." It's this type of pride that's worth fighting shy of because there's little you can do to build it and it's closely connected to narcissism or self-love. On the other hand, you can do a lot to increase authentic pride by increasing your effort, managing difficult situations, and learning new things. And all of these are connected to valuable feelings of self-worth.

Authentic pride has other benefits too. It:

- Means you maintain your organizational commitment.
- Encourages you to contribute to a group.
- Pushes you to go the extra mile.
- Helps you persevere.
- Enables you to select more challenging tasks.
- Spurs you on to think what else might be possible.
- Just feels good.

This list tells you that it's not only an outcome, it's also a resource that motivates you to go for bigger, better, and more. So motivation is a key feature of Pride as it applies to both individuals and organizations.

What has to be in place to experience Pride?

Pride is what's called a "self-conscious emotion" like shame, embarrassment, and guilt. You can only experience these complex and powerful feelings when you know who you are, what matters to you, and can measure external events against your internal standards.

To feel organizational Pride you need three more things.

Firstly, you need to feel you belong. If you're like most people, you'll have a psychological connection, an attachment to the place you work. And that means your job forms part of your identity and the organization fits with your self-image. That's why, when you meet someone new, one of the first questions you ask them is "What do you do?" You're investigating their identity and self-image.

If you can't identify with your organization, you won't be able to dig deep when you have to and you'll contribute less than you could. So if you can't connect with what an organization does, don't take a job there no matter how juicy it might look. A couple of years ago a close friend who was in this very position called me up. She'd been offered a global role in a worldwide burger chain. And now she had a dilemma. The role was everything she wanted, as was the expatriate package, and it was in a place she'd always wanted to live. In fact, it was all she had dreamed of. Except that it was working for an organization which she found hard to connect with. The thought that really stopped her from saying yes was the idea of sending her friends and colleagues her new email address. She knew she wouldn't feel pride in her employment so she didn't take the job.

> "I remember wandering around Tiananmen Square with John Simpson when they'd declared martial law. No-one was meant to be out but the crowd heard that we'd come from the BBC. There was a kind of rolling applause from over a million people. It was a rather unnerving large-scale response to two men just trying to avoid the People's Liberation Army. But of course it made us feel terrifically proud to be from the BBC."
>
> Mark Thompson, Director-General, BBC, London, UK

> "We have a test, which is when you're out having a drink and someone asks you what you do, how do you feel? Most people are very proud of what they do here and understand it's a privilege to work here."
>
> Adam Parr, CEO Williams Formula 1, Wantage, UK

Once you're clear that you identify with your organization and what it does, you'll then need to understand your Contribution and its effect. The closer you are to any main event, the prouder you'll obviously be. That's why working in a remote team or having corporate HQ based on the other side of the world can be so hard. As is working in a mega-institution. Of course you can feel proud by association, which is something that many organizations try to foster because they know how important it is. What they don't know is how closely associated Pride and happiness at work are.

Finally, to have a strong sense of Pride in your organization, you need to be able to make some sort of connection with the people that you are

"I've filmed the last three World Cups, European Championships, and the Olympics. I love doing FA Cup Finals, it's a huge buzz.

There are maybe 80,000 people in the stadium, but two billion people watching all over the world. I get a big kick out of that because even without my name on them, I know that people are seeing my pictures; I'm behind the camera."

Tony Dolce, BBC cameraman, London, UK

ultimately serving, even if they are all anonymous to you. It's hard to feel Pride because you deliver increased revenues to the shareholders; it's much more likely that you'll experience a strong sense of Pride when you know who you affect and how. When you've found some kind of personal understanding or link.

And although we all feel Pride in the same way, there are some cultural differences associated with how we feel it in an organizational setting. We've found much more Pride in India, Pakistan, and Africa, and much less in the USA or UK. That's probably because cultures which favor the group over the individual will automatically feel greater Pride. But either way it's possible for everyone to feel more proud of their workplace.

How to increase feelings of Pride in your organization

You may feel that it's up to the leadership of your organization to boost feelings of Pride for you. I disagree. Why is someone else responsible for how you feel? Or what you believe? So here are some questions to help you:

- Who are your organization's customers, clients, or users? How do you make a difference to them? What would it mean if your organization couldn't serve them or your function disappeared? How would their lives be changed for the worse?
- Cast your mind back to why you applied for your current role. What excited you about it at the time? Why did you select your organization? What did you come in wanting to achieve? How did this serve or connect to the wider remit of your organization?
- Ask yourself: what at this time would this organization have to demonstrate concretely to me if I were to feel 100 percent proud? Who would I have to see to be doing what? 0–10, how far away from this are they? Is this practical? Is it achievable? Am I being realistic? Who else other than me should also think about this? How could we set the ball rolling?

And instead of deleting internal newsletters and bulletins that pop into your in-box, try actually reading them. Look out for someone or something that you find newsworthy and follow them up. You'll learn something new and you might just feel interested and proud at the same time.

Concluding Pride

As you can see, this is a complex topic. It's not just about your workplace doing things right: they have to also do the right things, in the right circumstances, for the right people, and according to your lights. It's a dead cert that your organization is good at activities that do not generate any Pride in you whatsoever, even if they are important to its functioning. These activities don't matter to you because they don't attach to your identity, self-image, interests, standards, or constituents you care about. That's why Pride is so hard for organizations to build.

If you have really low Pride in your organization, my guess is you're stuck somewhere you don't want to be. My challenge to you is this: if you really don't want to try to improve your level of Pride in your organization, should you continue to be in your current role? Especially now you know how much it matters. Just as Trust does too.

Trust in Your Organization

I'm in a hot conference room with my business partner Julia. We're talking to a client about current and on-going work. It starts as a light and friendly conversation about partnership and an analysis of outcomes we've achieved so far. The figures look pleasingly high. But the conversation is quite frankly all balls.

We want to talk about how it's going, how to progress, and how to deal with issues. All Sam wants to do is grumble about costs and squeeze us for discounts. Partners? We might as well be robots except this would be doing robots a disservice. Julia tactfully steers the conversation to information we need to get the job done. Of course we can give you all of that once we've cleared up the issue of price. I can't look at him anymore and I can't stand this. Data to get a job done well isn't something to trade. And Sam hasn't ever delivered on anything he's promised. Not once.

Suppressing a sigh of irritation, the thought "you're known by the company you keep" flashes through my mind. Sam leans back, stroking his tie into place: it falls sideways again. The water is lukewarm and so is the coffee.

We've never fired a client yet but now seemed like a good time.

The real problem? It wasn't the money: it never is. The real issue was Trust. Sam was fundamentally unreliable; he simply didn't deliver. Because we couldn't trust him, we didn't believe him. Since he represented his organization, we didn't trust them either. And that meant we weren't happy to work with them.

The most important thing about low Trust is the high price everyone pays for it.

So what exactly is it and why is it so fragile?

What exactly is Trust?

Without Trust organizations simply wouldn't function, especially the flatter, less hierarchical organizations of today where change happens quickly. And it's often the unrecognized foundation on which remote, home and flexi-time employees work. Trust reduces costs, saves time, and means you can take a risk without worrying about hidden agendas and politics. In other words, Trust is a big social and psychological resource that allows you to focus on your job.

But it can be unstable, fragile, and tough to build.

Partly that's because you'll tend to think of your workplace as if it were a person. As if it were someone who understands you, has a character, and is capable of acting morally. Try this if you don't believe me and ask anyone the question, "What's your organization like?" I guarantee that 75 percent of their answer could apply to a person too. When you think about it, that's pretty ridiculous. But it explains why we believe that organizations should meet our personal expectations and standards just as a close friend would. Unfortunately, by doing this we're setting ourselves up for disappointment, especially in the Trust arena. An organization is not a person and will never understand you or deliver what you want, especially in challenging times.

It is, however, interesting to ask an interviewer when you're going for a job, "If your

"In what we do, we're prepared to risk our lives, so without a shadow of a doubt that's the final level of trust.

We're very different from other military organizations. Everyone wants to be there and everyone wants the toughest jobs. The more discreet the operation, the more sensitive it is, the more reward you tend to feel. But that reward is self-reward. To pull off a mission you have to pit yourself against the most difficult thing: the elements. It's physically challenging and life-threatening.

There are times when I've had to make a conscious leap that I'm doing what's right. You do things because you believe that someone somewhere is making the right decision. That takes an enormous amount of trust."

Senior officer, Special Forces, UK

organization were a person, could you describe its character?" By investigating the answers you get, you'll be able to get much more insight about a workplace – especially if you ask two or three people the same question. If you don't like the character you hear about, you probably won't like working there either.

Meanwhile, if you're in a job and experiencing doubts about Trust, try answering the following questions:

- Results: when they're not delivered, are messages real, fake, or fudged?
- Reliability: are words and deeds consistent everywhere?
- Reactions: are they real or false; stifled or accepted?
- Relations: is everyone treated as an equal partner, including people in the back office, janitors, suppliers, and vendors?
- Rumors: are there more than usual and where do they seem to come from?

Then ask yourself where the hard evidence for your answers is.

Trust is best built when the pressure is on, yet behavior throughout an organization is consistent. Consistency means you know you can take a risk and do what your organization asks. You'll be prepared to make yourself vulnerable, because you know that you can rely on it in return. In other words, you'll trust your organization.

But how does that happen? It starts with your colleagues. When you begin a new job you look to make trusting relationships. Those relationships are naturally extended to include allies of your allies; it's almost as if you extend your Trust by proxy, based on little more than hearsay.

And you learn about organizational Trust by assessing the actions of your senior leaders. To do that you need to believe that they are competent, have integrity, and keep your best interests at heart. You'll want to see your leaders doing what's right and moral rather than personally

"I worked for Baxter Healthcare and we had a tragic situation back in 2002 where unfortunately 55 people died while having treatment at our dialysis centers. My role was to represent Baxter and find out what had happened. But my mother read in *The New York Times* that her daughter was in Zagreb and responsible somehow for all these terrible deaths.

For the better part of three weeks I was locked up in a conference room with a pack of journalists camped outside the door while we tried to work out what had happened.

Although it was a really difficult time, it was very easy for me to speak from the heart. And to say from the heart that we would stay for as long as it takes and do the right thing. I could do that because my CEO believed in doing what was right and I had 100 percent trust that he meant it. So I knew that on behalf of the organization I could say that this was what our commitment would be."

Patricia O'Hayer, VP Communications, Unilever, The Netherlands

beneficial. In other words, integrity is part of the Trust package especially when times are tough or unfamiliar. That's when you'll go into over-drive looking for Trust, trying to predict what's going to happen next. And of course that's when leaders are most likely to screw up.

I'll never forget seeing the head of an investment bank running down a corridor, face anguished, muttering "Oh God" as he dashed past. It was extraordinary. And of course it was all over the business within about 20 minutes as everyone wondered what major catastrophe had taken place and who was for the chop. Coming over as calm and considered matters at every level if you want to inspire Trust, whatever position you hold in your organization.

Trust isn't just about appearances; it's also about doing the right thing strategically, logically, and emotionally inside and outside your workplace. Because even if you are not a leader, you can affect what others think and create Trust – or distrust. Most people start with high levels of Trust, which then gets worn away by the actions and inactions of others: it doesn't tend to work the other way round.

How is Trust eroded?

Trust is most eroded when you perceive that your organization shirks its responsibilities. Not because they can't fulfill them but because they just don't want to. When your workplace is unable to meet your expectations for valid and understandable reasons, you're much more likely to be forgiving. And you'll probably tolerate a maximum of two violations of Trust before you pull up the drawbridge and say enough's enough. Once and you'll give it the benefit of the doubt; twice indicates a trend in motion.

What causes most people to feel most enraged are those Trust-busting experiences that are unexpected, uncharacteristic, and unfair. And that's particularly true for people at the bottom of their organizational hierarchy. When Trust is fractured, organizations rely on threats or punishments, play favorites, and discourage input; when these are fueled by rumors, then fear, uncertainty, and doubt will mean greatly reduced Contribution.

But it's unrealistic to think that your organization will never, ever breach your Trust, or that you won't breach it in return. Any long-term relationship has to deal with Trust violations and how they are acknowledged, handled, and repaired is what seals the breach. Because, of course, there are major benefits to Trust in addition to adding to your happiness at work.

The benefits of Trust

Although there are lots of disagreements about what organizational Trust is and how it works, researchers do agree that it:

- Creates social capital.
- Predicts cooperation.
- Allows you to take risks.
- Facilitates knowledge and information sharing.
- Reduces feelings of personal pressure.
- Is a vital link between you and your organization.

"I tell everyone that I trust them to do things and then of course they do them. For example, there are almost no technical drawings here. The guys really blossom because they have such freedom that comes with high levels of trust.

It means we're really nimble, can experiment, and that our budget is one tenth of what it would be in a large organization."

Dr. Rafi Yoeli, President and CEO, Urban Aeronautics, Yavne, Israel

All of this shows that Trust simply makes your working life easier and more efficient. That in turn allows you to take risks with your personal resources, the most precious of which will be energy, effort, and reputation.

But the big issues with Trust ...

There are some really difficult issues for anyone trying to nurture organizational Trust. For example, getting a new working relationship off on the wrong foot is a real killer and is particularly difficult to recover from. Because once you have made your mind up, it will be almost impossible to shift it. You'll see what you expect to see, looking for evidence that confirms what you think, dismissing anything that doesn't. That's because your attitudes are anchored in heuristics, or rules of thumb that everyone uses when there's nothing solid. That's why investment banks are in such fabulous buildings. An inherently risky business wants to make you feel safe.

Another tough issue for leaders trying to build organizational Trust is that Trust-destroying events are more visible and noticeable than Trust-building events – and you're much more likely to hear about them too. When did anyone come running to tell you that the CEO followed through on her commitments for the 111th time that month? All that happens is your high expectations are confirmed. When things go well you just don't feel a strong positive reaction. Expecting a bonus and getting nothing will evoke a much stronger negative reaction than the positive opposite of expecting nothing and getting a bonus. That's because, typically, losses loom twice as large as gains.

Thirdly, sources of bad news are often seen as more credible than sources of good news. If you deliver bad news you're seen to be in the loop, connected to the heart of what's going on. People who deliver good news are sad saps who toe the corporate line.

How to build more Trust

Unfortunately, many organizations create low expectations of Trust by handling highly visible events appallingly badly. It's not that difficult to manage them well and it's something people really crave. Everyone wants to believe in their leaders and survey after survey reports that Trust is one of the things that employees rank and rate most highly. Because it means the rules of the game don't change, decisions aren't made arbitrarily, and there are clear reasons why things happen. What this takes is high-quality face-to-face communications that outline why decisions and choices have been made. And that takes time and thought along with a willingness to be honest.

Meanwhile, here are some basic rules to help build Trust no matter what level you are or where you work.

Rule 1: meeting and managing expectations
Doing what you commit to do is such a basic rule that it's almost banal to mention it. But it's extraordinary how often people don't. For example, not answering colleagues' or business partners' emails is not managing expectations. Everyone falls down from time to time: that's human nature. But dealing with repeated requests by ignoring them is not a way to build Trust. It's something simple that says a lot about you: that you're not 100 percent reliable. And reliability along with common business courtesy is the basis of Trust.

This leads on to part II of this rule: if you're not going to meet your expectations, tell people honestly without fudging the issue before you hit the buffers. Hiding something which then escalates behind the scenes and comes out at a later date is much, much worse. Ask Bernie Madoff.

Part III concerns creating realistic expectations in the first place. I love working with one executive because she will occasionally tell me, "I'm taking no actions as a result of this phone call; I'm swamped." I'm happy to know where I stand because she's setting up realistic expectations for us both.

Managing or changing beliefs may be easier than you think. If students can be persuaded to change their expectations of alcohol and reduce their consumption by a third after just one lecture, people can rethink their expectations about anything.

Rule 2: allocating resources

Trust is built one interaction at a time. And a central feature of every interaction that builds Trust is how you share and swap resources – whatever those resources are. When you do this consistently you build Trust because you're showing that you:

- Had free choice to decide to whom to give those resources.
- Settled on a particular person or group for specific reasons.
- Understand and appreciate their circumstances.
- Are willing to give something of clear benefit at a specific time.

Trust is built in the moment of giving because you show you have thought, analyzed, and acted. You've considered the whole context and done something positive for a particular person or group.

Rule 3: being wary of political hardball

The more politically Machiavellian you are, the less Trust will be invested in you and the less Trust you'll have in your organization. Politics exists everywhere but playing hard and fast is fatal in the Trust stakes because although it may bring you short-term wins, it will bring you long-term enemies too. How might this affect you further down the line? In the end people at the top always change and being in a polarized position is not useful. Divide and rule won't take and keep you there; it will ultimately just rule you out.

Rule 4: dismantling distrust

Dismantling distrust is different from building Trust. Both need to be taken care of because, like bullying at school, distrust is always present in any large organization. It needs constant vigilance because small things have such a large effect. Your salesperson who flouts all the rules because he or she "delivers the numbers" comes at a price: more undesirable behavior, resentment, and unrest. Clear and consistent signaling about what is and isn't acceptable is an organizational must for Trust. And from time to time that means honest conversations about your perceptions if you think that Trust is at risk.

Concluding Trust

It's not easy to help build organizational Trust. But if you want to feel it's there, you need to contribute to it too. Like anything that matters, it takes time and needs everyone's effort to achieve it. And it takes some strong virtues too. Like consistency, clear communications, and, most of all, a willingness to acknowledge and address difficult issues. And Recognition for those who build it because that will reinforce its importance.

Recognition for Your Achievements

It's usual today to be treated as a responsible and accountable individual who contributes to the overall well-being and progress of your organization. As someone who actively engages everything to make that happen. What you get in return is Recognition.

Recognition is when others inside or outside your organization acknowledge what you do and how you do it; it's the payback for your work that means much more to you than money. We know that because there's a strong negative correlation between Recognition and pay. This means the more you want Recognition, the less you want money in its place. In fact the effect was so strong that after we'd analyzed the data from over 1,000 respondents, we decided not to ask the question anymore because the results were so clear.

Then economic recession came along and we thought we ought to check and we asked another 1,000 people; the data hadn't budged. If you want Recognition, that's what you want and you won't find that money does it for you, no matter where you sit in the hierarchy of your organiza-

"When I was 19 or 20 I ran this project for the Board of Regents for the State of Florida. The idea was a consolidated data center that could register 35,000 kids over two universities in a week.

Registration was to start on Monday and on Friday the air-conditioning failed. To repair it would take a month. My boss said, 'This project's gonna fail.' I said, 'It can't fail.'

It dawned on me that something's got to keep airplanes cool when they're sitting on the ground. So I thought, 'Why not see if we can borrow one of those trucks and plug it into the side of the building.' Eastern Airlines said yes. We had to

Continued

tion. And this isn't just a generational thing: everyone from Baby Boomers to Gen Y-ers – born between 1977 and 2000 – want and need Recognition if they are going to be motivated to make and maintain their best Contribution.

That Recognition is crucial isn't exactly a new idea. Back in 1959, Herzberg published his Two-Factor Theory, which outlined the idea that it was a massive motivator along with things like achievement and responsibility. But this is an area where what we call the "knowing-doing gap" appears like a black hole. That's because far too many leaders feel that Recognition is unnecessary, difficult, embarrassing, time-consuming, or irrelevant. Or not part of their job. Therefore their team members do too and the effect is magnified and cascaded through an organization. And sometimes there's not enough Recognition because the mechanisms for it doesn't exist.

But here's why it needs to happen. It adds enormously to everyone's happiness at work, otherwise it wouldn't be connected to all the 5Cs.

But what, practically, does Recognition involve and how does it work?

The when and how of Recognition

You get Recognition at work in four different ways. You get it for:

get the trucks 300 miles, get the jet fuel, and think how to deal with the pressure so that the computers weren't blown away. And meantime we had to carve a hole in a building with no windows.

I was up all Friday night. On Saturday morning the head of all the computing centers comes in and he says, 'Bob, this is really amazing, people are running around doing everything.' Then he said, 'I want to tell you two things.' He points to the sun. 'That's going to come up tomorrow no matter what you do. You've done an amazing thing, now let these guys do their job. They will be so thrilled when you tell them it happened because of them and you make sure they get the right amount of credit. They'll feel so happy. They're here right now doing it for nothing, working all night long, and it's a great cause.'

Then he added, 'By the way, everybody will know you did this. You don't have to stand and take the credit. The right people, they know who did it.'

I've always remembered that."

Bob Cohn, entrepreneur, CEO and founder Octel Communications, San Francisco, CA, USA

- Who you are and what you do: this includes your industry, your job, and your status.
- What you achieve: this concerns what you deliver and the results you get.
- How you work: this encompasses working practices and relationships.
- How dedicated you are: this reflects the extra mile that you go to get things done.

"At Abercrombie & Fitch we were told our targets and how well we'd done individually. With a little more customer service and a little more push I got really good and it got noticed. My manager would buy me a Starbucks at the end of every day because 25 percent of my transactions would have a perfume in.

And you know, it was a really positive thing. It made me feel good about having done a good job. Their approach made me think that I was supporting a brand that I believed in; I took pride in dashing around the store helping the customer. I didn't feel expendable but that I'd been given an opportunity and that they were investing in me. It was a great place to work."

Isaac Bate, student, Oxford, UK

"Recognition for us comes with the community of particle physicists first of all. For me it also comes in the outreach work I do. When someone says to me, 'I don't understand what CERN is all about,' I organize a visit, they come and are fascinated. That for me is recognition."

Felicitas Pauss, Professor for Experimental Particle Physics, ETH Zurich, and External Relations Coordinator, CERN, France/Switzerland

Recognition is different from positive feedback in that it's public. Positive feedback happens mostly on a one-to-one basis, amongst your team or a small group of people. And it isn't appreciation, which takes place in a similar context; although they are strongly related, they are not the same thing.

Like food, everyone has preferences for how they like to be recognized. I'm sure you've heard anecdotes about employees who stood looking furious on a podium or walked out of reward ceremonies. They were being recognized in a way that meant nothing to them.

Dr. Gary Chapman says that there are five different ways that people like to be recognized. I've added a few more to his list: not all of them will work for you and you'll definitely have preferences for some and not others.

Words

If you're a words person, words in any form are how you prefer to be recognized. They can be delivered face to face or by email but are particularly important when they are delivered by someone you respect; this includes leaders in the field and both inside and outside your organization. Copying emails and telling third parties who report conversations back to you are both ways of really boosting feelings of Recognition.

Time

Time is what everyone's really short of: by giving this precious resource to or getting it from others, you have an implicit signal of value and worth. That's part of the equation. The other part aligns with the listening element of Contribution. Explaining or retelling events and having them acknowledged is a really powerful way of ensuring Recognition and making someone feel enormously valued. Doing this in a team setting benefits everyone in another way as well: it allows everyone to learn.

Gifts and treats

I used to work with someone who always gave beautifully thought through gifts. It gave her pleasure to put together boxes full of goodies that my family and I would enjoy. And though we haven't worked together for seven years, she still continues to send them to me. They're not expensive but they are personal and that's what matters most.

Gifts don't just apply to individuals: they can apply to teams and organizations too in the form of treats. Dinners that recognize effort, outings that bring everyone together by providing a shared experience. There's a lot of evidence that shows the best psychological capital is created when money is spent on common experiences. Common experiences are the stuff of memories, the things that individuals will talk about months and years later. Which of course adds to the overall Culture too.

> "When I was a child we had a house that was so cold that the goldfish used to freeze inside in winter. We had to put cardboard in our shoes to go to school: horrendous really.
>
> My dad was a laborer at an ironstone works. We'd pick potatoes in October, that sort of stuff. I left school at 15. When I look back I never would have dreamed that I would own houses abroad and boats.
>
> The biggest kick I get is the respect and recognition. I'm treated like people should be treated. I found myself invited by a client to a polo match and I was drinking champagne thinking, 'I never used to have shoes and here I am watching polo.'"
>
> Robert Tustain, builder and property developer, Banbury, UK

Acts of service

This is about doing things for others in a greater and a lesser sense. For example, I'm terrible at completing anything online. I don't know what it is but it seems to take me three times longer than anyone else. But Melissa, our Operations Director, knows my weakness and whisks anything online off me. And her acts of service for others are really remarkable because there are so many of them. She's the first to volunteer to do things for others because these acts mean a huge amount to her – and to us too.

Acts of service in an organizational setting include provision of child-care, gyms, restaurants at work, taxis home following late nights, and support for volunteering in the local community. All these are forms of Recognition in return for your Contribution.

Touch

At work we're trained not to touch others. It's simply not professional. And quite often it's cultural too. Once, when working in France, I held out my hand to introduce myself to someone who said, "I never shake a woman's hand." And he promptly gave me – no, not a French kiss – but one on both cheeks. I'll admit to being a little taken aback and having the thought, "This simply wouldn't happen in the USA." But if that's what it took for us to work more effectively together, that's what it took.

Symbols of achievement

This is a means of Recognition that I've added to Chapman's list. But it's what ceremonies, statuettes, medals, honors, certificates, trophies, and even parking spaces are all about: permanent or semi-permanent reminders of success.

Although such symbols are tools that are widely used by the military, sales teams, and anyone else who's customer-facing, it's rare to find such stuff dished out to anyone in a support role. When did you last hear of accounts clerk of the year? HR advisor or facilities person of the month? Has any assistant in any post-room ever received an award? Quite.

> "We do recognition well. You get your annual report, which is the drumbeat of how you're doing and impacts the likelihood of promotion.
>
> Then there are medals awarded when you serve, passing out parades, and young sailors get trade patches for technical training. All of that is just about recognition."
>
> Dr. Mike Young, Commander, Royal Navy, Portsmouth, UK

Checking in

Sometimes at work we don't want anything other than a call for no reason. It simply indicates that you have been in someone else's thoughts and that this person matters to you. Perhaps as a project progresses. Or because you've just not been in contact for a while. You're not offering appreciation, feedback, or thanks: you're just staying in touch. As he old saw has it, "it's the thought that counts."

> "Sometimes on a Friday afternoon it would be nice to have a checking-in call from your boss just to see how you are. The only reason they call now is to dump weekend work on you.
>
> We're in a tough environment, people don't like banks or bankers: our leaders could do so much just with a simple call or two. In my book that's not a big ask."
>
> Head of Leadership Development, British retail bank, London, UK

Promotions

Although this is last on the list, it's clearly not the least; being promoted is of course the biggest and most public form of Recognition. Because it says you've done such great work and achieved such success that you're ready for better things. It also signals that those at a more senior level are prepared to take a risk on you and that you're trusted to rise to it. And our data show that the higher up the hierarchy you go, the happier you become.

That's because, as we've found, you'll have more control, more respect – and more Recognition. On top of that, you'll strongly believe that you're fulfilling your potential.

Concluding Recognition

Sometimes the quiet internal satisfaction of a job well done is reward enough: but if you go out of your way and achieve something special, or someone does that for you, then it needs to be acknowledged. Because that's what brings happiness at work and means that everyone is willing to repeat that effort.

Just because you like to be recognized in a particular way doesn't mean that everyone wants what you do. By paying close attention to others' preferences, you'll recognize them in the way that means the most to them – as their effort did for you.

"Yes, I get a lot of recognition, name in the newspaper and all that stuff. Sometimes it's large but sometimes it's private. Then there's less recognition but enormous satisfaction.

I've represented politicians and big business people who've been under the government's microscope and didn't get charged and that's very satisfying. So is saving the existence of a company. I did two cases – Kidder Peabody and Salomon Brothers, who would have gone out of business if they'd been indicted. It was a great feeling, a terrific feeling when we saved them."

Gary P. Naftalis, Head of Litigation and Co-Chair, Partner, Kramer Levin Naftalis & Frankel LLP, New York, NY, USA

Concluding Pride, Trust, and Recognition

Pride, Trust, and Recognition are key indicators of happiness at work because they are connected to all the items within all the 5Cs. That's why they matter so much. Thinking through what you have, what you'd like more of, and how to go about getting it will definitely add to your happiness at work. With Pride, Trust, and Recognition you'll feel you're in the right place, doing the right thing, and without them you won't: you'll probably be looking for opportunities elsewhere. It's as simple as that.

Although they sound pretty nebulous, there are lots of concrete things that you can do to build them for yourself. It's important to remember and to reiterate that your happiness doesn't lie in others' hands; by seizing the initiative and taking action, you can manage and improve your situation.

Top take-aways for Chapter 9

- Pride, Trust, and Recognition map strongly onto all the 5Cs and are clear indicators of overall happiness at work.
- Pride and Trust work very similarly: if you have one, you'll have the other too.
- Pride in your organization comes from identifying with it, understanding your level of Contribution, knowing who your work affects, and being aware of its wider impact.
- Trust in your organization flows from two sources: your colleagues and your senior leaders.
- Recognition for your achievements comes from who you are, what you do, how you work, and how dedicated you are. It has nothing to do with money and lots to do with being recognized in the way you most prefer.

10

Achieving Your Potential

Introduction to Achieving Your Potential

Like, Pride, Trust, and Recognition, achieving your potential is very tightly connected to all the 5Cs and the elements within them. That's why it's so important: our findings reveal that people who are happiest at work achieve their potential 40 percent more than those who are unhappy in their job. It's something that sounds very esoteric and grandiose – possibly even pretentious. But work is likely to be the main context in which you get to stretch yourself and find out what you are capable of: dealing with domestic routine tests your patience, not your potential.

The hardest thing about this elusive concept is that you're most likely to think that you have got there only after the event. And at that precise moment the goal posts shift. To further develop it you'll once more have to push the edges of your comfort zone. That's because doing easy things, refining or repeating old stuff, isn't what achieving your potential is all about. It takes effort, persistence, and courage, all of which we've found to be closely associated with Confidence.

And it's also very strongly linked with:

- Feeling energized.
- Using your strengths.

"Achieving your potential is a concept you can only apply retrospectively because while you're doing it, you're slogging, you're busy, you're tense. Yes, you're mastering the craft, but it's not fun when you've lost your notebook or can't solve the problem or face any of the dozen things you have to deal with during the day. You have to bring that mastery to bear on all of it.

Sometimes you run up against a particularly tough nut but when you finally crack it, that's when you feel pretty good. That's when you have the sense of achieving your potential."

Marilyn Nissenson, writer, TV producer, and journalist, New York, NY, USA

- Using your skills.
- Learning new skills.
- Overcoming challenges at work.

We can see from our data that most people would rather feel that they are achieving their potential than stay in an unfulfilling job – despite economic recession. For example, when we compare data obtained before and after the collapse of Lehman's in September 2008, we can see that recession has only had a marginal effect on wanting to stay in your job. That figure has increased by only three months regardless of happiness level. Achieving your potential still matters more than hanging onto a job you don't like.

If you're like most people, you'll want to develop yourself, to learn and do new things: you want to invest in your human capital. And underlying this are some very practical things like honing strengths, extending skills, and adding to your knowledge. Which of course creates psychological capital too; you show yourself you can get better and improve. What's more uplifting than that?

"Mediocrity bores me. Pushing for excellence in the profession – that's how you reach your potential. When you work with others who want that too, it takes you all to the next level.

How do you do it? Look around you at the people you're working with and ask yourself, 'Do they want to do, and be, the best they can? And to achieve that not for the glory and vanity of it, but because they want to realize their full potential as a human being in terms of what they contribute?'

I struggle to get there – I think we all do to some extent – but that's truly what it's about."

Betsy Blair, COO, CJW Medical Center, Richmond, VA, USA

Feeling Energized

The most important thing you need to achieve your potential is energy. But where does that come from?

"Our profession suits people with high energy and rewards people who have visible amounts of it. If you're energetic you'll make more effort; then you stand out and get noticed. You can't plan everything in your career – but you can decide to put more in – whatever comes along."

Mark Thompson, Director-General, BBC, London, UK

Psychodynamic theorists, Freud, Jung, and their intellectual descendents, argued that you needed some kind of psychic energy to make your brain work. That energy was thought to come from two drives: the life and the death instinct. The Myers-Briggs Type Indicator, which took Jung's work on the conscious and unconscious mind into organizations, aims to clarify "natural" preferences, suggesting that you'll be psychically – rather than physically –

de-energized by working against those preferences. And the whole point is to bring this into
consciousness.

Maybe.

While I have my doubts about life, death, the
unconscious, or psychic energy, it's absolutely
clear that certain kinds of task are physically
draining for everyone alike. For example, work
that means going beyond the call of duty in
terms of time and effort; or drudgery – the stuff
that results in little reward. Both are very de-
energizing. As are constant interruptions or
blocks when you're trying to get something
done; they are de-energizing until you make a
breakthrough to get back on track. And that
takes persistence and self-control. Of course, the
more you're interrupted the harder it then is to
pick up the threads and the more energy it then
costs you.

So how does energy at work arise? I think it's
much simpler than life or death; I believe we're
energized at work when we're happy and we're
de-energized when we're not. And our data absolutely support this. In fact, happiness at work and
energy have one of the strongest relationships
we've found across all the data we've analyzed.
Here's some detail: people who are least happy
at work tell us they only feel energized 26 percent
of the time, while those who are happiest tell us
that they are energized 74 percent of the time.
We also asked everyone how much of the time
they felt de-energized at work. The people with
the lowest happiness levels say that they are de-
energized 39 percent of their time, while the
highest group are de-energized 11 percent of
their working day. That's an astonishing difference of more than 250 percent.

Nor will your low-energy colleagues be as
supportive as high-energy ones. In other words,

"Until the crash of 1998 I always
thought I was Superman, then
suddenly I saw some kryptonite. My
business was in difficulty and I
wanted to get back to my high
energy.

I realized that there were 15 toilet
associations without a headquarters
so I started the World Toilet
Organization. My employees were
angry: 'You're crazy, the business
needs you, we're in crisis and you're
running away half a day every day:
why?'

But I had to find my sanity, my
creative juice, and my energy. I
wasn't happy running a stressful
business doing turnaround
management. And 2.5 billion people
still don't have access to proper
sanitation and we want to solve that
problem.

Spiritually, the reward is much
higher than money: it's about
fulfillment, which is something
money can't buy. And breaking a
taboo has been very satisfying."

Jack Sim, social entrepreneur, CEO
and founder, World Toilet
Organization, Singapore

"I think work is about energy,
attacking things with vigor, about
thinking about what's possible rather
than what's not, and starting from a
point of 'yes,' not 'no.'

The hardest bit about starting
LastMinute.com was dealing with
such a culture of 'no, it's not
possible.' Every hotel said, 'No, the
web's not going anywhere, we're not
putting our product on the Internet.'
Seems extraordinary now but we

Continued

spent hours and hours calling individual hotels.

It was a constant mission about how this wasn't dangerous, it wasn't illegal, and actually could be handy and generate extra revenue."

Martha Lane Fox, co-founder and ex-CEO LastMinute.com; co-founder and chair Lucky Voice, London, UK

"I used to fly as a Captain with a low-cost airline and because of the scheduling I became really fatigued. It took me four months to fully recover my energy after I left; the rota meant you started on an early shift pattern and then moved to lates. Flight data collected across the airline showed that more errors were being made as a result. I believe that it's since been changed but the fatigue was insidious. There was just no time to recover from the physical and mental exhaustion of flying a plane six days a week."

Female First Officer, UK

you'll probably end up carrying the can for them. Because they're much less likely to deliver.

Now most people find that energy fluctuates during the day and that it's higher in the morning, lower at some point in the afternoon, rises again, and then drops off until you go to bed, by which time it's turned into fatigue. This points to the fact that energy really is a precious and limited resource that is quickly used up. That's why you'll feel particularly pressurized and negative when you waste it. And wasted energy has a knock-on effect on your time: the less energy you have, the less you can seize the initiative, the longer a task takes, the less productive you are. Then you wind up borrowing time from the hours when you should be relaxing and recuperating. Continually doing that can lead to burnout, which is just a long-lasting loss of energy.

On the other hand, you will feel energized when you make progress towards a goal. Or when you're with other people who are energized too. And very importantly, when you have had enough time to recharge outside work: Jim Loehr and Tony Schwartz's work with top-class athletes found that the key to success is recovery, which is something that most desk-bound professionals don't take seriously enough. In the short term this means moving location, changing activities, listening to music, gazing at something beautiful, even if it is onscreen, stretching, going outside to see the sky and get a breath of fresh air, or taking a brisk five-minute walk. Watching television, by the way, does not create positive energy, so don't expect it to: neither does drinking coffee or alcohol. And working long hours tells a mixed story.

Hours and hours

In our database of over 3,000 people, we've found working weeks range from 38 to over 100 hours a week. There's massive variation in the hours worked and how people feel about them. The story they tell is more complicated than we initially thought: either you'll hate your job because the hours are punishing, or you'll love your job and the hours don't feel like work. So in the final analysis, hours don't tell us very much.

But there are some interesting gender and cultural differences.

Women on the whole become unhappier at work as their hours get longer. Conversely, men become happier as they lengthen. And there are some interesting cultural differences too. Of course Americans, who work an average of 48 hours a week, show more consistent and extreme hours (over 60 hours a week) than any other nation. But they aren't the most productive with it. In fact, respondents in Europe who work on average 43 hours a week report levels of productivity that are 6 percent higher.

What's interesting from examining the data is that 48 hours a week seems to be a critical cutoff point. More than this and we can see that most reported productivity starts to decline quite dramatically. For example, when we look at employees in the financial or consulting sector, they tend to do longer hours, averaging about 52 per week. Their happiness scores put them in the second highest group, which means that they should be on task 72 percent of the time. They aren't. They are on task 63 percent of the time, so they are 13 percent less productive than they should be. And the quality of what they're doing could probably be higher too. The Whitehall II study which followed British civil servants over 20 years found that people who regularly worked over 55 hours a week scored lower in vocabulary and reasoning tests and that that effect wasn't a one-off but lasted over time.

So why do people regularly do long hours? There are two big reasons.

The first is that quite often we're not good at realizing when the energy we have is no longer up to the task we're doing. We're so enmeshed in it that we can't realize that it's better to stop.

> "What is the right amount of time to become a professional, to really ensure the best care for a patient and to provide job satisfaction? We haven't figured that out. I know 80 hours a week is too much but when you restrict the hours there are some negative outcomes.
>
> The problem is that we don't have cultural norms for reflection and rejuvenation in the USA; it's tied into the American Dream of hard work, which means we don't value vacation or leisure time."
>
> Professor Mark W. Babyatsky, Professor of Medicine, Mount Sinai Hospital, New York, NY, USA

> "I used to work really crazy hours. Around 80 a week but sometimes it would be 90 when I was director of a cardiac and transplant surgery department. I was managing about 160 people in a 24/7 operation.
>
> Then I decided to make better choices about my day, my projects, and priorities. What was really interesting was that I did 90 percent of my job on 30–40 percent fewer hours. By doing that I developed myself and developed others too, and that really served me in my subsequent roles."
>
> Diane Scott, President, Nursing Mentors Group, Midlothian, VA, USA

"You have to put in those hours at certain periods of time and I think that's OK. It's part of what builds a feeling of 'we'd do anything to make this better.' But once people move into the mode of doing that on a regular basis then it becomes self-fulfilling, because there's nothing to go back to, there's nothing else to do, and those hours give you a sense of purpose. And that's really unhealthy. I've rarely seen that quality of work is influenced by how many hours you put in."

Shikhar Ghosh, CEO Appex, entrepreneur, Senior Lecturer Harvard Business School, Boston, MA, USA

"It's not about balance but it is about energy. I'm very protective of my energy and I'm very careful how I spend my evenings so I don't push the limits. I know there's a danger point and I don't need to do standing around a room with another glass of champagne."

Lynne Franks, PR guru, visionary, and author, London, UK

"Hunter-gatherers don't work much by our standards. Even in difficult places like the Kalahari people work about 12–15 hours to get food and shelter. Then they're sensible enough to get on with the real business of life, which is discussing things, telling stories, and socializing."

Chris Gosden, Professor of European Archaeology, Oxford University, UK

The second big reason is that when everyone else is doing long hours it's tough to breeze out. We all like group members to conform and behave in the same way or we feel threatened. I realized that quite early in my career when I found myself doing silly hours mostly because everyone else was. One day I made the conscious decision that I was going to have a life outside work and go to the theater, films, and see friends. All it would take was doing an hour less at my desk every day. The first time I left earlier one of my colleagues said, "Leaving early are we?" And he continued to make sarcastic comments about my Commitment for months afterwards.

This attitude is hard to crack: we can clearly see from our consulting and coaching work that others judge your Commitment level by watching the hours you do because it's an obvious and visible measure of it. On the other hand, there's a negative relationship between hours and Culture: no-one likes working in organizations where long hours are the norm. In other words, we look at hours as good for others but not for ourselves. The only way round this conundrum is some honest conversations and some different ways of behaving: and that takes courage, which is of course part of achieving your potential.

Using Your Strengths

Strengths are today's big management and leadership trend. Put "strengths at work" into Google and you'll come up with 51 million hits. Look on any management publications and you'll find racks of new books and lots of articles about them. So what are they? Broadly speaking, a strength is something that you have a natural disposition for and that you enjoy using. And at face value what's not appealing about that? Here's how you can find and recognize them. And it's important to do that because it's much easier and far more enjoyable to do more of what you do easily and well.

Recognizing your strengths

One of the easiest ways is to go online, pay to do Gallup's Strength-Finder, the VIA survey, or Realise2. Or try any of these three routes instead.

Route 1

Think about three or four times when you felt that you were the best you could possibly be at work. What were you doing? Who were you with? What led to this? Then consider the strengths that lay behind these experiences. And think about your levels of motivation and energy. If these were high, I'm guessing you'll have been really successful in what you were doing.

Route 2

Look for other people who display the strengths you also have. What do they do? How do they do it? In what ways are you similar or different? If you feel you can, go and talk to them to understand how they do what they do. Benchmarking yourself is a way of conducting a reality check and helping you to develop too.

Route 3

Contact people who worked with you in the past and ask them what strengths they saw in you during that period. Talking to several ex-colleagues, mentors, and family members means that you'll get a more balanced picture, especially if you ask them about your weaknesses too. That's important because strengths-based feedback alone doesn't generate positive actions or feelings: in fact quite the opposite – they appear to shrink. You'll pay more attention to negative feedback because it directs your attention to what you can do to improve and you'll work out positive actions as a result.

"When I thought about teaching medicine, I decided to go back to my roots and to talk to people who had mentored me as early as elementary school.

A couple of teachers remembered that I used to gather groups of students at school and tutor them. I learned quickly that by teaching you have to be very confident of your knowledge. I did it because it was a great learning tool for me. And it was something I'd been doing from a young age."

Professor Mark W. Babyatsky, Professor of Medicine, Mount Sinai Hospital, New York, NY, USA

This meshes with my experience working with senior leaders who I've seen become frustrated by only strengths-based feedback. They are hungry to know what to grow and improve because this is how their organizations grow and improve too.

This isn't the only problem with strengths. The truth is that they are in the happiness equation but they aren't *that* important. When we crunched our data we found that there are 23 elements that are more important than strengths. For example, being respected, raising issues that matter to you, feeling effective and resilient, helping your colleagues for starters, and most crucially motivation matter more. Then we wondered if strengths are really important for productivity. Once more we found that motivation was top of the list and there were seven other elements ahead of strengths. Strengths contribute to happiness at work and to productivity but they don't appear to be pivotal, probably because they are linked with several tricky issues.

Some of the issues with a strengths-based approach

One of the major difficulties with strengths is that most people don't have a good understanding of what their strengths are. We know this because we've found that there's an 85 percent data cross-over between what people think of their skills and what they think of their strengths. And when you ask individuals up and down organizations what their strengths are, they frequently refer to skills. In other words, they think that they are the same thing. That implies it will be hard for people to tell the difference between strengths and other concepts too. Nor is the situation improved by the confusion generated by practitioners and pundits. Strengths are not only referred to as skills but also as aptitudes, traits, talents, values, and virtues. Then there's the language used to identify them.

If you thought happiness was a tough word to say at work, try telling a prospective employer that you are bringing a lot of playfulness and humor to the workplace. Or a love of temperance and a yearning to exercise your courage.

Then there are cultural issues associated with the kinds of conversations that are okay to have at work. Although strengths-based conversations may be acceptable in some organizations

> "What are my strengths? Brilliant organizational and influencing skills combined with very strong empathy and fantastic commercial insight. I am an unusually commercial HR Director.
>
> I've always been detailed and compartmentalized: even as a little boy I'd lay my things out in a certain order. It's the way my mind has always worked. It means I'm on top of the detail; I've got my finger on the button. It's what makes me successful."
>
> HR Director, service industry, Hong Kong/London, UK

and especially in the USA, they are clearly not in others. One of the funniest exchanges I ever had was with a French female senior executive who, when I asked her about strengths and whether she ever talked about them with her boss, told me she would rather "spit in my eye" than do so. The vehemence of her answer says it all.

But however much you pat yourself on the back when you think about your strengths, here's the bald truth. Weakness counts for much more. Simply because a weakness carries a lot more negative weight than its equivalent strength carries a positive one. Take rapport, something which is recognized as a strength everywhere.

Failure to build rapport is much more likely to block your career than success is likely to bring you a promotion. Work is a social activity and rapport is an essential social skill. If you find it tough, there is simply no way round it. You can't delegate rapport building, you can't partner with someone so that they do it for you, and you can't use a different strength to overcome your lack of it. If you want career success, you just have to learn to manage this weakness. Weakness is more salient because that's what others notice in you; juicy projects and promotions are allocated by a process of exclusion, not inclusion, and most organizations can't risk a big failure. That's why weaknesses will always matter especially as you climb the greasy pole.

The best way to look at strengths

It's not clear from the literature whether your strengths are fixed or not, whether you have lots of them, or whether they are context-specific. Professor Linda Ginzel at Chicago Booth Business School believes that you have a "pool of strengths" to draw from depending on what you're being asked to do. That pool contains lots of potential that floats to the top depending on the opportunities you're presented with.

I agree. I think that you'll experience your strengths when internal capacity is combined with external opportunity. The implication of this is that you'll never fully experience all your strengths, because the potential you have is as wide as your possible experiences. In short, the great news is there'll always be more. And in fact regarding them as fixed may not only be limiting, it can also be dangerous. Because over-using your strengths is a common route to personal catastrophe. Ironically, having a good understanding of your strengths is important because one of the most important things you can do is understand when not to use them.

"I was promoted really fast and I found myself at 32 in charge of a global team, responsible for hundreds of millions in revenues. It seemed to all fall into my lap and I was the golden boy. I got fast-tracked up the organization because I'd been a great salesman with an instinctive knack for it. I was a hands-on guy, good with CIOs because I understood the detail of their projects.

But it didn't mean that I was a strategic thinker. Working at board level was a whole new game, fraught with politics, and I was in way over my head. My forthrightness, which is what clients had valued, made me some enemies; and the hotter, pacier style of sales didn't suit the cooler nature of the boardroom.

I knew it wasn't working and even with a coach I couldn't seem to fix it. Especially the politics. So I jumped before I was pushed. The last 12 months have been the toughest I've been through. Derailed? It feels more like a train-smash."

General Manager, IT, Mountain View, CA, USA

When strengths result in downfall

It's easy to overuse a strength and to not even know that's what you're doing. Kaplan and Kaiser, who researched strength over-use, found that 55 percent of managers' colleagues thought that they used too much of one strength. More worryingly, those managers were simply unaware that this was the case. It's worrying because some of the biggest personal crashes come about when people can't stop using a particular set of strengths and can't see that what they do just doesn't work anymore. That's what derailing is all about and it happens most often during times of transition such as getting a promotion, working for a new boss, or finding yourself in a changed economic environment. In other words. derailing is all about failing to adapt.

If you face transition, one of the things that really matters is to take stock and see if you need to dive into that pool of strengths and try something new if you want to succeed. And in those circumstances it may be particularly important to use or develop some new skills too.

Using Your Skills

Although skills and strengths are similar, there's been a lot more research into the importance of skills. They matter in generating flow experiences and building happiness at work, and not using them can generate feelings of depression.

Skills, unlike strengths, aren't based on something innate; they are acquired through opportunity, instruction, practice, and support. And the more you do, the better you get, which means one of the most important qualities you'll have is the grit and determination to practice. That's what produces expertise.

The terrific news about skills is that research over the past 30 years has found that, other than in sport, you don't need an innate ability to become a top performer. And this is true in music, mathematics, medical diagnosis, scientific output, and social science amongst others. If you give yourself enough time and have enough motivation, you can become an expert in almost any field. In fact this is precisely the premise that the Suzuki method of teaching music is based on – that all children have an ability to learn music just by learning and deliberately practicing from a young age.

Deliberate practice

Deliberate practice is a term coined by Professor Anders Ericsson, who observed and researched it. He and his colleagues noticed that the key to expertise is practicing what you struggle to do. The good news is that this means experts are usually made and rarely born. The bad news is that it takes time. And that a fundamental part of deliberate practice is doing difficult things, like watching videos of screw-ups if you're a sportsman or woman, or spending hours rehearsing tricky passages if you're a musician. Or practicing that presentation one more time if the content is complex.

But whatever you want to develop expertise in, the basic parameters for deliberate practice include:

- Having a well-defined task.
- Receiving immediate informative and detailed feedback.
- Getting the detail right through repetition.
- Taking the time for self-reflection and evaluation.
- Keeping endurance and motivation high over time.

That's how you push yourself to attain the next level of performance. It isn't about performing a skill a large number of times over a long period, but about doing this with improvement and growth in mind. To do that means breaking a skill down into its component parts in order to focus on excelling at all the detail.

Many people aiming to get to or stay at the top of their game work with a coach. And a coach is anyone who you feel can challenge and help you learn. Their main job is to point out what's wrong and push you to then get it right. Because detailed feedback is the name of the game if you want to progress. That's the kind of feedback which has the most effect or accelerates your ability to learn a task. Now this doesn't rule out positive feedback: it just means remembering the 3:1 rule outlined in Chapter 4. And understanding that feedback which has the weakest effect on performance is that which threatens someone else's self-esteem. Feedback that has the

"I got the feedback that I wasn't communicating my thought process and wasn't in tune enough with the office. That was hard to hear. I'd always thought that water-cooler time was wasted time. But then I thought about the fact that being in my office might not be the best way to be and that I could involve others more.

At first it felt awkward and that I had to be someone else at work. But now I realize that people want to talk to me and that I enjoy talking to them. Doing this has made me feel more connected and happier at work."

Amanda Felt, Director, Executive Education, Chicago Booth, London, UK

best result is task- and performance-specific and given to you by an expert in the field who pushes you to deliver your best by improving and adapting what you do.

The faster you adapt, the faster you'll develop the neural pathways that make this enhanced performance automatic. That was shown in a now famous study of London cab drivers done by Eleanor Maguire.

To become a London cabbie you have to do "The Knowledge," which requires learning 25,000 London streets over about 2–3 years. Maguire looked at 16 cabbies who'd been driving for an average time of about 14 years to investigate how their brains might be different from those of normal drivers. And she found that a cab driver's right hippocampus, which fires up when thinking through routes, was bigger. The longer a cabbie had been driving, the larger their right hippocampus. But as you've already noticed, it takes a serious amount of time to develop this level of skill.

Ericsson's research suggests that it takes about 10 years or 10,000 hours of deliberate practice to become an expert. And it's the final 2,500 hours that make the difference between being an expert and being a good performer; those are best built up by rehearsing between 2 and 4 hours a day when you feel most fresh.

Now this research into expertise was done by looking at world-class performers; most of the rest of us are content to do something a little more modest than that, and have to work within much tighter time frames. We don't have the luxury of a decade at our disposal. But even deliberate practice for an hour a day over three months makes a difference to a skill.

So what are you going to practice to make sure it's perfect? Because it will extend your potential – just as learning a new skill will too.

Learning New Skills

Learning is the fastest, easiest, and safest way to develop your potential; it builds self-belief and Confidence, which add to your psychological capital.

That in turn enhances your Contribution: you're growing your ability to meet current and future goals.

Some people take it seriously and learn all the time; others wait until opportunity or failure suddenly stares them in the face. Now new opportunities that require you to learn are just a gap between what you can deliver and what you want to do. Failure is a similar opportunity where you didn't bridge the gap because you hadn't learned enough. But those failures are often a spur to learning. That means any regrets or "if only" thoughts should act as a red flag: what do you need to learn to avoid the same thing happening again?

Interestingly, learning is another of the few areas where we've found some big gender differences: women are much happier than men when they can learn and develop at work. This is a serious issue: learning is fundamental to developing strong human capital. Without continuous learning an organization simply won't be able to deliver its strategy. That means organizations need to sell the benefits of development much better and ensure that learning and sharing knowledge is something that's officially supported and seen to be important right at the top. Or there's a big risk of wasting resources – because learning doesn't come cheap.

"When I first started teaching I thought, 'I'll do this for a few years and then I'll get it. I'll master it and move on.'

That's a little embarrassing when I look back on it. The longer you do something, the more you realize how complex it is and how hard to become really excellent at it.

I like the feeling of having something to add to a conversation but I still feel I haven't exhausted everything that I have to contribute. And I still feel that there's personal growth and learning there, both personally and professionally."

Kate Scott, Assistant Headmaster, Neighborhood House Charter School, Dorchester, MA, USA

"HIV has really taken a toll on our country: a generation ahead of me was almost wiped out so the best talent rises fast. We have had to learn quickly and without too many role models. I've got a name for it: crash learning. Crash learning is about stretching without breaking."

Dr. Matthews Mtumbuka, Head of Operations, Malswitch, Blantyre, Malawi

Courses, conferences, coaching, mentoring, and apprenticeships are very expensive and time-consuming. And often very poorly and unimaginatively delivered with not enough practical application, covering lots of "what" and little "how." That's in a formal setting.

In an informal setting, those supposedly showing you the ropes frequently don't have the time or ability. My second "placement" as a graduate trainee involved six months in a windowless old meat safe, reorganizing and reordering the contents and structure of over 2,000 files. That would have been okay except that I'd been expecting to learn about asset allocation within the pension fund division of the business. And I was enrolled to sit professional exams based on what I'd learned at the end of my stint.

For informal education to work you need to have a few formal guidelines and structure. If they don't exist, you'll need to try to put some in place: if I'd done that my life at that time would have been a lot easier.

Informal learning is much more fluid and can range from talking to a mentor, mastering a skill under the guidance of a colleague or friend, to reading up or doing web-based research about the area you want to improve. Or by purposefully asking others inside and outside of work how they tackle similar stuff.

Doing this virtually is of course the most cost- and time-efficient way to learn. And the big plus is that it's an easy way to connect with others to get support. That in turn builds enthusiasm and motivation to learn because being a member of a social network is all about belonging and feeling instantly connected to a specific group of people. And it explains why virtual problem-solving tools like intranets, user groups, internal wiki sites, blogs, or instant messaging are so popular and useful.

But whether learning is formal or informal, everyone needs to understand why developing and sharing knowledge matters if they're going to support it. Because the best learning experiences result in great things for organizations and individuals. Other than knowledge and understanding, you also get a reinforced sense of competence, self-belief, energy, and enjoyment, and it even adds to finding meaning at work. Plus it boosts your aspirations; knowing how to do something better means you'll extend your goals as a result – and you'll be able to overcome the challenges you'll inevitably face at work.

Overcoming Challenges at Work

Most people assume that anything tough at work must be stressful. That's because the "stress" word, borrowed from engineering, has been hijacked and applied liberally to anything that anyone simply doesn't like. And it's absolutely not the case. In reality happiness at work often comes out of doing difficult things, as our data clearly show. Challenges, particularly ones you feel in control of and that you feel supported in, actually contribute a huge amount to your levels of happiness at work. But curiously, we can see from our results that there's a big paradox around challenges.

No-one likes challenges coming their way or being given things that are difficult to do. But everyone likes sorting out problems once they have them and managing matters on the way. And the happier you are, the more you enjoy it.

In our statistics we can identify that those who have the highest levels of happiness at work also overcome 27 percent more challenges. And overcoming challenges is one of the main ways you signal to yourself that you are developing your potential.

A defining characteristic of those who take on and overcome big challenges is a strong sense of curiosity – or a desire to look for what's different and new. If you have this character trait you'll embrace uncertainty, jump on difficult things, and get absorbed by them. That leads to additional knowledge and experience, which in turn deepens and builds curiosity over time. What you end up with is a lovely virtuous circle that motivates curious people to learn even more and look for ever greater challenges in their field.

Now pop psychology tells you that one person's challenge is another's walk in the park. But it actually looks as if challenges at work fall into two groups which we all respond to in similar ways.

Easier-to-manage challenges
Easier-to-manage challenges include time pressure, high workload, and high levels of responsibility. They are easier to manage because getting them signals that someone thinks you are capable and resourceful enough to deal with them, and that affects your self-belief. And usually the more responsibility you have, the more choice you get in how to do what you've been tasked with.

Time-pressure is interesting because most people think that it's negative; actually it results

> "Curiosity is something which helps to increase the quality of our attention and level of our engagement. In this age of information overload, human attention has become a scarce resource. Our curiosity has become a necessary foil to the attention deficit created by that overload.
>
> I never look at things from one discipline only, I'm always looking how things interconnect, how one can solve problems by bringing surprising elements together. Curiosity has relevance in almost every area I explore; as an enabler of my own learning and also as a way to enter territory I am unfamiliar with."
>
> Elaine Rumboll, Director, Executive Education Graduate School of Business, University of Cape Town, South Africa

> "I've been able to do things where I really challenge myself to the extent that I do things I never possibly thought I could achieve. To know that I've gone to the edge of my capabilities and further without giving in is an amazing feeling. Those challenges drive me to succeed, to prove myself. I couldn't have come back here and say, 'You know, I couldn't do it; it was too foul.'
>
> If I failed the challenges I'd accepted, I'd fail myself."
>
> Ann Daniels, polar explorer, Exeter, UK

in using your initiative to manage your challenges differently to find new ways of doing things. Unless you're pushed into a corner, you'll keep on doing things the same old way. The minute you have to do more with less is the moment you'll be developing your potential: you have no choice but to devise a new way of delivering.

> "I really, really push the limits. It's more than accepting challenges: I look for something beyond what I can do and then I do it. That's what's involved in building a machine that's a cross between a Harrier Jump jet and a helicopter.
>
> If you're with your back to the wall you can do so much more than when you're comfortable. There's so much more that everyone can try that they aren't even aware of, especially when there's an urgent need. And there is for what we're building."
>
> Rafi Yoeli, President and CEO, Urban Aeronautics, Yavne, Israel

> "If you control people you get a lot of efficiency, but then you find that they aren't innovative or creative. It's very wasteful if you have talented people not using their sense of enterprise.
>
> When you employ a person you employ the entire person. I coined this word 'bureaucrazy' which is something you find in large organizations and government. It's when the rules become so heavy they start to impede progress and you can't fulfill the vision. It's very self-defeating."
>
> Jack Sim, social entrepreneur, CEO and founder, The World Toilet Organization, Singapore

Harder-to-manage challenges
On the other hand, harder-to-manage challenges actively reduce feelings of accomplishment and achievement. They typically include things that you have very little control or influence over, for example red tape or an ambiguous and unclear role. But it's guaranteed that at some point in your career you'll face both of them.

Red tape is the toughest of all because it actively prevents you achieving your goals and reduces your Contribution as you battle to deal with it. That's if you bother at all. Now every organization needs processes, but they don't need them gone wild: that's not process but red tape, which banishes common sense and leads to labyrinths of despair.

The danger with red tape is that learned helplessness sets in. That's when you and all your co-workers know that nothing can be changed through any effort that you make. So you make no effort. And a self-fulfilling downward spiral sets in which is boring, depressing, exhausting, numbing, and very unproductive. And very typical when working in large bureaucracies.

Unlike red tape, role ambiguity is something that you have to get to grips with in any new job. Understanding what's expected of you and how you achieve success is vital if you're going to be really productive. But sometimes that can be tricky. For example, when a new position has been created which has multiple and unclear demands; or when you feel less capable and confident than others want you to be; or when you get a new boss who has different expectations and demands. But it's no surprise that clarity about what you have to achieve makes you happier: you know what you have to deliver.

One of the most important ways that you can deal with harder-to-manage challenges is by getting support, which might include resources, funding, technology, equipment, and education. And most importantly, you'll get your best support from like-minded friends and colleagues.

Here's the caveat: overcoming challenges is not about working inside your comfort zone. You may well be doing things that you are unsure of in a complex and uncertain situation which requires courage because you don't know what the outcomes will be. But it's exactly how you achieve your potential.

Concluding Achieving Your Potential

Feeling that you are achieving your potential is something that's central to being happy at work. We know that because it's very strongly connected to the 5Cs and to Pride, Trust, and Recognition. Now you don't want it all day every day; if your home life requires lots of effort and energy there'll be little left over for work. But it's rare to find people who have absolutely no desire to grow and develop because it's such a basic human drive.

What's interesting is our data show that few people think that they are maxed out on the potential front. Which is good news and bad news. It's good news because there's a lot more to offer and tap into: it's bad news because it means that organizations are not taking advantage of a huge amount of talent, goodwill, and energy which lies at their disposal. There's a massive resource at hand which, with a little effort, could easily be developed for everyone's benefit.

If you think you have a lot more to offer than you are being asked to deliver, I recommend that you think big. Connect your unused potential to specific organizational goals and then go and grab the bull by the horns. Doing what's big,

"I did the Race Across America in 2007, 2008, and 2009. Most of us are not professional cyclists but we cross America in under 12 days. This time I did it in 10 days and 20 hours on 13½ hours sleep.

I'm just a normal guy who's proving that anything's possible with the right mindset. With the right mindset you can do a lot more than you know. I have a passionate belief that we all have greatness inside us and that most of us are only just scratching our full potential."

Jim Rees, author, speaker, and coach, London, UK

brave, and difficult and practicing as you go is how you're most likely to find success. And increase your happiness at work.

Top take-aways for Chapter 10

- Achieving your potential is strongly associated with feeling energized, using your strengths and skills, learning new skills, and overcoming challenges.
- Start to pay attention and be mindful of what energizes you: it's a good internal marker of your happiness. Doing long hours may mean you don't have enough recovery time, and a 48-hour week looks like it's the maximum number of hours you should work before your productivity rapidly starts to fall off.
- Work with strengths but don't lose sight of weakness: successful people are aware of both. And they spend time boosting and refining their skills too.
- Remember that the fastest way to develop your potential is to learn.
- Recognize that if you're like most people, you won't like being given challenges but will like overcoming them. It's normal to experience less happiness when you start tackling a big project and more as you work your way through it.

Happiness at Work
A Conclusion

A few months ago I was going through airport security at London's Heathrow airport and I was pulled aside to have my hand luggage checked. Waiting and watching the woman riffling through my belongings, I asked her if she was happy in her work. She drew herself up and standing tall replied, "I'm really scared of flying and what I do is take that little bit of fear away for people. Nothing and no-one is going to get past me, so in my own way I'm helping keep Britain safe. Eight hours a day, five days a week, I love being here, doing what I do and I do it really well."

At that moment I was reminded of the CEO in that multinational boardroom. She had what he did not and as a result was an asset to her employers: he was a liability. She worked hard; really believed in what she did; liked the place she worked; knew she was there for the long haul; and understood that she truly delivered. From that brief encounter, it was clear she had the 5Cs as well as huge Pride in what she did.

Those 5Cs, Contribution, Conviction, Culture, Commitment, and Confidence, all consist of individual elements each of which is underpinned and supported by Pride, Trust, Recognition, and the concept that you are achieving your potential. Rather like a Jenga block tower, you can take a few blocks away and the tower will still be there; but remove a cornerstone and the whole edifice tumbles down.

That kind of collapse matters for personal and professional reasons: if you're really happy at work you'll be 180 percent happier with life overall, have 180 percent more energy, and be nearly 50 percent more productive than your least happy colleagues. You might think that it's your energy or productivity that leads to happiness and it doesn't work the other way round. Of course one affects the other, but the process has to start somewhere and it's clear that happiness comes first. That's why it's worth nurturing and managing this complex emotion.

Happiness is complex because people and the organizations in which they work are complicated. So a simplistic answer was never going to fit the bill. But it's worth remembering that work has had and continues to have a bad press; even when people are miserable in their jobs, they still estimate that they enjoy 30 percent of their day.

Now recession has of course affected everyone and has decreased happiness levels at work. That's hardly a big surprise. The consequences are that people intend to stay longer in their jobs, take less time off sick, and are working longer hours. That might be good news for employers but here's the flipside: energy and productivity have decreased significantly across the board, so you might feel that you're doing more but you'll be feeling worse and delivering less. And as a result you may want out as soon as economic upturn comes along. Yet the fact is you don't have to quit to change: you can make your working day better and your job more personally sustainable, and there are lots of practical and simple things that you can do to help yourself.

The easiest place to start is by being more mindful and aware of your situation. All that involves is stepping back to recognize how you feel in any given moment – and why. Doing this is one of the easiest ways to build your psychological capital and to protect it too. But that psychological capital is not going to be banked in a vacuum; other people have an effect on how you feel and you'll have an effect on them too. Being mindful of that is the first step towards understanding that although work can't "make" you happy, you can make yourself happier at work.

What Next?

If you'd like to explore happiness at work further, here are some ways to do it.

- Come to a happiness at work seminar: the website www.iopener.com has a list of what's happening and when.
- Get your own personal report by clicking on www.iopener.com/ippqreport and take the iOpener People and Performance Questionnaire. It will take you about five minutes and you'll get a free and personalized report about your happiness at work. If you think a friend would like to do it too, forward them the link. You can send this link as often and as many times as you like because we believe that something as valuable as this should be available to everyone.
- Think about getting a company or team report too: email me at jess.prycejones@iopener.com or visit the website to download a sample report.
- Sign your company up at www.happycompaniesindex.com, an index that is monitoring and measuring the happiest organizations everywhere.

And if you'd like to read more, download a webcast, sign up to my blog, and visit our website – www.iopener.com.

Finally, I'd love to hear about your personal experiences in using these tools and techniques, so please do contact me and let me know.

References

1 Why Happiness at Work? Why Now?

p. 2 "Get promoted faster ..." (Boehm, J.K., & Lyubomirsky, S., 2008. Does happiness promote career success? *Journal of Career Assessment, 16*(1), 101–116).

p. 2 "Earn more ..." (Diener, E., & Biswas-Diener, R., 2002. Will money increase subjective well-being? A literature review and guide to needed research. *Social Indicators Research, 57*(2), 119–169).

p. 2 "Get more support ..." (Iverson, R.D., Olekalns, M., & Erwin, P.J., 1998. Affectivity, organizational stressors and absenteeism: A causal model of burnout and its consequences. *Journal of Vocational Behavior, 52*(1), 1–23; Staw, B.M., Sutton, R.I., & Pelled, L.H., 1994. Employee positive emotion and favorable outcomes at the workplace. *Organization Science, 5*(1), 51–71).

p. 2 "Generate better ideas ..." (Fredrickson, B., & Branigan, C., 2005. Positive emotions broaden the scope of attention and thought–action repertoires. *Cognition and Emotion, 19*(3), 313–332).

p. 2 "Generate more creative ideas ..." (Baas, M., De Dreu, C.K.W., & Nijstad, B.A., 2008. A meta-analysis of 25 years of mood-creativity research: Hedonic tone, activation, or regulatory focus? *Psychological Bulletin, 134*(6), 779–806).

p. 2 "Achieve your goals ..." (Sheldon, K.M., & Houser-Marko, L., 2001. Self-concordance, goal attainment, and the pursuit of happiness: Can there be an upward spiral? *Journal of Personality and Social Psychology, 80*(1), 152–165).

p. 2 "Interact better ..." (Forgas, J.P., 2002. Feeling and doing: Affective influences on interpersonal behavior. *Psychological Inquiry, 13*(1), 1–28).

p. 2 "Receive superior reviews ..." (Cropanzano, R., & Wright, T.A., 1999. A 5-year study of change in the relationship between well-being and job performance. *Consulting Psychology Journal: Practice and Research, 51*(4), 252–265).

p. 2 "Learn more" (Goetz, M.C., Goetz, P.W., & Robinson, M.D., 2007. What's the use of being happy? Mood states, useful objects, and repetition priming effects. *Emotion, 7*(3), 675–679).

p. 2 "Achieve greater success ..." (Isen, A.M., 1970. Success, failure, attention, and reaction to others: The warm glow of success. *Journal of Personality and Social Psychology*, 15(4), 294–301).

p. 2 "Are healthier ..." (Watson, D., 1988. Intraindividual and interindividual analyses of positive and negative affect: Their relation to health complaints, perceived stress and daily activities. *Journal of Personality and Social Psychology*, 54(6), 1020–1030; Kobasa, S.C., 1979. Personality and resistance to illness. *American Journal of Community Psychology*, 7(4), 413–423).

p. 2 "You'll be less affected by stress hormones ..." (Kubzansky, L.D., Sparrow, D., Vokonas, P., & Kawachi, I., 2001. Is the glass half empty or half full? A prospective study of optimism and coronary heart disease in the normative aging study. *Psychosomatic Medicine*, 63, 910–916).

p. 2 "In fact happiness looks ..." (Danner, D.D., Snowdon, S.A., & Friesen, W.V., 2001. Positive emotions in early life and longevity: Findings from the nun study. *Journal of Personality and Social Psychology*, 80(5), 804–813).

p. 3 "Happiness leads to all these positive outcomes ..." (Boehm, J.K., & Lyubomirsky, S., 2008. Does happiness promote career success? *Journal of Career Assessment*, 16(1), 101–116).

p. 3 "Nor does it work ..." (Ng, W., & Diener, E., 2009. Feeling bad? The "power" of positive thinking may not apply to everyone. *Journal of Research in Personality*, 43(3), 455–463).

p. 5 "Psychologists, philosophers ..." (His Holiness The Dalai Lama & Cutler, H., 1999. *The art of happiness: A handbook for living*. London: Hodder and Stoughton).

p. 7 "Human capital isn't new ..." (Smith, A., 1776. *An inquiry into the nature and causes of the wealth of nations*).

p. 9 "Thought to be the opposite of burnout ..." (Schaufeli, W.B., Salanova, M., González-Romá, V., & Bakker, A.B., 2002. The measurement of engagement and burnout: A two-sample confirmatory factor analytic approach. *Journal of Happiness Studies*, 3(1), 71–92).

p. 9 "... it's been broadly defined ..." (Schaufeli, W.B., Salanova, M., González-Romá, V., & Bakker, A.B., 2002. The measurement of engagement and burnout: A two-sample confirmatory factor analytic approach. *Journal of Happiness Studies*, 3(1), 71–92).

p. 9 "... it's even been described ..." (Wefald, A.J., & Downey, R.G., 2009. The incubator. Job engagement in organizations: Fad, fashion, or folderol? *Journal of Organizational Behavior*, 30(1), 141–145).

p. 9 "At its best engagement ..." (Csikzentmihalyi, M., 2003. *Good business: Leadership, flow and the making of meaning*. Hodder and Stoughton).

p. 10 "If happiness indicates job satisfaction ..." (Stajkovic, A.D., 2006. Development of a core confidence-higher order construct. *Journal of Applied Psychology*, 91(6), 1208–1224).

p. 11 "Twin studies show …" (Lykken, D., 1999. *Happiness: The nature and nurture of joy and contentment*. New York: St. Martin's Press).

p. 11 "We know that …" (Tellegen, A. et al., 1988. Personality similarity in twins reared apart and together. *Journal of Personality and Social Psychology, 54*(6), 1031–1039).

p. 11 "He said, 'It's now clear … '" (Wallis, C., 2005. The new science of happiness. *Time*, January 9, A1–A9).

p. 11 "You'll be delighted …" (Boswell, W.R., Boudreau, J.W., & Tichy, J., 2005. The relationship between employee job change and job satisfaction: The honeymoon–hangover effect. *Journal of Applied Psychology, 90*(5), 882–892).

p. 11 "What's interesting is that …" (Bruce, H., 2008. Life goals matter to happiness: A revision of set-point theory. *Social Indicators Research, 86*(2), 213–231).

p. 11 "That's backed up by further research …" (Oswald, A.J., & Powdthavee, N., 2008. Does happiness adapt? A longitudinal study of disability with implications for economists and judges. *Journal of Public Economics, 92*(5), 1061–1077).

p. 11 "A recent study in the USA …" (Tkach, C., & Lyubomirsky, S., 2006. How do people pursue happiness? Relating personality, happiness-increasing strategies and well-being. *Journal of Happiness Studies, 7*(2), 183–225).

p. 12 "That's the question that Commander Dr. Mike Young …" (Young, M., 2008. *Life leadership* [online]. Available at www.consultmike.com/2.html [accessed December 18, 2008]).

2   The Research Journey

p. 17 "That stage involved asking 418 executives …" (60 percent were men, 40 percent were women; 73 percent were aged between 31–50).

p. 18 "Time and again psychological research over 40 years …" (Rotter, J.B., 1971. External control and internal control. *Psychology Today, 5*(1), 37–58).

p. 20 "Work more discretionary hours …" (Wegge, J., Schmidt, K.-H., Parkes, C., & van Dyke, R., 2007. Taking a "sickie": Job satisfaction and job involvement as interactive predictors of absenteeism in a public organization. *Journal of Occupational and Organizational Psychology, 80*(1), 77–89).

p. 20 "Take less sick leave …" (Lyubomirsky, S., King, L., & Diener, E., 2005. The benefits of frequent positive effect: Does happiness lead to success? *Psychological Bulletin, 131*(6), 803–855).

p. 20 "Stay longer in your job …" (Clarke, A.E., 2001. What really matters in a job? Hedonic measurement using quit data. *Labour Economics, 8*(2), 223–242).

p. 21 "To test our assumptions we carried out two surveys on two different groups of 193 and 403 people respectively" (in press).

p. 21 "And now we had some really serious data" (Edmunds, L.D., & Pryce-Jones, J., 2007. Relationships between employee happiness, overtime, sick leave and intention to stay or leave. *Selection and Development Review, 24* (2), 8–12).

p. 21 "We then divided the answers into five groups using a validated general happiness scale" (Lyubomisky, S., & Lepper, H.S., 1999. A measure of subjective happiness: Preliminary reliability and construct validation. *Social Indicators Research*, 46(2), 137–155).

p. 22 "She told us that the process we'd followed …" (Stewart-Brown, S., & Edmunds, L., 2007. Assessing emotional intelligence in children: A review of existing measures of emotional and social competence. In R. Bar-On, J.G. Maree, & M.J. Elias (Eds.), *Educating people to be emotionally intelligent*. Westport, CT: Praeger/Greenwood).

p. 23 "And it means you start with content that has validity from the outset" (Nunnally, J.C., 1978. *Psychometric theory*. New York: McGraw-Hill College).

p. 23 "What we found has been further consolidated by over 3,000 respondents from 79 countries …" (The number of executive MBA students makes up about 9 percent of the total database. They show a normal distribution and are not a large enough group to skew or alter the data).

p. 25 "Finally, lying at the heart of all of this …" (Rogers, Carl R., 1980. *A way of being*. Boston: Houghton-Mifflin).

p. 26 "Happier people are more productive …" (Zelenski, J.M., Murphy, S.A., & Jenkins, D.A., 2008. The happy-productive worker thesis revisited. *Journal of Happiness Studies*, 9(4), 521–537).

p. 27 "Now take a look at the percentage of people …" (Categorized by standard deviation not raw scores).

p. 28 "In the UK and the USA the average employee takes 6 days off sick a year …" (*The Economist*, 2009. Sick of it [online]. (Updated February 2, 2009). Available at www.economist.com/daily/chartgallery/displaystory.cfm?story_id=13051301 [accessed October 1, 2009]).

p. 28 "We know that happiness is the cause of this …" (Boehm, J.K., & Lyubomirsky, S., 2008. Does happiness promote career success? *Journal of Career Assessment*, 16(1), 101–116).

p. 29 "Secondly, other researchers have found that happiness is an area in which people don't fake good results" (Peterson, C., Park, N., & Seligman, M.E.P., 2005. The VIA: Constructs don't correlate with social desirability constructs. Assessment of character strengths. In G.P. Koocher, J.C. Norcross, and S.S. Hill III (Eds.), *Psychologists' desk reference*. New York: Oxford University Press).

p. 29 "… to appear 'better' than they are" (Jang, D., & Kim, D.-Y., 2009. Two faces of human happiness: Explicit and implicit life satisfaction. *Asian Journal of Social Psychology*, 12(3), 185–198).

p. 29 "For example, if you're asked to assess how much time you've had off sick …" (Johns, G., 1994, How often were you absent? A review of the use of self-reported absence data. *Journal of Applied Psychology*, 79, 574–591).

p. 29 "We knew that we were looking at the same concept whoever you were …" (Oishi, S., Diener, E., Napa Scollon, C., & Biswas-Diener, R., 2004. How was happiness assessed – they just asked them … several times. *Journal of Personality and Social Psychology*, *86*(3), 460–472).

3   Contribution from the Inside-Out

p. 33 "Not to mention make you feel good" (Job, V., Langens, T.A., & Brandstätter, V., 2009. Effects of achievement goal striving on well-being: The moderating role of the explicit achievement motive. *Personality and Social Psychology Bulletin*, *35*(8), 983–996).

p. 34 "Then you'll work harder towards them …" (Emmons, R.A., 2003. Personal goals, life meaning, and virtue: Wellsprings of a positive life. In C.L.M. Keyes & J. Haidt (Eds.), *Flourishing: Positive psychology and the life well-lived*. Washington, DC: American Psychological Association).

p. 34 "… because you'll want to invest more time and energy …" (Sagiv, L., Roccas, S., & Hazan, O., 2004. Congruence: Positive psychology in practice. In A. Linley & S. Joseph (Eds.), *Positive psychology in practice*. Hoboken, NJ: John Wiley & Sons).

p. 35 "The first and most common goal trap …" (Ordóñez, L.D., Schweitzer, M.E., Galinsky, A.D., & Bazerman, M.H., 2009. Goals gone wild: The systematic side effects of overprescribing goal setting. *Academy of Management Perspectives*, *23*(1), 6–16).

p. 36 "Finally, goals that you work towards positively …" (Carver, C.S., & Scheier, M.F., 1999. Themes and issues in the self-regulation of behaviour. In R.S. Wyer, Jr (Ed.), *Perspectives on behavioural self-regulation: Advances in social cognition* (Vol. *12*, pp. 1–105). Mahwah, NJ: Erlbaum).

p. 37 "It's only difficult goals that increase happiness over time …" (Wiese, B.S., & Freund, A.M., 2005. Goal progress makes one happy, or does it? Longitudinal findings from the work domain. *Journal of Occupational and Organizational Psychology*, *78*(2), 287–304).

p. 37 "Of course it's true that impossible goals aren't motivating …" (Cron, W.L., Slocum, J.W., VandeWalle, D., & Fu, F.Q., 2005. The role of goal orientation on negative emotions and goal setting when initial performance falls short of one's performance goal. *Human Performance*, *18*(1), 55–80).

p. 37 "That's why the concept of 'stretched goals … '" (Ordóñez, L.D., Schweitzer, M.E, Galinsky, A.D., & Bazerman, M.H., 2009. Goals gone wild: The systematic side effects of overprescribing goal setting. *Academy of Management Perspectives*, *23*(1), 6–16).

p. 37 "What everyone wants is variety" (Warr, P.B., 1987. *Work, unemployment and mental health*. Oxford: Oxford University Press).

p. 37 "Constantly doing the same thing gets boring …" (Frederick, S., & Loewenstein, G., 1999. Hedonic adaptation. In D. Kahneman, E. Diener, & N.

Schwarz (Eds.), *Well-being: The foundations of hedonic psychology*. New York: Russell Sage Foundation).

p. 37 "What really matters is calibrating it ..." (Melamed, S., Ben-Avi, I., Luz, J., & Green, M.S., 1995. Objective and subjective work monotony: Effects on job satisfaction, psychological distress, and absenteeism in blue-collar workers. *Journal of Applied Psychology, 80*(4), 29–42).

p. 37 "Lack of realism about what's possible ..." (Nesse, R., 2000. Is depression an adaptation? *Archives of General Psychiatry, 57*(1), 14–20).

p. 39 "That's how you'll not only develop your potential ..." (Sheldon, K.M., & Houser-Marko, L., 2005. Self-concordance, goal attainment, and the pursuit of happiness: Can there be an upward spiral? *Journal of Personality and Social Psychology, 80*(1), 152–165).

p. 43 "As well as being an important element of Contribution ..." (LePine, J.A., & Van Dyne, L., 1998. Predicting voice behavior in work groups. *Journal of Applied Psychology, 83*(6), 853–868).

p. 44 "And then there's the tension you can create ..." (Premeaux, S.F., & Bedeian, A.G., 2003. Breaking the silence: The moderating effects of self-monitoring in predicting speaking up in the workplace. *Journal of Management Studies, 40*(6), 1537–1562).

p. 44 "... or feeling that you're stepping out of line ..." (Asch, S.E., 1956. Studies of independence and conformity: A minority of one against a unanimous majority. *Psychological Monographs, 70*(9), no. 416).

p. 45 "The situation I experienced ..." (Hu, S.-M., & Zuo, B., 2007. Impact of job insecurity on job pressure, job satisfaction and performance. *Chinese Journal of Clinical Psychology, 15*(2), 142–145).

p. 45 "And your levels of psychological capital are likely to be low ..." (Lau, B., & Knardahl, S., 2008. Perceived job insecurity, job predictability, personality and health. *Journal of Occupational and Environmental Medicine, 50*(2), 72–181).

p. 45 "At its worst, job insecurity ..." (Mauno, S., Kinnunen, U., Mäkikangas, A., & Nätti, J., 2005. Psychological consequences of fixed-term employment and perceived job insecurity among health care staff. *European Journal of Work and Organizational Psychology, 14*(3), 209–237).

p. 46 "So make sure that this is how you talk about yourself ..." (Casciaro, T., & Lobo, S.L., 2005. Competent jerks, lovable fools and the formation of social networks. *Harvard Business Review, 83*(6), June 92–99).

4 Contribution from the Outside-In

p. 49 "Feelings and behaviors are catching ..." (Barsade, S.G., 2002. The ripple effect: Emotional contagion and its influence on group behavior. *Administrative Science Quarterly, 47*(4), 644–675).

p. 49 "There's clear research showing that negative behavior ..." (Yang, J., 2008. "Can't serve customers right? An indirect effect of co-workers' counterproductive behavior in the service environment. *Journal of Occupational and Organizational Psychology*, *81*(1), 29–46).

p. 49 "But a *positive* ripple effect ..." (Fowler, J.H., & Christakis, N.A., 2009. Dynamic spread of happiness in a large social network: Longitudinal analysis over 20 years in the Framingham Heart Study. *British Medical Journal*, *338*(7685), 1–13).

p. 49 "And we're not alone ..." (Alvesson, M., & Sveningsson, S., 2003. Managers doing leadership: The extra-ordinarization of the mundane. *Human Relations*, *56*(12), 1435–1459).

p. 50 "What everyone agrees is that listening ..." (Cronin, M.W., 1993. Teaching listening skills via interactive videodisc. *Technical Horizons in Education Journal*, *21*, 62–68).

p. 50 "Language is a notoriously poor way of doing that ..." (Keysar, B., & Henly, A.S., 2002. Speakers' overestimation of their effectiveness. *Psychological Science*, *13*(3), 207–212).

p. 50 "... that they express themselves more clearly ..." (Keysar, B., & Henly, A.S., 2002. Speakers' overestimation of their effectiveness. *Psychological Science*, *13*(3), 207–212).

p. 50 "... and they fail to remember ..." (Wu, S., & Keysar, B., 2007. The effect of information overlap on communication effectiveness. *Cognitive Science*, *31*(1), 169–181).

p. 51 "When you're listened to at a gold standard ..." (Huwe, R.A., 1996. Informative supervisory feedback and supervisory listening: An examination of effects on productivity and satisfaction. *Abstracts International Section A: Humanities and Social Sciences*, *56*(12-A), 4852).

p. 53 "Positive feedforward can really help clarify your role ..." (Whitaker, B.G., 2008. Explicating the links between the feedback environment, feedback seeking, and job performance. *Dissertation Abstracts International: Section B: The Sciences and Engineering*, *68*(9-B), 6376).

p. 53 "... improve productivity ..." (Pritchard, R.D., et al., 2008. The productivity measurement and enhancement system: A meta-analysis. *Journal of Applied Psychology*, *93*(3), 540–567).

p. 53 "... validate your work ..." (Bakker, A.B., et al., 2003. A multigroup analysis of the job demands–resources model in four home care organizations. *International Journal of Stress Management*, *10*(1), 16–38).

p. 53 "... increase your sense of control ..." (Sparr, J.L., & Sonnentag, S., 2008. Feedback environment and well-being at work: The mediating role of personal control and feelings of helplessness. *European Journal of Work and Organizational Psychology*, *17*(3), 388–412).

p. 53 "… reduce negative feelings …" (Rosen, C.R., Levy, P.E., & Hall, R.J., 2006. Placing perceptions of politics in the context of the feedback environment, employee attitude, and job performance. *Journal of Applied Psychology, 91*(1), 211–230).

p. 54 "… while other studies have demonstrated that badly managed feedback is strongly associated with burnout …" (Bakker, A.B., et al., 2003. A multigroup analysis of the job demands–resources model in four home care organizations. *International Journal of Stress Management, 10*(1), 16–38).

p. 54 "… and wanting to leave your job …" (Sparr, J.L., & Sonnentag, S., 2008. Feedback environment and well-being at work: The mediating role of personal control and feelings of helplessness. *European Journal of Work and Organizational Psychology, 17*(3), 388–412).

p. 55 "In fact, up to 70 percent of managers find talking about performance tough …" (Sulkowicz, K., 2008. Straight talk at review time. *Business Week*, September 16).

p. 55 "The best ratio of positive to negative is thought to be 3:1" (Fredrickson, B.L., & Losada, F., 2005. Positive affect and the complex dynamics of human flourishing. *American Psychologist, 60*(7), 678–686).

p. 57 "It also increases output …" (cited in www.businessweek.com/magazine/content/09_62/s0902044518985.htm).

p. 57 "Psychologist Carol Dweck …" (Dweck, C., 1999. Caution – praise can be dangerous. *American Educator, 23*(1), 4–9).

p. 59 "You absolutely know when you have it …" (Matsumoto, D., 1992. More evidence for the universality of a contempt expression. *Motivation and Emotion, 16*(4), 363–368).

p. 59 "Paul Ekman, who has done decades of research into facial expressions …" (Ekman, P., 2007. *Emotions revealed: Recognizing faces and feelings to improve communication and emotional life*, 2nd ed. New York: Henry Holt).

p. 59 "That glue will mean that you want to work – and work well – with your team members" (Festinger, L., 1950. Informal social communication. *Psychological Review, 57*(5), 271–282; Mullen, B., & Copper, C., 1994. The relationship between group cohesiveness and performance: An integration. *Psychological Bulletin, 115*, 210–277).

p. 61 "That way you'll decrease conflict …" (Barsade, S.G., 2002. The ripple effects: Emotional contagion and its influence on group behavior. *Administrative Science Quarterly, 47*(4), 644–675).

p. 61 "In the same vein, what you don't want to do is lots of bitching and moaning …" (Wu, T.-Y., & Hu, C., 2009. Abusive supervision and employee emotional exhaustion: Dispositional antecedents and boundaries. *Group and Organization Management, 34*(2), 143–169).

5 Conviction

p. 64 "Looked at from the opposite perspective, the more you're demotivated, the less interest you show in your job, the less value you find in your work ..." (Seligman, M.E.P., 1995. *Helplessness*. San Francisco: Freeman).

p. 64 "... and the less effort you make too ..." (Ryan, R.M., & Connell, J.P., 1989. Perceived locus of causality and internalization: Examining reasons for acting in two domains. *Journal of Personality and Social Psychology, 57*(5), 749–761).

p. 64 "Then you feel less competent" (Bandura, A., 1986. *Social foundations of thought and action: A social cognitive theory*. Englewood Cliffs, NJ: Prentice-Hall).

p. 65 "Think Playstations and Nintendos ..." (Koepp, M.J., et al., 1998. Evidence for striatal dopamine release during a video game. *Nature, 393,* 266–268).

p. 66 "But the one that's best researched and most validated is Self Determination Theory" (Deci, E.L., & Ryan, R.M., 2000. The "what" and "why" of goal pursuits: Human needs and the self-determination of behavior. *Psychological Inquiry, 11*(4), 227–268).

p. 66 "Choice entails actively deciding on experiences and behavior ..." (Iyengar, S.S., & Lepper, M.R., 1999. Rethinking the value of choice: A cultural perspective on intrinsic motivation. *Journal of Personality and Social Psychology, 76*(3), 349–366).

p. 66 "It's about your freedom to align yourself ..." (Ryan, R.M., & Deci, E.L., 2000. Self-determination theory and the facilitation of intrinsic motivation, social development, and well-being. *American Psychologist, 55*(1), 68–78).

p. 66 "Which will mean that your overall motivation levels will be high ..." (Sheldon, K.M., Ryan, R., & Reis, H.T., 1996. What makes for a good day? Competence and autonomy in the day and in the person. *Personality and Social Psychology Bulletin, 22*(12), 1270–1279).

p. 67 "Mihaly Csikszentmihalyi, the psychologist ..." (Csikszentmihalyi, M., 2003. *Good business: Leadership, flow and the making of meaning*. London: Hodder and Stoughton).

p. 68 "What's interesting about flow ..." (Salanova, M., Bakker, A.B., & Llorens, S., 2006. Flow at work: Evidence for an upward spiral of personal and organizational resources. *Journal of Happiness Studies, 7*(1), 1–22).

p. 68 "The second telltale sign is reciprocity ..." (Cialdini, R.B., 2007. *Influence: The psychology of persuasion*. Fort Worth, TX: Harcourt Brace).

p. 68 "And that could include ... doing something kind" (Sills, J., 2009. Workwise: Kindness and co-operation. *Psychology Today*, Mar–Apr 2009, Article ID 4786).

p. 69 "Because it's much more often a cause of downfall ..." (Manzoni, J.F., & Barsoux, J.L., 2002. *The set-up-to-fail syndrome: How good managers cause great people to fail*. Cambridge, MA: Harvard Business School Press).

p. 69 "All attitude is expressed through behavior ..." (Ajzen, I., 1991. The theory of planned behavior. *Organizational Behavior and Human Decision Processes*, *50*(2), 179–211).

p. 70 "You can try savoring the moment ..." (Bryant, F.B., 2003. Savoring beliefs inventory (SBI): A scale for measuring beliefs about savoring. *Journal of Mental Health*, *12*(2), 175–196).

p. 70 "Thinking positively about the future is correlated with general happiness ..." (MacLeod, A.K., & Conway, C., 2005. Well-being and the anticipation of future positive experiences: The role of income, social networks, and planning ability. *Cognition and Emotion*, *19*(3), 357–373).

p. 70 "Working through the precise process that leads to success ..." (Greitemeyer, T., & Würz, D., 2005–6. Mental simulation and the achievement of health goals: The role of goal difficulty. *Imagination, Cognition and Personality*, *25*(3), 239–251).

p. 71 "Richard Easterlin wrote a seminal paper ..." (Easterlin, R.A., 1974. Does economic growth improve the human lot? Some empirical evidence. In P. David and M. Reder (Eds.), *Nations and households in economic growth: Essays in honor of Moses Abramovitz*. New York and London: Academic Press).

p. 71 "The blogosphere has it that you only need a very low income to be happy: once you've earned between $10,000 and $15,000 a year ..." (Layard, R., 2006. *Happiness: The lessons from a new science*. Harmondsworth: Penguin).

p. 71 "Of course you'll get a temporary hike in happiness levels when you get a pay rise ..." (Kahneman, D. et al., 2006. Would you be happier if you were richer? A focusing illusion. *Science*, *312*(5782), 1908–1910).

p. 72 "But there's some conflicting evidence too" (Diener, E., & Biswas-Diener, R., 2002. Will money increase subjective well-being? *Social Indicators Research*, *57*(2), 119–169).

p. 72 "And it also found that in the USA 90 percent of people earning at least $250,000 call themselves very happy ..." (Leonhardt, D., 2008. Maybe money does buy happiness after all. *The New York Times*, April 16).

p. 72 "In fact this finding about income and happiness is so clear that German researchers ..." (Schimmack, U., November 2008. *Measuring wellbeing in the socio-economic panel study*. Berlin: SOEP).

p. 72 "And to crown it all, psychologists and economists ..." (Stevenson, B., & Wolfers, J., 2008. Economic growth and subjective well-being: Reassessing the Easterlin Paradox. *Brookings Papers on Economic Activity*, *1*, 1–87).

p. 72 "If you want cash to do good things with it ..." (Dunn, E.W., et al., 2008. Spending money on others promotes happiness. *Science*, *319*(5870), 1687–1688).

p. 72 "It will help you build self-awareness ..." (Salanova, M., et al., 2006. Flow at work: Evidence for an upward spiral of personal and organizational resources. *Journal of Happiness Studies*, *7*(1), 1–22).

p. 74 "Shortly after the attacks, it was estimated that 7.5 percent of residents …" (Galea, S., et al., 2002. Psychological sequelae of the September 11 terrorist attacks in New York City. *New England Journal of Medicine*, *346*(13), 982–987).

p. 74 "After 4 months only 1.7 percent of the population reported PTSD symptoms …" (Galea, S., et al., 2002. Posttraumatic stress disorder in Manhattan, New York City, after the September 11th terrorist attacks. *Journal of Urban Health Studies*, *79*, 40–353).

p. 74 "You aren't necessarily damaged by being at the epicenter of something awful" (Silver, R.C., et al., 2004. Exploring the myths of coping with a national trauma: A longitudinal study of responses to the September 11th terrorist attacks. *Journal of Aggression, Maltreatment and Trauma*, *9*(1–2), 129–141).

p. 75 "Just as some people are tall or short, some people are hardier" (Kobasa, S.C., 1979. Stressful life events, personality and health: An inquiry into hardiness. *Journal of Personality and Social Psychology*, *37*(1), 1–11).

p. 75 "… and more resilient" (Luthar, S.S., Cicchetti, D., & Becker, B., 2000. The construct of resilience: Implications for interventions and social policies. *Development and Psychopathology*, *12*(4), 857–885).

p. 75 "Your levels of resilience are therefore part of who you are" (McManus, C., 2005. Myers and medicine, 2005. *The Psychologist*, *18*(12), 748–751; Scheier, M.F., Weintraub, J.K., & Carver, C.S., 1986. Coping with stress: Divergent strategies of optimists and pessimists. *Journal of Personality and Social Psychology*, *51*(6), 1257–1264).

p. 75 "Glen Elder, the ground-breaking American sociologist …" (Elder, G.H., & Conger, R.D., 2000. *Children of the land: Adversity and success in rural America*. Chicago: University of Chicago Press).

p. 76 "Randomized controlled trials clearly show that immediate post trauma counseling does not reduce distress" (Wessely, S., Bisson, J., & Roes, S., 2000. A systematic review of brief psychological interventions ("debriefing") for the treatment of immediate trauma-related symptoms and the prevention of post-traumatic stress disorder. In M. Oaklet-Browne, R. Churchill, D. Gill, M. Triveid, & S. Wessely (Eds.), *Depression, anxiety and neurosis module of the Cochrane Database of Systematic Reviews*, 3rd ed. Oxford: Update Software).

p. 76 "… or promote resilience" (Gist, R., 2002. What have they done to my song? Social science, social movements and the debriefing debates. *Cognitive and Behavioral Practice*, *9*(4), 273–279).

p. 76 "But there's more and more evidence to show …" (Wortman, C.B., & Boerner, K., 2007. Beyond the myths of coping with loss: Prevailing assumptions versus scientific evidence. In H.S. Friedman & R.C. Silber (Eds.), *Foundation of health psychology*. New York: Oxford University Press).

p. 76 "For example, a recent study showed …" (Seery, M.D., et al., 2008. Expressing thoughts and feelings following a collective trauma: Immediate responses to 9/11 predict negative outcomes in a national sample. *Journal of Consulting and Clinical Psychology, 76*(4), 657–667).

p. 77 "And they're happier as a result because they know they'll manage ..." (Greenglass, E.R., & Fiksenbaum, L., 2009. Proactive coping, positive affect and well-being: Testing for mediation using path analysis. *European Psychologist, 14*(1), 29–39).

p. 77 "Secondly, proactive copers interpret events in a more upbeat way ..." (Tugade, M.M., & Fredrickson, B.L., 2004. Resilient individuals use positive emotions to bounce back from negative emotional experiences. *Journal of Personality and Social Psychology, 86*(2), 320–333).

p. 79 "The important thing about finding positive meaning is that you'll recover faster physiologically" (Tugade, M.M., & Fredrickson, B.L., 2004. Resilient individuals use positive emotions to bounce back from negative emotional experiences. *Journal of Personality and Social Psychology, 86*(2), 320–333).

p. 79 "... and decrease your chances of depression too" (Watkins, P.C., Cruz, L., Holben, H., & Kolts, R.L., 2008. Taking care of business? Grateful processing of unpleasant memories. *Journal of Positive Psychology, 3*(2), 87–99).

p. 80 "Doing this has been shown to help bring closure ..." (Watkins, P.C., Cruz, L., Holben, H., & Kolts, R.L., 2008. Taking care of business? Grateful processing of unpleasant memories. *Journal of Positive Psychology, 3*(2), 87–99).

p. 82 "You've accessed what's important about what you do" (King, L.A., Hicks, J.A., Krull, J.L., & Del Gaiso, A.K., 2006. Positive affect and the experience of meaning in life. *Journal of Personality and Social Psychology, 90*(1), 179–196).

p. 82 "Of course, this is a lot easier to do after years of experience ..." (Miller, C.S., 2009. Meaningful work over the life course. *Dissertation Abstracts International: Section B: The Sciences and Engineering, 69*(8-B), 5078).

6 Culture

p. 87 "Articles refer to 'killing' ..." (Mintzberg, H., 2007. Productivity is killing American enterprise. *Harvard Business Review, 85*(7–8), 25–29); "front lines" (Levy, M., 2007. Look to your front line for the future. *Harvard Business Review, 85*(7–8), 55–56); "battles" (Dillon, K., 2009. The coming battle over executive pay. *Harvard Business Review, 87*(9), 96–103); "fight" (Kumar, N., 2006. Strategies to fight low-cost rivals. *Harvard Business Review, 84*(12), 104–113); "firing" (Sonnenfeld, J., & Ward, A.J., 2007. Firing back: How great leaders rebound after career disasters. *Harvard Business Review, 85*(1), 76–84); "arsenal" (Buehler, K., Freman, A., & Hulme, R., 2008. The new arsenal of risk management. *Harvard Business Review, 86*(1), 93–100); "defusing land mines" (Goldsmith, M., 2009. How not to lose the top job. *Harvard Business Review, 87*(1), 74–80).

p. 87 "Look once more at *Harvard Business Review* and you'll find articles that refer to boxing ..." (Sull, D., 2009. How to thrive in turbulent markets. *Harvard Business Review, 87*(2), 80–88); "Olympian experience" (Jones, G., 2008. How the best of the best get better and better. *Harvard Business Review, 86*(6), 123–127); "racing" (Ready, D.A., Hill, L.A., & Conger, J.A., 2008. Winning the race for talent in emerging markets. *Harvard Business Review, 86*(11), 62–70); "baseball" (Anthony, S.D., 2009. Major league innovation. *Harvard Business Review, 87*(10), 51–54).

p. 87 "As one article asserts, 'Winning is everything'" (Malhotra, D., Ku, G., & Murnighan, J.K., 2008. When winning is everything. *Harvard Business Review, 86*(5), 78–86).

p. 94 "Since ancient times tracts have been written about why comradeship mattered" (Thucydides, *The History of the Peloponnesian War*, 431 BC).

p. 94 "And the benefit of that is less conflict, more cooperation ..." (Jehn, K.A., Chadwick, C., & Thatcher, S.M.B., 1997. To agree or not to agree: The effects of value congruence, individual demographic dissimilarity, and conflict in workgroup outcomes. *International Journal of Conflict Management, 8*(4), 287–305).

p. 94 "... and better teamwork" (Jordan, P.J., Lawrence, S.A., & Troth, A.C., 2006. The impact of negative mood on team performance. *Journal of Management and Organization, 12*(2), 131–145).

p. 94 "It matters in the long term too: research over time has found that lack of support ..." (Leader, D., & Corfield, D., 2007. *Why do people get ill?* London: Hamish Hamilton).

p. 94 "People with better social networks and close relationships live longer" (Eriksson, B.G., Hessler, R.M., Sundh, V., & Steen, B., 1999. Cross-cultural analysis of longevity among Swedish and American elders: The role of social networks in the Gothenburg and Missouri longitudinal studies compared. *Archives of Gerontology and Geriatrics, 28*(2), 131–148).

p. 94 "... have better mental health" (Kawachi, I., & Berkman, L.F., 2001. Social ties and mental health. *Journal of Urban Health, 78*(3), 458–467).

p. 94 "... are better teamworkers" (Murillo, A.G., 2006. A longitudinal study of the development of team member exchange. *Dissertation Abstracts International: Section B: The Sciences and Engineering, 67*(2-B), 1191).

p. 95 "Focusing on similarities bridges differences ..." (Epstude, K., & Mussweiler, T., 2009. What you feel is how you compare: How comparisons influence the social induction of affect. *American Psychologist, 9*(10), 1–14).

p. 95 "People who disclose more tend to be liked more" (Collins, N.L., & Miller, L.C., 1994. Self-disclosure and liking: A meta-analytic review. *Psychological Bulletin, 116*(3), 457–475).

p. 95 "... and they get more help as a result" (Blickle, G., et al., 2008. The roles of self-disclosure, modesty and self-monitoring in the mentoring relationship: A longitudinal multi-source investigation. *Career Development International,* *13*(3), 224–240).

p. 95 "Broadly speaking, values are important guiding principles" (Cable, D.M., & Edwards, J.R., 2004. Complementary and supplementary fit: A theoretical and empirical integration. *Journal of Applied Psychology, 89*(5), 822–834).

p. 95 "In organizations they provide the norms ..." (Edwards, J.R., & Cable, D.M., 2009. The value of value congruence. *Journal of Applied Psychology, 94*(3), 654–677).

p. 96 "It boosts your psychological capital" (Cable, D.M., & Edwards, J.R., 2004. Complementary and supplementary fit: A theoretical and empirical integration. *Journal of Applied Psychology, 89*(5), 822–834).

p. 96 "... because fundamental beliefs that you hold precious ..." (Allport, G.W., 1961. *Pattern and growth in personality.* New York: Holt, Rinehart, & Winston).

p. 97 "It results in reduced misunderstanding" (Kalliath, T.J., Bluedorn, A.C., & Strube, M.J., 1999. A test of value congruence effects. *Journal of Organizational Behavior, 20*(7), 1175–1198).

p. 97 "People just do communicate better when their values are aligned ..." (Edwards, J.R., & Cable, D.M., 2009. The value of value congruence. *Journal of Applied Psychology, 94*(3), 654–677).

p. 97 "And that results in better team performance" (Chou, L.-F., et al., 2008. Shared work values and team member effectiveness: The mediation of trustfulness and trustworthiness. *Human Relations, 61*(12), 1713–1742).

p. 97 "... as well as better relations with your colleagues and with your boss" (Meglino, B.M., Ravlin, E.C., & Adkins, C.L., 1989. A work values approach to corporate culture: A field test of the value congruence process and its relationship to individual outcomes. *Journal of Applied Psychology, 74*(3), 424–432).

p. 97 "Actively working with values ..." (Schmeichel, B.J., & Vohs, K., 2009. Self-affirmation and self-control: Affirming core values counteracts ego depletion. *Journal of Personality and Social Psychology, 96*(4), 770–782).

p. 98 "But actively thinking about and expressing values ..." (Fujita, K., Trope, Y., Liberman, N., & Levin-Sagi, M., 2006. Construal levels and self-control. *Journal of Personality and Social Psychology, 90*(3), 351–367).

p. 98 "Although happiness at work is generally pretty stable ..." (Judge, T.A., Scott, B.A., & Ilies, R., 2006. Hostility, job attitude and workplace deviance: Test of a multilevel model. *Journal of Applied Psychology, 91*(1), 126–138).

p. 99 "The well-known Whitehall study of public sector employees undertaken over a ten-year time period showed that lack of fairness was associated with poorer thinking, sleeplessness" (Elovainio, M., et al., 2009. Organizational justice and sleeping problems: The Whitehall II study. *Psychosomatic Medicine, 71*(3), 334–340.)

p. 99 "… and a significantly increased risk of heart attack" (De Vogli, R., et al., 2007. Unfairness and health: Evidence from the Whitehall II study. *Journal of Epidemiology and Community Health*, *61*(6), 513–518).

p. 99 "In all of these areas, fairness is the topic that crops up most" (Mikula, G., Petri, B., & Tanzer, N., 1990. What people regard as unjust: Types and structures of everyday experiences of injustice. *European Journal of Social Psychology*, *20*(2), 133–149).

p. 99 "… and has the biggest effect on happiness, especially when it concerns your boss" (Loi, R., Yang, J., & Diefendorff, J.M., 2009. Four-factor justice and daily job satisfaction: A multilevel investigation. *Journal of Applied Psychology*, *94*(3), 770–781).

p. 100 "But worst-case scenarios result in outright sabotage" (Ambrose, M.L., Seabright, M.A., & Schminke, M., 2002. Sabotage in the workplace: The role of organizational justice. *Organizational Behavior and Human Decision Processes*, *89*(1), 947–965).

p. 101 "The more control – real or otherwise – you perceive you have in your job …" (Karasek, R.A., 1979. Job demands, job decision latitude, and mental strain. *Administrative Science Quarterly*, *24*(2), 285–311).

p. 101 "Feelings of low control have been shown to be connected to lethargy" (Seligman, M.E.P., 1975. *Helplessness: On depression, development, and death.* San Francisco: W.H. Freeman); "burnout" (Taris, T.W., et al., 2001. Job control and burnout across occupations. *Psychological Reports*, *97*(3), 955–961); "time off sick" (North, F.M., et al., 1996. Psychosocial work environment and sickness absence among British civil servants: The Whitehall II study. *American Journal of Public Health*, *86*(3), 332–340); "conflict at home" (Butler, A.B., Grzywacz, J.G., Bass, B.L., & Linney, K.D., 2005. Extending the demands–control model: A daily diary study of job characteristics, work–family conflict and work–family facilitation. *Journal of Occupational and Organizational Psychology*, *78*(2), 155–169); "heart disease" (Bosma, H., et al., 1997. Low job control and risk of coronary heart disease in Whitehall II (prospective cohort) study. *British Medical Journal*, *314*, 558–565).

p. 101 "For example, something as simple as just deciding the order in which you do a list of tasks …" (Glass, D.C., & Singer, J.E., 1972. *Stress and adaptation: Experimental studies of behavioral effects of exposure to aversive events.* New York: Academic Press).

p. 103 "Research over the past 50 years …" (Rotter, J.B., 1966. Generalized expectancies for internal versus external control of reinforcement. *Psychological Monographs*, *80*(1), 1–28).

p. 103 "And this is applicable whatever culture you come from" (Spector, P.E., et al., 2002. Locus of control and well-being at work: How generalizable are Western findings? *Academy of Management Journal*, *45*(2), 453–466).

p. 103 "All three reactions arise because everyone wants to make the 'right' decision" (Meier, L.L., Semmer, N.K., Elfering, A., & Jacobshagen, N., 2008. The double meaning of control: Three-way interactions between internal resources, job control and stressors at work. *Journal of Occupational Health Psychology*, *13*(3), 244–258).

p. 104 "Mentors help you build career success" (Allen, T.D., Lentz, E., & Day, R., 2006. Career success outcomes associated with mentoring others: A comparison of mentors and nonmentors. *Journal of Career Development*, *32*(3), 272–285).

p. 104 "The best mentors do that by balancing challenge with support" (Shernoff, D.J., & Nakamura, J., 2006. Balancing challenge and support in effective mentoring relationships. *Annual Meeting of the American Psychological Association*. New Orleans: American Psychological Association).

p. 104 "A third way of enhancing your sense of control …" (Spector, P.E., 1986. Perceived control by employees: A meta-analysis of studies concern autonomy and participation at work. *Human Relations*, *39*(11), 1005–1016).

7   Commitment

p. 109 "Big projects and goals which create a lasting sense of happiness …" (Warr, P., 2007. *Work, happiness and unhappiness*. Mahwah, NJ: Erlbaum).

p. 110 "Desire for meaning is quite simply a basic human motivation" (Frankl, V.E., 1963. *Man's search for meaning: An introduction to logotherapy*. New York: Washington Square Press).

p. 110 "And there are health benefits" (Ryff, C.D., & Singer, B.H., 2008. Know thyself and become what you are: A eudaimonic approach to psychological well-being. *Journal of Happiness Studies*, *9*(1), 13–39); " … which include less depression" (Debats, D.L., Van der Lubbe, P.M., & Wezeman, F.R., 1993. On the psychometric properties of the Life Regard Index (LRI): A measure of meaningful life. *Personality and Individual Differences*, *14*(2), 337–345); "reduced cortisol levels … and less heart disease" (Friedman, E.M., et al., 2007. Plasma interleukin-6 and soluble IL-6 receptors are associated with psychological well-being in aging women. *Health Psychology*, *26*(3), 305–313).

p. 111 "Karl Marx (who in 1844 wrote that meaning was important …" (Marx, K., 1844. *Economic and philosophic manuscripts of 1844*. New York: International Publishers (December 1980)).

p. 111 "Meanwhile, psychologists have provided answers … which include making daily decisions and taking action" (Maddi, S.R., 1970. The search for meaning. In M. Page (Ed.), *Nebraska symposium of motivation*. Lincoln, NE: University of Nebraska Press); "finding the right goals" (Klinger, E., 1977. *Meaning and void*. Minneapolis, MN: University of Minnesota Press); "creating the right relationships, self improvement" (Ebersole, P., 1998. Types and depths of written life meanings. In P.T.P. Wong & S.P. Fry (Eds.), *The human quest for meaning: A handbook of psychological research and clinical application*. Mahwah, NJ: Erlbaum); "meeting personal needs" (Baumeister, R.F., 1991. *Meanings of life*. New York: Guilford Press); "finding coherence" (Battista, J., & Almond, R., 1973. The development of meaning in life. *Psychiatry*, *36*(4), 409–427); "transcending oneself" (Allport, G.W., 1961. *Pattern and growth in personality*. New York: Holt, Rinehart, & Winston).

p. 111 "In 1943 Abraham Maslow ..." (Maslow, A.H., 1943. A theory of human motivation. *Psychological Review*, *50*(4), 370–396).

p. 111 "From all the coaching and consulting work that I've done, I believe that you start to create meaning by making decisions – as Frankl proposed" (Frankl, V.E., 1963. *Man's search for meaning: An introduction to logotherapy*. New York: Washington Square Press).

p. 113 "This is important: one of the underlying causes of burnout is when you don't find meaning for yourself in what you do" (Loonstra, B., & Tomic, W., 2005. Work pressure, existential meaning and burn-out among ministers in orthodox reformed denominations. *Psyche en Geloof*, *16*(2), 66–81).

p. 113 "Purpose in life is important because it helps manage anxiety" (Ruini, C., & Fava, G.A., 2009. Well-being therapy for generalized anxiety disorder. *Journal of Clinical Psychology*, *65*(5), 510–519).

p. 113 "... while lack of it has been linked to depression" (Turner, N., et al., 2007. What influences purpose in life in first-episode psychosis? *British Journal of Occupational Therapy*, *70*(9), 401–406).

p. 113 "So according to Carol Ryff's research ..." (Ryff, C.D., & Burton, S., 1998. The role of purpose in life and personal growth in positive human health. In P.T.P. Wong & S.P. Fry (Eds.), *The human quest for meaning: A handbook of psychological research and clinical application*. Mahwah, NJ: Erlbaum).

p. 115 "According to psychologist Amy Wrzesniewski ..." (Wrzesniewski, A., McCauley, C., Rozin, P., & Schwartz, B., 1997. Jobs, careers, and callings: People's relations to their work. *Journal of Research in Personality*, *31*(1), 21–33).

p. 115 "Maybe you volunteer, something which is well known for increasing happiness" (Borgonovi, F., 2008. Doing well by doing good: The relationship between formal volunteering and self-reported health and happiness. *Social Science and Medicine*, *66*(11), 321–334).

p. 116 "Job crafting implies that there are tasks and relationships which can be expanded ..." (Berg, J.M., Dutton, J.E., & Wrzesniewski, A., *What is job crafting and why does it matter?* From the Center of Positive Organizational Scholarship, 2008).

p. 116 "The first step is to ensure that those tasks and relationships fit your needs ..." (Wrzesniewski, A., & Dutton, J.E., 2001. Crafting a job: Revisioning employees as active crafters of their work. *Academy of Management Review*, *26*(2), 179–201).

p. 117 "Vital engagement is something that Jeanne Nakamura and Mihalyi Csikszentmihalyi have been investigating" (Nakamura, J., & Csikszentmihalyi, M., 2003. The construction of meaning through vital engagement. In C.L.M. Keyes & J. Haidt (Eds.), *Flourishing: Positive psychology and the life well-lived* (pp. 83–104). Washington, DC: American Psychological Association).

p. 117 "When you're vitally engaged, you're doing something which is profoundly important to you ..." (Nakamura, J., & Csikszentmihalyi, M., 2003. The construction of meaning through vital engagement. In C.L.M. Keyes & J. Haidt (Eds.), *Flourishing: Positive psychology and the life well-lived* (pp. 83–104). Washington, DC: American Psychological Association).

p. 118 "For example, there's good evidence that clear and appropriate vision statements ..." (Iseri-Say, A., Toker, A., & Kantur, D., 2008. Do popular management techniques improve performance? Evidence from large businesses in Turkey. *Journal of Management Development*, *27*(7), 660–677).

p. 119 "According to Kouzes and Posner ..." (Kouzes, J.M., & Posner, B.Z., 1995. *The leadership challenge: How to keep getting extraordinary things done in organizations*, 2nd ed. San Francisco: Jossey-Bass).

p. 120 "How you feel affects what you do and the effort you put in" (Grant, A.M., & Ashford, S.J., 2008. The dynamics of proactivity at work. In A.P. Brief & B.M. Staw (Eds.), *Research in organizational behavior*. Greenwich, CT: JAI Press).

p. 120 "and the better you feel, the harder you try both now and in the immediate future" (Foo, M.-D., Uy, M.A., & Baron, R.A., 2009. How do feelings influence effort? An empirical study of entrepreneurs' affect and venture effort. *Journal of Applied Psychology*, *94*(4), 1086–1094).

p. 120 "They create what Barbara Fredrickson calls a broaden and build model ..." (Cohn, M.A., & Fredrickson, B.L., 2006. Beyond the moment, beyond the self: Shared ground between selective investment theory and the broaden-and-build theory of positive emotions. *Psychological Inquiry*, *17*(1), 39–44; Fredrickson, B.L., 2006. The broaden-and-build theory of positive emotions. In M. Csikszentmihalyi & I.S. Csikszentmihalyi (Eds.), *A life worth living: Contributions to positive psychology*. New York: Oxford University Press).

p. 123 "Like lots of psychological concepts, hope is both a trait ..." (Snyder, C.R., 1994. *The psychology of hope*. New York: Free Press).

p. 123 "Whatever it comes from, it's valuable because ... it's clearly associated with higher job performance" (Peterson, S.J., & Byron, K., 2008. Exploring the role of hope in job performance: Results from four studies. *Journal of Organizational Behavior*, *29*(6), 785–803); " ... and happiness" (Youssef, C.M., & Luthans, F., 2007. Positive organizational behavior in the workplace: The impact of hope, optimism, and resilience. *Journal of Management*, *33*(5), 774–800).

p. 123 "For example, pessimists achieve incredible goals ..." (Lopes, M.P., & Cunha, M.P., 2008. Who is more proactive, the optimist or the pessimist? Exploring the role of hope as a moderator. *Journal of Positive Psychology*, *3*(2), 100–109).

p. 123 "According to positive psychologist Rick Snyder …" (Lopez, S.J., et al., 2004. Strategies for accentuating hope. In P.A. Linley & S. Joseph (Eds.), *Positive psychology in practice*. Hoboken, NJ: John Wiley; Snyder, C.R., 1994. *The psychology of hope*. New York: Free Press).

8 Confidence

p. 128 "And it's particularly affected when you don't have the skill to cope …" (Stankov, L., & Lee, J., 2008. Confidence and cognitive test performance. *Journal of Educational Psychology, 100*(4), 961–976).

p. 129 "Most of us over-estimate our abilities from time to time and think that we're much better than we are" (Kruger, J., & Dunning, D., 1999. Unskilled and unaware of it: How difficulties in recognizing one's own incompetence lead to inflated self-assessments. *Journal of Personality and Social Psychology, 77*(6), 1121–1134).

p. 129 "… especially when the task at hand is a tough one" (Stankov, L., Lee, J., & Paek, I., 2009. Realism of confidence judgments. *European Journal of Psychological Assessment, 25*(2), 123–130).

p. 129 "If you had accurate thoughts about what you could do, you'd never set the bar any higher …" (Bandura, A., 1997. *Self-efficacy: The exercise of control*. New York: Freeman).

p. 129 "And although both the experienced and inexperienced do this" (McKenzie, C.R.M., Liersch, M.J., & Yaniv, I., 2008. Overconfidence in interval estimates: What does expertise buy you? *Organizational Behavior and Human Decision Processes, 107*(2), 79–191).

p. 129 "… it's particularly true of people who don't know their personal limitations" (Ehrlinger, J., et al., 2008. Why the unskilled are unaware: Further explorations of (absent) self-insight among the incompetent. *Organizational Behavior and Human Decision Processes, 105*(1), 98–121).

p. 129 "… or can't do anything about them" (Kruger, J., & Dunning, D., 1999. Unskilled and unaware of it: How difficulties in recognizing one's own incompetence lead to inflated self-assessments. *Journal of Personality and Social Psychology, 77*(6), 1121–1134).

p. 130 "By the way, it's not only humans who do this: chimps, orangutans …" (Osvath, M., & Osvath, H., 2008. Chimpanzee (*Pan troglodytes*) and orangutan (*Pongo abelii*) forethought: Self-control and pre-experience in the face of future tool use. *Animal Cognition, 11*(4), 661–674).

p. 130 "… and even bees" (Cheng, K., Pena, J., Porter, M.A., & Irwin, J.D., 2002. Self-control in honeybees. *Psychonomic Bulletin and Review, 9*(2), 259–263).

p. 130 "But even a single act of self-control …" (Vohs, K.D., et al., 2008. Making choices impairs subsequent self-control: A limited-resource account of decision making, self-regulation, and active initiative. *Journal of Personality and Social Psychology*, *94*(5), 883–898).

p. 130 "Amazingly, some kids could wait for more than an hour" (Mischel, W., & Ebbesen, E.B., 1970. Attention in delay of gratification. *Journal of Personality and Social Psychology*, *16*(2), 329–337).

p. 130 "Those who'd managed to wait the 15 minutes could plan better …" (Mischel, W., Shoda, Y., & Peake, P.K., 1988. The nature of adolescent competencies predicted by preschool delay of gratification. *Journal of Personality and Social Psychology*, *54*(4), 687–696).

p. 131 "Procrastination takes place when you don't like doing something because it's too tough …" (Lonergan, J.M., & Maher, K.J., 2000. The relationship between job characteristics and workplace procrastination as moderated by locus of control. *Journal for Social Behavior and Personality*, *15*(5), 213–224).

p. 131 "In one study more than 90 percent of students reported that they procrastinated" (Schouwenburg, H.C., 1995. Academic procrastination: Theoretical notions, measurement and research. In J.R. Ferrari, J.L. Johnson, & W.G. McGown (Eds.), *Procrastination and task avoidance: Theory, research and treatment*. New York: Plenum Press).

p. 131 "… a number that holds true outside student life too" (Harriott, J., & Ferrari, J.R., 1996. Prevalence of procrastination among samples of adults. *Psychological Reports*, *78*(2), 611–616).

p. 131 "Professional workers are more likely to procrastinate than unskilled workers" (Hammer, C.A., & Ferrari, J.R., 2002. Differential incidence of procrastination between blue- and white-collar workers. *Current Psychology*, *21*(4), 333–338).

p. 131 "The cleverer you are, the more you procrastinate" (Ferrari, J.R., 1991. Self-handicapping by procrastinators: Protecting self-esteem, social-esteem or both? *Journal of Research in Personality*, *25*(3), 245–261).

p. 131 "Age, gender, and education don't affect time spent procrastinating" (Hammer, C.A., & Ferrari J.R., 2002. Differential incidence of procrastination between blue- and white-collar workers. *Current Psychology*, *21*(4), 333–338).

p. 131 "The average employee spends a staggering 80 minutes a day doing personal activities as a way of avoiding the tough stuff" (D'Abate, C.P., & Eddy, E.R., 2007. Engaging in personal business on the job: Extending the presenteeism construct. *Human Resource Development Quarterly*, *18*(3), 361–383).

p. 132 "You're more likely to take action when your choices are limited, you're working to externally imposed deadlines" (Ariely, D., & Wertenbroch, K., 2002. Procrastination, deadlines, and performance: Self-control by precommitment. *Psychological Science*, *13*(3), 219–224).

p. 132 "You're the kind of person that finds pulling a rabbit out of a hat …" (Lay, C., Edwards, J.M., Parker, J.D., & Endler, N.S., 1989. An assessment of arousal, anxiety, coping and procrastination during an examination period. *European Journal of Personality*, *3*(3), 195–208).

p. 132 "And active procrastinators believe that they incubate ideas better, maximize time" (Schraw, G., Wadkins, T., & Olafson, L., 2007. Doing the things we do: A grounded theory of academic procrastination. *Journal of Educational Psychology*, *99*(1), 12–25); "are more efficient" (Vacha, E.F., & McBride, M.J., 1993. Cramming: A barrier to student success, a way to beat the system or an effective learning strategy? *College Student Journal*, *27*(1), 2–11); "and create more flow experiences as a result" (Schraw, G., Wadkins, T., & Olafson, L., 2007. Doing the things we do: A grounded theory of academic procrastination. *Journal of Educational Psychology*, *99*(1), 12–25).

p. 132 "And most importantly have been shown to increase Confidence" (Rogerson, L.J., & Hryciako, D.W., 2002. Enhancing competitive performance of ice hockey goaltenders using centering and self-talk. *Journal of Applied Sport Psychology*, *14*(1), 14–26).

p. 133 "Feeling swamped and acting out of a pressurized negative place ..." (Weinberg, R.S., & Gould, D., 2006. *Foundations of sport and exercise psychology*, 4th ed. Champaign, IL: Human Kinetics Europe).

p. 133 "'Not thinking' causes more thinking ..." (Wenzlaff, R.M., & Wegner, D.M., 2000. Thought suppression. *Annual Review of Psychology*, *51*, 59–91).

p. 133 "Dan Wegner has done decades of experiments ..." (Wegner, D.M., 1994. Ironic processes of mental control. *Psychological Review*, *101*(1), 34–52).

p. 133 "The consequences of doing a task like this ..." (Kozak, M., Sternglanz, R.W., Viswanathan, U., & Wegner, D.M., 2008. The role of thought suppression in building mental blocks. *Consciousness and Cognition: An International Journal*, *17*(4), 1123–1130).

p. 133 "In the same way pressure to avoid a pitfall or pratfall ..." (Wegner, D.M., 2009. How to think, say, or do precisely the worst thing for any occasion. *Science*, *325*, 48–50).

p. 134 "It's a technique that sports psychologists have been working with for a couple of decades ..." (Hardy, J., Gammage, K., & Hall, C.R., 2001. A descriptive study of athlete self-talk. *Sports Psychologist*, *15*(3), 306–318).

p. 134 "It works because it helps you ..." (Rogerson, L.J., & Hrycaiko, D.W., 2002. Enhancing competitive performance of ice hockey goaltenders using centering and self-talk. *Journal of Allied Sport Psychology*, *14*(1), 14–26; Theodorakis, Y., Hatzigeorgiadis, A., & Chroni, S., 2008. Self-talk: It works but how? Development and preliminary validation of the functions of Self-Talk Questionnaire. *Measurement in Physical Education and Exercise Science*, *12*(1), 10–30).

p. 135 "Interestingly, athletes and psychologists say that of all the different types of self-talk ..." (Hatzigeorgiadis, A., Zourbanos, N., Mpoumpaki, S., & Theodorakis, Y., 2009. Mechanisms underlying the self-talk–performance relationship: The effects of motivational self-talk on self-confidence and anxiety. *Psychology of Sport and Exercise*, *10*(1), 185–192).

p. 135 "The second aspect is to connect this to self-control ..." (Nideffer, R.M., 1992. *Psyched to win*. Champaign, IL: Human Kinetics).

p. 135 "And there's lots of evidence showing that mental images ..." (Taylor, S.E., Pham, L.B., Rivkin, I.D., & Armor, D.A., 1998. Harnessing the imagination: Mental stimulation, self-regulation and coping. *American Psychologist*, 53(4), 429–439).

p. 135 "Possibly because the very act of imagining ..." (Sherman, S.J., Skov, R.B., Hervitz, E.F., & Stock, C.B., 1981. The effects of explaining hypothetical future events: From possibility to actuality and beyond. *Journal of Experimental Social Psychology*, 17(2),142–158).

p. 136 "Research suggests that people who do the former feel more intense emotions" (Holmes, E.A., Coughtrey, A.E., & Connor, A., 2008. Looking at or through rose-tinted glasses? Imagery perspective and positive mood. *Emotion*, 8(6), 875–879).

p. 136 "... while those who do the latter find broader meaning, significance, and increased motivation" (Vasquez, N.A., & Buehler, R., 2007. Seeing future success: Does imagery perspective influence achievement motivation? *Personality and Social Psychology Bulletin*, 33(10), 1392–1405).

p. 136 "There's amazing evidence that mental rehearsal triggers the same connections in your brain as actually doing the activity itself" (Wohldmann, E.L., 2006. Pushing the limits of imagination: The effectiveness of motor imagery for acquiring and maintaining a sequential motor skill. *Dissertation Abstracts International: Section B: The Sciences and Engineering*, 67(2-B), 1178).

p. 136 "... so it helps you learn faster" (Sanders, C.W., et al., 2008. Learning basic surgical skills with mental imagery: Using the simulation centre in the mind. *Medical Education*, 42(6), 607–612).

p. 136 "And increases your Confidence" (Munroe, K.J., Giacobbi, P., Hall, C.R., & Weinberg, R.S., 2000. The four Ws of imagery use: Where, when, why and what. *Sport Psychologist*, 14(2), 119–137).

p. 137 "So although it originates from external sources" (Carr, A., 2004. *Positive psychology: The science of happiness and human strengths*. Hove: Brunner-Routledge).

p. 137 "Self-worth is how you feel about yourself given your accumulated experiences; it may vary ..." (Ferris, D.L., Brown, D.J., Lian, H., & Keeping, L.M., 2009. When does self-esteem relate to deviant behavior? The role of contingencies of self-worth. *Journal of Applied Psychology*, 94(5), 1345–1353).

p. 137 "Self-belief is what you think about your personal capabilities to perform certain tasks ..." (Bandura, A., 1994. Self-efficacy. In V.S. Ramachaudran (Ed.), *Encyclopedia of human behavior*. New York: Academic Press).

p. 137 "Albert Bandura, the foremost researcher in the field ..." (Bandura, A., 1994. Self-efficacy. In V.S. Ramachaudran (Ed.), *Encyclopedia of human behavior*. New York: Academic Press).

p. 138 "That's why it's good to compare up ..." (Warr, P.B., 2007. *Work, happiness, and unhappiness*. Mahwah, NJ: Erlbaum).

p. 139 "This kind of knowing divides into two groups ..." (Sadler-Smith, E., 2008. *Inside intuition*. New York: Routledge).

p. 140 "For example, one study found that nurses in a neonatal intensive care unit ..." (Crandell, B., & Gamblian, V., 1991, as cited in Kahneman, D., & Klein, G., 2009. Conditions for intuitive expertise, a failure to disagree. *American Psychologist*, 64(6), 515–526).

p. 140 "Another looked at diagnoses made by psychiatrists ..." (Srivastava, A., & Grube, M., 2009. Does intuition have a role in psychiatric diagnosis? *Psychiatric Quarterly*, 80(2), 99–106).

p. 140 "The same goes for intuition in education" (Burke, L.A., & Sadler-Smith, E., 2006. Instructor intuition in the educational setting. *Academy of Management Learning and Education*, 5(2), 169–181); "management consulting" (Coman-Johnson, C., 1985. Intuition: A bona fide occupational requirement in the management consulting profession? *Consultation: An International Journal*, 4(3), 189–198); "and leadership" (Agor, W.H., 1986. The logic of intuition: How top executives make important decisions. *Organizational Dynamics*, 14(3), 5–18).

p. 140 "In short, it may play a much larger role in effective decision making ..." (Andersen, J.A., 2000. Intuition in managers: Are intuitive managers more effective? *Journal of Managerial Psychology*, 15(1–2), 46–67).

p. 142 "Role clarity is something that contributes to your overall happiness ..." (Moynihan, D.P., & Pandey, S.K., 2007. Finding workable levers over work motivation: Comparing job satisfaction, job involvement, and organizational commitment. *Administration and Society*, 39(7), 803–832).

p. 145 "In fact the numbers are simply incredible in statistical terms" (Pride 0.6; Trust 0.6; Recognition, 0.4; $p = < .000$).

9   Pride, Trust, and Recognition

p. 150 "We can see this in our data because they map very closely ..." (0.84; $p = < .000$).

p. 151 "There'll be lack of motivation" (Williams, L.A., & DeSteno, D., 2008. Pride and perseverance: The motivational role of pride. *Journal of Personality and Social Psychology*, 94(6), 1007–1017).

p. 151 "That's why they matter so much in underpinning psychological ... capital" (Clapp-Smith, R., Vogelgesang, G.R., & Avey, J.B., 2009. Authentic leadership and positive psychological capital: The mediating role of trust at the group level of analysis. *Journal of Leadership and Organizational Studies*, 15(3), 227–240).

p. 151 "Recent studies show that pride in any sense ..." (Tracy, J.L., & Robins, R.W., 2008. The nonverbal expression of pride: Evidence for cross-cultural recognition. *Journal of Personality and Social Psychology*, 94(3), 516–530).

p. 151 "People who are proud are seen as more likeable …" (Williams, L.A., & DeSteno, D., 2009. Pride: Adaptive social emotion or seventh sin? *Psychological Science, 20*(3), 284–288).

p. 152 "Means you maintain your organizational commitment" (Boezeman, E.J., & Ellemers, N., 2008. Pride and respect in volunteers' organizational commitment. *European Journal of Social Psychology, 38*(1), 159–172).

p. 152 "Encourages you to contribute to a group" (Boezeman, E.J., & Ellemers, N., 2007. Volunteering for charity: Pride, respect, and the commitment of volunteers. *Journal of Applied Psychology, 92*(3), 771–785).

p. 152 "Pushes you to go the extra mile" (Belschak, F., & Verbeke, W., 2004. On the wings of pride: The effects of pride on salespeople's performance. *Gedrag en Organisatie, 17*(6), 430–447).

p.152 "Helps you persevere" (Williams, L.A., & DeSteno, D., 2008. Pride and perseverance: The motivational role of pride. *Journal of Personality and Social Psychology, 94*(6), 1007–1017).

p. 152 "Enables you to select more challenging tasks" (Conroy, D.E., Elliot, A.J., & Pincus, A.L., 2009. The expression of achievement motives in interpersonal problems. *Journal of Personality, 77*(2), 495–526).

p. 152 "Spurs you on to think what else might be possible" (Fredrickson, B., & Branigan, C., 2005. Positive emotions broaden the scope of attention and thought–action repertoires. *Cognition and Emotion, 19*(3), 313–332).

p. 152 "Just feels good" (Zell, A.L., 2008. Pride and humility: Possible mediators of the motivating effect of praise. *Dissertation Abstracts International: Section B: The Sciences and Engineering, 68*(9-B), 6396).

p. 152 "You can only experience these complex and powerful feelings when you know who you are" (Lewis, M., Alessandri, S.M., & Sullivan, M.W., 1992. Differences in shame and pride as a function of children's gender and task difficulty. *Child Development, 63*(3), 630–638).

p. 153 "And that means your job forms part of your identity" (Ellemers, N., de Gilder, D., & Haslam, S.A., 2004. Motivating individuals and groups at work: A social identity perspective on leadership and group performance. *Academy of Management Review, 29*(3), 459–478).

p. 153 "If you can't identify with your organization …" (Tyler, T.R., & Robert, I., 1999. Why people cooperate with organizations: An identity-based perspective. In R.I. Sutton & B.M. Staw (Eds.), *Research in organizational behavior.* Greenwich, CT: Elsevier Science/JAI Press).

p. 154 "That's probably because cultures which favor the group over the individual …" (Neumann, R., Steinhäuser, N., & Roeder, U.R., 2009. How self-construal shapes emotion: Cultural differences in the feeling of pride. *Social Cognition, 27*(2), 327–337).

p. 155 "You'll learn something new and you might just feel proud …" (Webster, J.M., Duval, J., Gaines, L.M., & Smith, R.H., 2003. The roles of praise and social comparison information in the experience of pride. *Journal of Social Psychology*, *143*(2), 209–232).

p. 156 "Trust reduces costs" (Fukuyama, F., 1995. *Trust: The social virtues and the creation of prosperity*. New York: Free Press).

p. 156 "... and means you can take a risk without worrying about hidden agendas and politics" (Mayer, R.C., & Gavin, M.B., 2005. Trust in management and performance: Who minds the shop while the employees watch the boss? *Academy of Management Journal*, *48*(5), 874–888).

p. 156 "As if it were someone who understands you, has a character ..." (Coleman, J.S., 1993. The rational reconstruction of society. *American Sociological Review*, *58*(1), 1–15).

p. 157 "Those relationships are naturally extended to include allies of your allies; it's almost as if you extend your Trust by proxy ..." (Burt, R.S., & Knez, M., 1996. Trust and third-party gossip. In R.M. Kramer & T.R. Tyler (Eds.), *Trust in organizations: Frontiers of theory and research*. Thousand Oaks, CA: Sage Publications).

p. 157 "To do that you need to believe that they are competent ..." (Mayer, R.C., Davis, J.H., & Schoorman, F.D., 1995. An integrative model of organizational trust. *Academy of Management Review*, *20*(3), 709–734).

p. 158 "That's when you'll go into over-drive looking for Trust ..." (Shapiro, D.L., & Kirkman, B.L., 1999. Employees' reaction to the change to work teams: The influence of anticipatory justice. *Journal of Organizational Change Management*, *12*(1), 51–67).

p. 158 "Most people start with high levels of Trust, which then gets worn away" (Elangovan, A.R., Auer-Rizzi, W., & Szabo, E., 2007. Why don't I trust you now? An attributional approach to erosion of trust. *Journal of Managerial Psychology*, *22*(1), 4–24).

p. 158 "... it doesn't tend to work the other way round" (Berg, J., Dickhaut, J., & McCabe, K., 1995. Trust, reciprocity, and social history. *Games and Economic Behavior*, *10*(1), 122–142).

p. 158 "And you'll probably tolerate a maximum of two violations of Trust ..." (Elangovan, A.R., Auer-Rizzi, W., & Szabo, E., 2007. Why don't I trust you now? An attributional approach to erosion of trust. *Journal of Managerial Psychology*, *22*(1), 4–24).

p. 158 "What causes most people to feel most enraged ..." (Bell, B.S., Wiechmann, D., & Ryan, A.M., 2006. Consequences of organizational justice expectations in a selection system. *Journal of Applied Psychology*, *91*(2), 455–466).

p. 158 "And that's particularly true for people at the bottom ..." (De Vogli, R., et al., 2007. Unfairness and health: Evidence from the Whitehall II study. *Journal of Epidemiology and Community Health*, *61*(6), 513–518).

p. 158 "When Trust is fractured, organizations rely on threats or punishments, play favorites, and discourage input" (Cangemi, J.P., Rice, J., & Kowalski, C.J.,

1990. The development, decline and renewal of trust in an organization: Some observations. *Psychology: A Journal of Human Behavior, 27*(3), 46–53).

p. 158 "… when these are fueled by rumors" (DiFonzo, N., & Bordia, P., 2007. *Rumor psychology: Social and organizational approaches.* Washington, DC: American Psychological Association).

p. 159 "Creates social capital" (Fussell, H., Harrison-Rexrode, J., Kennan, W.R., & Hazleton, V., 2006. The relationship between social capital, transaction costs, and organizational outcomes: A case study. *Corporate Communications, 11*(2), 148–161).

p. 159 "Predicts cooperation" (Dirks, K.T., & Ferrin, D.L., 2002. Trust in leadership: Meta-analytic findings and implications for research and practice. *Journal of Applied Psychology, 87*(4), 611–628).

p. 159 "Allows you to take risks" (Colquitt, J.A., Scott, B.A., & LePine, J.A., 2007. Trust, trustworthiness, and trust propensity: A meta-analytic test of their unique relationships with risk taking and job performance. *Journal of Applied Psychology, 92*(4), 909–927).

p. 159 "Facilitates knowledge and information sharing" (Chowdhury, S., 2005. The role of affect- and cognition-based trust in complex knowledge sharing. *Journal of Managerial Issues, 17*(3), 310–326; Lucas, L.M., 2005. The impact of trust and reputation on the transfer of best practices. *Journal of Knowledge Management, 9*(4), 87–101).

p. 159 "Reduces feelings of personal pressure" (Harvey, S., Kelloway, E.K., & Duncan-Leiper, L., 2003. Trust in management as a buffer of the relationships between overload and strain. *Journal of Occupational Health Psychology, 8*(4), 306–315).

p. 159 "Is a vital link between you and your organization" (Lind, E.A., 2001. Fairness heuristic theory: Justice judgements as pivotal cognitions in organizational relations. In J. Greenberg & R. Cropanzano (Eds.), *Advances in organizational justice.* Stanford, CA: Stanford University Press).

p. 159 "For example, getting a new working relationship off on the wrong foot is a real killer …" (Lount, Jr., R.B., Zhong, C.-B., Sivanathan, N., & Murnighan, J.K., 2008. Getting off on the wrong foot: The timing of a breach and the restoration of trust. *Personality and Social Psychology Bulletin, 34*(12), 1601–1612).

p. 159 "You'll see what you expect to see, looking for evidence that confirms what you think" (Choi, J., 2008. Event justice perceptions and employees' reactions: Perceptions of social entity justice as moderator. *Journal of Applied Psychology, 93*(3), 513–528).

p. 159 "… dismissing anything that doesn't" (Higgins, E.T., & Bargh, J.A., 1987. Social cognition and social perception. *Annual Review of Psychology, 38,* 369–425).

p. 159 "Expecting a bonus and getting nothing will evoke a much stronger negative reaction …" (Bell, B.S., Wiechmann, D., & Ryan, A.M., 2006. Consequences of organizational justice expectations in a selection system. *Journal of Applied Psychology, 91*(2), 455–466).

p. 160 "That's because, typically, losses loom twice as large as gains" (Tversky, A., & Kahneman, D., 1991. Loss aversion in riskless choice: A reference-dependent model. *Quarterly Journal of Economics, 106*, 1039–1061).

p. 160 "Thirdly, sources of bad news are often seen as more credible ..." (Slovic, P., 1993. Perceived risk, trust and democracy. *Risk Analysis, 13*(6), 675–682).

p. 160 "If you deliver bad news you're seen to be in the loop ..." (Slovic, P., 1993. Perceived risk, trust and democracy. *Risk Analysis, 13*(6), 675–682).

p. 161 "If students can be persuaded to change their expectations of alcohol ..." (Lau-Barraco, C., & Dunn, M.E., 2008. Evaluation of a single-session expectancy challenge intervention to reduce alcohol use among college students. *Psychology of Addictive Behaviors, 22*(2), 168–175).

p. 161 "And a central feature of every interaction that builds Trust is how you share and swap resources" (Nugent, P.D., & Abolafia, M.Y., 2006. The creation of trust through interaction and exchange: The role of consideration in organizations. *Group and Organization Management, 31*(6), 628–650).

p. 161 "The more politically Machiavellian you are ..." (Albrecht, S., 2008. The direct and indirect influence of organizational politics on organizational support, trust and commitment. In E. Vigoda-Gadot & A. Drory (Eds.), *Handbook of organizational politics*. Northampton, MA: Edward Elgar).

p. 161 "Clear and consistent signaling about what is and isn't acceptable ..." (Six, F., & Sorge, A., 2008. Creating a high-trust organization: An exploration into organizational policies that stimulate interpersonal trust building. *Journal of Management Studies, 45*(5), 857–884).

p. 163 "And this isn't just a generational thing: everyone from Baby Boomers ..." (Curry, C.J., 2008. Predicting the effects of extrinsic and intrinsic job factors on overall job satisfaction for Generation X and Baby Boomers in a regional healthcare organization. *Dissertation Abstracts International: Section B: The Sciences and Engineering, 68*(12-B), 8435).

p. 163 "... to Gen Y-ers" (Na'Desh, F.D., 2009. Grown up digital: Gen-Y implications for organizations. *Dissertation Abstracts International Section A: Humanities and Social Sciences, 69*(9-A), 3625).

p. 163 "Back in 1959, Herzberg published his Two-Factor Theory ..." (Herzberg, F., 1959. *The motivation to work*. New York: John Wiley).

p. 163 "You get Recognition at work in four different ways" (Brun, J.-P., & Dugas, N., 2008. An analysis of employee recognition: Perspectives on human resources practices. *International Journal of Human Resource Management, 19*(4), 716–730).

p. 164 "Dr. Gary Chapman says that there are five different ways ..." (Chapman, G., 2007. *The five love languages*, 2nd ed. Chicago: Northfield).

p. 165 "There's a lot of evidence that shows the best psychological capital …" (Tatzel, M., 2003. The art of buying: Coming to terms with money and materialism. *Journal of Happiness Studies, 4*(4), 405–435).

10 Achieving Your Potential

p. 171 "For example, work that means going beyond the call of duty in terms of time and effort …" (Kinman, G., & Jones, F., 2008. Effort–reward imbalance and overcommitment: Predicting strain in academic employees in the United Kingdom. *International Journal of Stress Management, 15*(4), 381–395).

p. 171 "As are constant interruptions or blocks when you're trying to get something done" (Zohar, D., Tzischinski, O., & Epstein, R., 2003. Effects of energy availability on immediate and delayed emotional reactions to work events. *Journal of Applied Psychology, 88*(6), 1082–1093).

p. 171 "… you're de-energized then because getting back on track takes such high levels of energy and self-control" (Vohs, K.D., et al., 2008. Making choices impairs subsequent self-control: A limited-resource account of decision making, self-regulation, and active initiative. *Journal of Personality and Social Psychology, 94*(5), 883–898).

p. 171 "Of course, the more you're interrupted the harder it then is to pick up the threads" (Monk, C.A., Trafton, J.G., & Boehm-Davis, D.A., 2008. The effect of interruption duration and demand on resuming suspended goals. *Journal of Experimental Psychology: Applied, 14*(4), 299–313).

p. 171 "In fact, happiness at work and energy have one of the strongest relationships we've found …" ($.767, p = .000$).

p. 172 "That's why you'll feel particularly pressurized and negative when you waste it" (Hobfoll, S.E., & Shirom, A., 2001. Conservation of resources theory: Applications to stress and management in the workplace. In R.T. Golembiewski (Ed.), *Handbook of organizational behavior*, 2nd ed. New York: Marcel Dekker).

p. 172 "Continually doing that can lead to burnout …" (Shirom, A., et al., 2005. Burnout and health review: Current knowledge and future research directions. *International Review of Industrial and Organizational Psychology, 20*, 269–307).

p. 172 "And very importantly, when you have had enough time to recharge outside work" (Sonnentag, S., 2003. Recovery, work engagement and proactive behavior: A new look at the interface between nonwork and work. *Journal of Applied Psychology, 88*(3), 518–528).

p. 172 "Jim Loehr and Tony Schwartz's work with top class athletes …" (Loehr, J., & Schwartz, T., 2001. The making of a corporate athlete. *Harvard Business Review*, January, 120–128).

p. 173 "The Whitehall II study which followed British civil servants over 20 years …" (Virtanen, M., et al., 2009. Long working hours and cognitive function. The Whitehall II study. *American Journal of Epidemiology*, *169*(5), 596–605).

p. 174 "We all like group members to conform …" (Asch, S.E., 1956. Studies of independence and conformity: A minority of one against a unanimous majority. *Psychological Monographs*, *70*(9), No. 416).

p. 175 "Contact people who worked with you in the past …" (Roberts, L.M., et al., 2005. How to play your strengths. *Harvard Business Review*, January, *83*(1)).

p. 175 "That's important because strengths based feedback alone doesn't generate positive actions or feelings …" (Spreitzer, G., Stephens, J.P., & Sweetman, D., 2009. The reflected best self field experiment with adolescent leaders: Exploring the psychological resources associated with feedback source and valence. *Journal of Positive Psychology*, *4*(5), 331–348).

p. 175 "You'll pay more attention to negative feedback because it directs your attention to what you can do to improve" (Baumeister, R.F., Bratslavsky, E., Finkenauer, C., & Vohs, K., 2001. Bad is stronger than good. *Review of General Psychology*, *5*(4), 323–370).

p. 177 "It's not clear from the literature whether your strengths are fixed or not …" (in addition I can't find empirical evidence addressing a possible Hawthorne effect).

p. 177 "Professor Linda Ginzel at Chicago Booth Business School …" (private communication, September 2009).

p. 178 "Kaplan and Kaiser, who researched strength over use …" (Kaplan, R.E., & Kaiser, R.B., 2009. Stop overdoing your strengths. *Harvard Business Review*, February).

p. 178 "That's what derailing is all about" (Prince, D.W., 2005. Avoiding executive derailment: Individual and organizational responsibilities. *Business Leadership Review*, *2*(1)).

p. 178 "They matter in generating flow experiences" (Csikszentmihalyi, M., 1997. *Finding flow: The psychology of engagement with everyday life*. New York: Basic Books).

p. 178 " … and building happiness at work" (Kornhauser, A.W., 1965. *Mental health of the industrial worker: A Detroit study*. Oxford: John Wiley).

p. 178 " … and not using them can generate feelings of depression" (Warr, P., 2007. *Work, happiness and unhappiness*. Mahwah, NJ: Erlbaum).

p. 178 "And this is true in music" (Sloboda, J.A., & Howe, M.J.A., 1991. Biographical precursors of musical excellence: An interview study. *Psychology of Music*, *19*, 3–21); "mathematics" (Gustin, W.C., 1985. The development of exceptional research mathematicians. In B.S. Bloom (Ed.), *Developing talent in young people*. New York: Ballantine Books); "medical diagnosis" (Moulaert, V., et al., 2004. The effects of deliberate practice in undergraduate medical education. *Medical*

Education, *38*(10), 1044–1052); "scientific output" (Lehman, H.C., 1953. *Age and achievement*. Princeton, NJ: Princeton University Press); "social science" (Voss, J.F., Greene, T.R., Post, T.A., & Penner, B.C., 1983. Problem-solving skill in the social sciences. In G.H. Bower (Ed.), *The psychology of learning and motivation: Advances in research and theory* (Vol. *17*, pp. 165–213). San Diego, CA: Academic Press).

p. 179 "Deliberate practice is a term coined by Professor Anders Ericsson …" (Ericsson, K.A., 1996. *The road to excellence: The acquisition of expert performance in the arts, sciences, sports and games*. Hillsdale, NJ: Erlbaum).

p. 179 "He and his colleagues noticed that the key to expertise …" (Ericsson, K.A., Prietula, M.J., & Cokely, E.T., 2007. The making of an expert. *Harvard Business Review*, June).

p. 179 "That's the kind of feedback which has the most effect …" (Kluger, A.N., & DeNisi, A., 1996. The effects of feedback interventions on performance: A historical review, a meta-analysis and a preliminary feedback intervention theory. *Psychological Bulletin*, *119*(2), 254–284).

p. 179 "And understanding that feedback which has the weakest effect on performance …" (Kluger, A.N., & DeNisi, A., 1996. The effects of feedback interventions on performance: A historical review, a meta-analysis and a preliminary feedback intervention theory. *Psychological Bulletin*, *119*(2), 254–284).

p. 180 "That was shown in a now famous study of London cab drivers …" (Maguire, E.A., et al., 2000. Navigation-related structural change in the hippocampi of taxi drivers. *Proceedings of the National Academy of Sciences of the United States of America*, *97*(8), 4398–4403).

p. 180 "Ericsson's research suggests that it takes about 10 years or 10,000 hours of deliberate practice …" (Ericsson, K.A., Krampe, R.T., & Tesch-Römer, C., 1993. The role of deliberate practice in the acquisition of expert performance. *Psychological Review*, *100*(3), 363–406).

p. 180 "And it's the final 2,500 hours that make the difference between being an expert and being a good performer; those are best built up …" (Ericsson, K.A., Krampe, R.T., & Tesch-Römer, C., 1993. The role of deliberate practice in the acquisition of expert performance. *Psychological Review*, *100*(3), 363–406).

p. 180 "But even deliberate practice for an hour a day …" (Farmer, L.C., & Williams, G.R., 2005. *The rigorous application of deliberate practice methods in skills courses*. Prepared for LCLA/IALS Sixth International Clinical Conference Enriching Clinical Education, cdn.law.ucla.edu/SiteCollectionDocuments/workshops%20and%20colloquia/clinical%20programs/larry%20farmer%20and%20gerald%20williams.pdf).

p. 181 "But those failures are often a spur to learning" (Markman, K.D., McMullan, M.N., & Elizaga, R.A., 2008. Counterfactual thinking, persistence and performance: A test of the reflection and evaluation model. *Journal of Experimental Social Psychology*, *44*(2), 421–428).

p. 181 "That means organizations need to sell the benefits of development much better and ensure that learning and sharing knowledge is something that's officially supported" (Noe, R.A., & Wilk, S.L., 1993. Investigation of the factors that influence employees' participation in development activities. *Journal of Applied Psychology*, 78(2), 291–302).

p. 182 "And the big plus is that it's an easy way to connect with others to get support" (Daniels, K., et al., 2009. An experience sampling of learning, affect and the demands control support model. *Journal of Applied Psychology*, 94(4), 1003–1017).

p. 182 "But whether learning is formal or informal, everyone needs to understand why developing and sharing knowledge matters ..." (Noe, R.A., & Wilk, S.L., 1993. Investigation of the factors that influence employees' participation in development activities. *Journal of Applied Psychology*, 78(2), 291–302).

p. 182 "Other than knowledge and understanding, you also get a reinforced sense of competence ..." (Kets de Vries, M.F.R., 2001. Creating authentizotic organizations: Well-functioning individuals in vibrant companies. *Human Relations*, 54, 101–111).

p. 182 "Challenges, particularly ones you feel in control of ..." (Cavanaugh, M.A., Boswell, W.R., Roehling, M.V., & Boudreau, J.W., 2000. An empirical examination of self-reported work stress among US managers. *Journal of Applied Psychology*, 85(1), 65–74).

p. 182 " ... and that you feel supported in ..." (Wallace, J.C., et al., 2009. Work stressors, role-based performance, and the moderating influence of organizational support. *Journal of Applied Psychology*, 94(1), 254–262).

p. 183 "A defining characteristic of those who take on and overcome big challenges ..." (Gallagher, M.W., & Lopez, S.J., 2007. Curiosity and well-being. *Journal of Positive Psychology*, 2(4), 236–248).

p. 183 "If you have this character trait you'll embrace uncertainty" (Kashdan, T.B., & Silvia, P.J., 2009. Curiosity and interest: The benefits of thriving on novelty and challenge. In S.J. Lopez & C.R. Snyder (Eds.), *Oxford handbook of positive psychology*, 2nd ed. New York: Oxford University Press).

p. 183 "That leads to additional knowledge and experience ..." (Svoboda, E., 2006. Cultivating curiosity. *Psychology Today* [online]. Available at www.psychology-today.com/articles/200608/cultivating-curiosity [accessed September 29, 2009]).

p. 183 "But it actually looks as if challenges at work fall into two groups ..." (Cavanaugh, M.A., Boswell, W.R., Roehling, M.V., & Boudreau, J.W., 2000. An empirical examination of self-reported work stress among US managers. *Journal of Applied Psychology*, 85(1), 65–74).

p. 183 "Time-pressure is interesting because most people think that it's negative; actually it results in using your initiative ..." (Fay, D., & Sonnentag, S., 2002. Rethinking the effects of stressors: A longitudinal study on personal initiative. *Journal of Occupational Health Psychology*, 7(3), 221–234).

p. 185 "But it's no surprise that clarity about what you have to achieve makes you happier ..." (Lang, J., Thomas, J.L., Bliese, P.D., & Adler, A.B., 2007. Job demands and job performance: The mediating effect of psychological and physical strain and the moderating effect of role clarity. *Journal of Occupational Health Psychology*, *12*(2), 116–124).

p. 185 "One of the most important ways that you can deal with harder to manage challenges is by getting support" (Hochwarter, W.A., Witt, L.A., Treadway, D.C., & Ferris, G.R., 2006. The interaction of social skill and organizational support on job performance. *Journal of Applied Psychology*, *91*(2), 482–489).

Happiness at Work: A Conclusion

p. 187 "Of course one affects the other ..." (Boehm, J.K., & Lyubomirsky, S., 2008. Does happiness promote career success? *Journal of Career Assessment*, *16*(1), 101–116).

Dramatis Personae

The thing I really loved about writing this book was doing the interviews. Data are fun but people are much more exciting. Listening to all their stories was a fantastic experience – and it was thrilling how everyone added so much color and detail to the pieces of the happiness puzzle.

In all, over 80 interviews took place. I did all of them except for five: four were done by my colleague Barbara Fölscher in South Africa. She interviewed Monwabisi Maqogi, Dr. Iqbal Surve, Elaine Rumboll, and George Steyn. Jack Shukman, my son, interviewed Jack Sim in Singapore.

I did three interviews on the phone: with George Pappas in Melbourne, Dr. Matthews Mtumbuka in Blantyre, and Alan Macdonald in Kabul.

Otherwise I wanted to meet everyone face to face: happiness at work is rarely done in a vacuum, it's a collegiate experience.

So where and when possible I wanted to meet people. Their stories and illustrations make everything come alive and I'm hugely grateful for the time and effort they took with me.

Name	Date and location	Background
Babyatsky, Mark W.	New York, NY, USA June 2009	Professor, Head of the School of Medicine, Professor of Gastroenterology, Mount Sinai Hospital, New York, NY
Bate, Isaac	Oxford, UK March 2009	Student studying journalism in London
Beattie, Juli	Oxford, UK June 2009	Director and founder of The Art Room, a charity to help children learn through art
Bhandari, Romesh	Delhi, India September 2009	Foreign minister under Indira and Rajiv Gandhi. Ex-Governor of Uttar Pradesh and author

Name	Date and location	Background
Blair, Betsy	Richmond, VA, USA June 2009	COO, CJW Medical Center in Richmond, VA, providing care for Richmond and Central Virginia. One of HealthGrades America's 50 Best Hospitals (2007–2008)
Blanco, Dianne	London, UK October 2009	CEO Orteq, a biotech organization that makes replacement meniscuses for knee injuries
Boissier, Paul	Poole, UK October 2009	CEO Royal National Lifeboat Institution (the charity that saves lives at sea); ex-Deputy Commander-in-Chief Fleet (COO of the Royal Navy)
Bonham Carter, Edward	London, UK February 2009	CEO Jupiter Asset Management, one of the UK's most successful investment groups
Botton, Alain de	Oxford, UK July 2009	Philosopher, writer, and founder of the School of Life in London
Brick, Anita	Chicago, IL, USA June 2009	Founder of the Encouragement Institute whose aim is to foster appreciation
Briner, Rob	London, UK June 2009	Professor of Organizational Psychology at Birkbeck, University of London
Bywaters, Alan	London, UK October 2009	Founder of the UK-based consultancy The Mindful Capitalist, explorer, and author
Cauvy, Christophe	Oxford, UK May 2009	Regional Digital Director, EMEA, McCann WorldGroup – the global advertising agency
Chilcott, Martin	Oxford, UK May 2009	Social and environmental entrepreneur; CEO Meltwater Ventures, Chairman 2degrees Ltd, Director The Zero Carbon Company
Cohn, Bob	San Francisco, CA, USA June 2009	Founder of Octel Communications, the company that commercialized voicemail and was sold to Lucent Technologies; former partner with Sequoia Capital; tech-company advisor
Coleridge, Sir Paul	Exeter, UK June 2009	High Court judge, Family Division, UK
Daniels, Ann	Exeter, UK June 2009	Foremost British polar explorer; member of first all-woman team to North Pole; led all-woman team to the South Pole; solo adventurer; navigator on the Catlin expedition

Name	Date and location	Background
Das, Mohammad	New York, NY, USA June 2009	Moroccan-born New York cab driver
Davis, David	Gwenddwr, UK August 2009	Sheep farmer working 120 acres in Mid-Wales
Dipofi, Leah	Midlothian, VA, USA June 2009	Server in Carrabba's Italian grill, Richmond, VA, USA
Dolce, Tony	London, UK April 2009	News cameraman for BBC TV
Dorje, Trinley Thaye, His Holiness, The 17th Gyalwa Karmapa	Delhi, India September 2009	Head of the Kagyu school, one of the four main schools of Tibetan Buddhism. Also known as the Black Hat Lama.
Felt, Amanda	London, UK March 2009	Director of Business Development, Executive Education, Europe, Chicago Booth Business School, London Campus
Franks, Lynne	London, UK October 2009	British PR guru, visionary, and author
Ghosh, Shikhar	Boston, MA, USA June 2009	Founder of eight tech-based entrepreneurial companies; CEO Appex, which built the infrastructure for the US mobile phone industry. Named as "Master of the Internet Universe" by Forbes. Senior lecturer in entrepreneurial management at Harvard Business School
Gosden, Chris	Oxford, UK October 2009	Professor of Archaeology and Anthropology Oxford; discovered Papua New Guinea had been settled 30,000 years ago
Gowers, Andrew	London, UK February 2009	Ex-Head of Communications, Lehman's; ex-editor of *The Financial Times*; currently interim Head of Communications at London Business School
Hefes, Sylvain	London, UK May 2009	Investment banker; Chairman of the executive board, Paris-Orleans Bank S.A. France (holding company of N.M. Rothschild); ex-head of European Wealth Management, Goldman Sachs

Name	Date and location	Background
Hirsi, Habibo	Boston, MA, USA June 2009	Server in Au Bon Pain, Boston, MA
House, Paul	Delhi, India September 2009	Managing Director, SGS India; SGS provides global testing, inspecting, and certification to ensure quality standards
Johnston, Alan	London, UK October 2008	BBC journalist; kidnapped in Gaza in 2007 by Palestinian militants and held hostage for 4 months
Juniper, Tony	Cambridge, UK May 2009	Activist, environmentalist, author; ex-head of Friends of the Earth, advisor to the His Royal Highness the Prince of Wales
Lane Fox, Martha	London, UK May 2009	Co-founder and ex-CEO LastMinute.com; co-founder and chair Lucky Voice; co-founder of Antigone
Lapid, Yair	Tel Aviv, Israel September 2009	Israeli journalist, author, and television presenter. Host of *Ulpan Shishi*, the TV news-magazine program
Legarda, Loren	London, UK July 2009	Senator and presidential candidate in the 2010 election, The Philippines
Leland, Olivia	Carpentras, France July 2009	Senior Program Officer, Bill and Melinda Gates Foundation
Liao, Bill	London, UK October 2009	CEO Xing AG. First entrepreneur to monetize a web 2.0 business. CEO of Neo.org and WeForest.com
Macdonald, Alan	Phone October 2009	Chief of Staff, Mine Action Coordination Centre of Afghanistan (MACCA), Kabul, Afghanistan
Makin, Dr. Louise	London, UK May 2009	CEO BTG plc, the UK's largest pharmaceutical company
Maqogi, Monwabisi	Cape Town, South Africa March 2009	Ex-freedom fighter, ANC activist, entrepreneur, Khyalitsha, South Africa
Mawson, Lord Andrew	London, UK December 2008	Founder and President Community Action Network and a leading British social entrepreneur
Mtumbuka, Dr. Matthews	Phone October 2009	Head of Operations, Malswitch, Blantyre, Malawi
Munthe, Nelly	London, UK June 2009	Philanthropist and social entrepreneur

Name	Date and location	Background
Naftalis, Gary P.	New York, NY, USA June 2009	Leading American trial lawyer, Head of Litigation and Co-Chair, Kramer Levin Naftalis and Frankel. Named as one of the 100 most influential lawyers in the USA
Nasheed, Mohamed	London, UK April 2009	President of the Maldives; MP for Malé; Amnesty International Prisoner of Conscience
Nissenson, Marilyn	New York, NY, USA June 2009	Writer, television producer, and journalist
O'Hayer, Patricia	London, UK October 2008	Vice-President Communications Europe, Unilever, The Netherlands
Palmer, Jeremy	Oxford, UK September 2009	Partner, Beaumont Street Partners; ex-CEO UBS EMEA
Pappas, George	Phone May 2009	Ex-Managing Partner, The Boston Consulting Group, Australasia
Parr, Adam	Wantage, UK April 2009	CEO Williams Formula 1 team
Pauss, Felicitas	Geneva, Switzerland July 2009	Professor for Experimental Particle Physics, ETH Zurich; External Relations Coordinator, CERN
Pillai, Nisha	London, UK June 2009	BBC World news anchor and journalist
Rees, Jim	London, UK October 2009	Athlete, iron man, and speaker. Participated in Across America Race 2007, 2008, 2009
Robson, Mark	Oxford, UK May 2009	Children's author who writes fantasy fiction for young adults
Rumboll, Elaine	Delhi, India September 2009	Head of Executive Education, Graduate School of Business, Cape Town, South Africa
Schultz, William	Delhi, India September 2009	President and CEO Coca-Cola Bottlers, The Philippines
Scott, Diane	Midlothian, VA, USA June 2009	President, Nursing Mentors Association, USA
Scott, Kate	Dorchester, MA, USA June 2009	Assistant Headmaster, Neighborhood House Charter School, Dorchester, MA, USA (yes, that is headmaster)
Senior officer, Special Forces	June 2009	Confidential

Name	Date and location	Background
Shukman, Henry	Oxford, UK July 2009	Poet and writer based in Santa Fe, New Mexico
Sikka, Marut	Delhi, India September 2009	Celebrity chef and CEO Marut Sikka Team India
Sills, Eileen	London, UK February 2009	COO, Guy's and St. Thomas's NHS Foundation Trust; Chief Nurse and Joint Director of Clinical Leadership
Sim, Jack	Singapore June 2009	CEO World Toilet Organization, Singapore
Smith, Malcolm	London, UK July 2009	Chairman, GT Tools Ltd and consultant
Steyn George	Cape Town, South Africa September 2009	Managing Director, Pep Stores, largest retailer in Southern Africa
Stocking, Barbara	Oxford, UK October 2009	CEO Oxfam. Oxfam is a leading charity working to end poverty; it focuses on global emergency response, development, and advocacy work
Surve, Dr. Iqbal	Cape Town, South Africa June 2009	Doctor, anti-apartheid campaigner, social entrepreneur, and CEO Sekunjalo Investments
Terwitte, Brother Paulus	Oxford, UK July 2009	German Capuchin monk, writer, and Gestalt therapist
Thompson, Mark	London, UK October 2009	Director-General, BBC
Tomlinson, Charlotte	Oxford, UK October 2009	Pianist
Tustain, Robert	Banbury, UK April 2009	Builder and property developer
Walsh, Willie	London, UK October 2008	CEO British Airways
Wild, Matt	Delhi, India September 2009	Head of Operations, British Gas India
Willenz, Avigdor	Herzliya, Israel September 2009	CEO and founder of Galileo Technology Ltd; sold to Marvell Technology Group in 2001. Philanthropist
Yoeli, Rafi	Tel Aviv, Israel September 2009	CEO and President of Urban Aeronautics. Chief engineer of revolutionary flying vehicles, both manned and unmanned
Young, Commander Mike	Plymouth, UK December 2008	Head of Organizational Development in the Royal Navy

The following interviews were done anonymously: all these organizations required permission for people to speak, with the exception of one person whose anonymity I chose to protect.

Name	Date and location	Background
Entomologist	Oxford, UK June 2009	Entomologist, based in Belgium
IT general manager	Oxford, UK July 2009	Based in Mountain View, CA, USA
Business development	London, UK March 2009	Head of business development currently based in Denmark
Three senior female bankers	London, UK April/May 2009	Three senior female bankers who preferred to remain anonymous; two worked for investment banks, the other was happy to be identified with RBS because she had left
Two learning and development specialists	London, UK March/May 2009	Both men worked in different high-profile Footsie 100 financial institutions
HR Director	Oxford, UK May 2009	HR Director, service industry, Hong Kong/London
Female First Officer	London, UK October 2009	Previously a Captain with a low-cost airline
Cleaner	Boston, MA, USA June 2009	
BAA employee	Heathrow airport, UK June 2009	Not allowed to speak to anyone without permission

Index

Note: page numbers in italics denote figures or tables